"... A POET OR NOTHING AT ALL"

"… A Poet or Nothing at All"

The Tübingen and Basel Years of Hermann Hesse

Richard C. Helt

Berghahn Books
Providence • Oxford

Published in 1996 by

Berghahn Books
Editorial offices:
165 Taber Avenue, Providence, RI 02906, USA
Bush House, Merewood Avenue, Oxford, OX3 8EF, UK

Library of Congress Cataloging-in-Publication Data
Helt, Richard C.
--A poet or nothing at all : the Tübingen and Basel years of
Hermann Hesse / Richard C. Helt.
    p.   cm.
Includes bibliographical references and index.
ISBN 1-57181-049-8 (alk. paper). -- ISBN 1-57181-075-7 (pbk.)
    1. Hesse, Hermann, 1877–1962--Homes and haunts--Germany--
Tübingen. 2. Hesse, Hermann, 1877–1962--Homes and haunts--
Switzerland--Basel. 3. Tübingen (Germany)--Intellectual life.
4. Basel (Switzerland)--Intellectual life.   I. Title.
PT2617.E85Z72153 1996
838'.91209--dc20
[B]   96-11390
                                    CIP

British Library Cataloguing in Publication Data
A CIP catalogue record for this book is available from
the British Library.

Printed in the United States on acid-free paper

Front cover: *Hermann Hesse Around 1902.* Permission granted by Volker
Michels, Offenbach.

In Memoriam

Ruby Elizabeth Räuber Berg Helt
(1912–1995)

CONTENTS

ILLUSTRATIONS

PREFACE

During the several years of research and writing that have resulted in this book, I had the assistance and cooperation of dozens of people and institutions in Europe and North America, and I would be remiss not to acknowledge many of them by name. Nearly all of the people mentioned here have granted me permission to use previously unpublished material and photographs, and most have also provided additional information that was helpful in the completion of this study.

I am deeply indebted to my former student, Adelheid Leube, and her father, Dr. Herbert Leube, of Ludwigshafen for first bringing Hesse's *Notturni* to my attention and for presenting me with a copy of the Mezger-Leube *Notturni*. For repeatedly providing new material and valuable information about Hesse's relationship with Karl Ernst Knodt, I wish to thank Dr. Manfred Knodt of Darmstadt, as well as Ilse Knodt of Nassau and her late husband, Wolfgang Knodt. Cesco Como's daughter, Josefa Michaelis-Como of Seeheim-Jugenheim, contributed indispensable information on the friendship between her father and Hesse. Princess Renata von Schoenaich-Carolath of Haseldorf (Uetersen) graciously made available previously unknown correspondence between Hesse and her grandfather, Prince Emil von Schoenaich-Carolath, along with additional letters from the latter to Karl Ernst Knodt. Prof. em. Dr. Hans-Felix Piper of Lübeck and his wife deserve my special thanks, not only for allowing me to peruse documents and manuscripts inherited from his uncle, Dr. Kurt Piper, but for inviting me into their home to view those papers. I am similarly grateful to Ludwig Finckh's daughter, Haile Finckh von Kutzleben of Hemmenhofen, who also invited me to her home for a personal interview and provided me with a copy of another unknown set of Hesse's *Notturni*. During the 1992 Hesse Colloquium in Calw, it was my great honor to meet Hesse's sons, Bruno and Heiner, who enthusiastically encouraged my research on their father's early poetry and granted me permission to publish many of the *Notturni* poems. For permission to include those poems here and to quote from other Hesse writings, both published and unpublished, I am also most grateful to Dr. Siegfried Unseld of the Suhrkamp Verlag in Frankfurt am Main.

My very fruitful research in the Hesse Archives of the Swiss National Library in Bern was facilitated by Dr. Thomas Feitknecht, who has repeatedly honored requests for information and material. I was also aided by a perusal of the Hesse holdings in the Technical University in Zürich. Prof. Dr. Dieter Lohmeier of the State Library of Schleswig-Holstein in Kiel generously assisted me in the search for Kurt Piper's correspondence.

I extend my most sincere gratitude to Dr. Bernhard Zeller, who has devoted decades to the organization of the Hesse papers and documents at the German Literary Archives in Marbach, and to Dr. Jochen Meyer, who granted permission for the publication of previously unpublished materials from the Hesse Archives. The competent and always helpful staff of the German Literary Archives also deserves my heartfelt thanks, in particular Winfried Feifel, Viktoria Fuchs, Jutta Salchow, and Ingrid Grüninger.

The considerable financial support that I have enjoyed during these years is acknowledged here with the utmost gratitude: from the National Endowment for the Humanities in Washington for a Travel to Collections grant in 1988 and a Summer Stipend in 1991; from the German Academic Exchange Service for a three-month grant in fall, 1991; and from the German Schiller Society for a four-month Marbach stipend in spring, 1992. I also express my sincere appreciation to Northern Arizona University for supporting my sabbatical leave in 1991–92, and I am particularly indebted to Dr. Henry Hooper, Associate Provost for Research and Graduate Studies at Northern Arizona University, for his steadfast and continuing support of my research endeavors.

Without the work of other Hesse scholars, my research on Hermann Hesse's life could well have taken several years longer to complete. The invaluable two-volume collection of Hesse's correspondence before 1900, *Kindheit und Jugend vor 1900*, edited and richly annotated by Ninon Hesse and Gerhard Kirchhoff, made my research significantly more achievable. Ralph Freedman, Professor Emeritus at Princeton University, graciously provided key information from his own research materials during the final year of my research. My special thanks goes to Professor Joseph Mileck of the University of California, Berkeley, who supported and encouraged my research from beginning to end and whose own monumental studies of Hermann Hesse provided indispensable information, material, and inspiration.

For his support and keen scrutiny of my manuscript through every stage of its preparation, I am very grateful to my colleague and friend, Professor Nicholas Meyerhofer of Northern Arizona University. Finally, my most heartfelt gratitude is reserved for Volker Michels and Ursula Michels-Wenz, who vigorously assisted me in the search for unpublished letters and poems and painstakingly proofread the final manuscript, and who, on numerous occasions, opened their home to me and my family.

Flagstaff, Arizona   February 1996

INTRODUCTION

Hermann Hesse's biographers have uniformly emphasized his firm, if youthful, resolve to become a writer, quoting from the author's retrospective autobiographical sketch, *Kurzgefaßter Lebenslauf* (1924):

> Die Sache war so: von meinem dreizehnten Jahr an war mir das eine klar, daß ich entweder ein Dichter oder gar nichts werden wolle.[1]
>
> [It was this way: from the time I was thirteen years old, I knew that I would become a poet or nothing at all.]

Rarely, however, has a Hesse scholar noted the author's subsequent insight, articulated in that same passage:

> Zu dieser Klarheit kam aber allmählich eine andere, peinliche Einsicht. Man konnte Lehrer, Pfarrer, Arzt, Handwerker, Kaufmann, Postbeamter werden, auch Musiker, auch Maler oder Architekt, zu allen Berufen der Welt gab es einen Weg, gab es Vorbedingungen, gab es eine Schule, einen Unterricht für den Anfänger. Bloß für den Dichter gab es das nicht![2]
>
> [Gradually, however, another insight came to me, a quite uncomfortable one. You could train to become a teacher, a pastor, a physician, a craftsman, a salesman, a postal employee, even a musician, a painter, or an architect. There were qualifying guidelines, there was a school or some kind of training for every occupation in the world, save for that of writer!]

---

1. Hermann Hesse, *Kurzgefaßter Lebenslauf* (1924), in *Gesammelte Werke* (Frankfurt/M., 1970), 6: 393–94. See, for example, Ralph Freedman, *Hermann Hesse: Pilgrim of Crisis* (New York, 1978), 39; Joseph Mileck, *Hermann Hesse: Biography and Bibliography*, 2 vols. (Berkeley, 1977), 1: 11. [Unless otherwise noted, all English translations are the author's.]

2. Ibid., 394. See, in particular, Hugo Ball, *Hermann Hesse – Sein Leben und sein Werk* (Berlin, 1927), 59–60.

It was most likely this realization that provided the strongest impetus for Hesse's essentially autodidactic study of German (and European) literature and art. By 1895, as Joseph Mileck notes, Hesse had already "steeped himself in German literature of the eighteenth and nineteenth centuries and had become well acquainted with many of the major English, French, Scandinavian, and Russian authors of the same period."[3] From October 1895 until August 1898, while completing his three-year apprenticeship as a bookseller at Heckenhauer's in Tübingen (and working as a salaried employee there the following year), Hermann Hesse devoted much of his free time – evenings, Sundays, and the few vacations days he was allowed – to a sustained schedule of reading and formal analysis of German prose and poetry, especially of post-Enlightenment writing. Although he was in the bookstore twelve hours a day, six days a week, Hesse held doggedly to a rigorous and methodical program of reading. As Gotthilf Hafner has keenly observed, Hesse's early prose writings – especially *Hermann Lauscher* (1900) – demonstrate clearly "how stubbornly logical was the writer's development and autodidactic training."[4]

The young bookseller's letters, especially those to his parents and siblings, also bear vivid witness to the rigor and conscientiousness of his Tübingen *Privatstudien*, as he called them:

> Meine Freunde flüchten sich abends ins Wirtshaus, zu Bier und Karten; ich flüchte mich vom Äußern der Bücher ins Innere und betreibe planmäßig größere literaturhistorische und überhaupt geistesgeschichtliche Studien, die, wie ich hoffe, sich später werden verwerten lassen.[5]

> [My friends take refuge in the evening in the pub, drinking beer and playing cards. I escape the exterior world of books and enter their interior realm, where I am conducting an extensive study of literary history, indeed of intellectual history in general, which, I hope, will pay off grandly later on.]

These missives also served Hesse as a forum for the evaluation and analysis of his reading, as well as for the articulation of his own system of literary aesthetics, even though the latter was increasingly at odds with the strict, religiously informed aesthetic

---

3. Joseph Mileck, *Hermann Hesse: Life and Art* (Berkeley, 1978), 15.
4. Gotthilf Hafner, *Hermann Hesse – Werk und Leben* (Nürnberg, 1970), 17.
5. Letter to Johannes and Marie Hesse, 2 October 1898, in *Hermann Hesse – Kindheit und Jugend vor Neunzehnhundert*, 2 vols. eds. Ninon Hesse and Gerhard Kirchhoff (Frankfurt, 1966 and 1978), 2: 286.

notions of his parents and repeatedly strained their relationship, particularly that between Hermann and his mother.

After the intense difficulties between parents and son in the early 1890s, however, the Hesses were relieved that Hermann's life finally seemed to be stabilizing, and Johannes Hesse offered an insightful assessment of the value of his son's self-education:

> Ich glaube, Du kommst mehr zum Lesen und Studieren als mancher Student.[6]
>
> [I think you are doing more reading and learning than many a student at the university.]

While it was pure coincidence that the eighteen-year-old Hesse came to the university town of Tübingen – his father had placed a random advertisement in a Stuttgart newspaper on 3 October 1895, seeking an apprenticeship in a bookstore, and Hesse received an offer from Heckenhauer's dated the following day[7] – his daily contact with students and professors in the store made him feel a part of the university community in Tübingen. Gradually, Hesse developed a small circle of five or six friends (who called themselves the *petit cénacle*), all of whom were students. Although he more than occasionally criticized students and student life in letters to family members and close friends, there can be little doubt that Hesse was also sometimes envious of them and dearly valued the friendship of those in his own circle.[8] Indeed, in a 1948 letter to Ludwig Finckh, Hesse referred to himself, Finckh, and "dozens of *other students*"[9] back in Tübingen, an inaccuracy that may well be interpreted as an indication of his

---

6. Letter from Johannes Hesse to Hermann Hesse, 26 January 1898, in *Kindheit und Jugend*, 2: 234.

7. *Kindheit und Jugend*, 2: 17.

8. Hesse's most acerbic critique of the German university of the time is contained in a letter to the poet, dramatist, and editor Alfons Paquet dated 20 March 1903: "Weder war ich Student noch habe ich je mit dem Studentenleben sympathisiert. Mir sind sowohl die gelehrten wie die burschikosen Studenten zumeist ein Greuel, ich fand den Universitätsbetrieb läppisch und halte es für schade, daß ein so großer Teil der jungen Generation das Studium für die einzig anständige und rechte Berufswahl hält." In Hermann Hesse, *Gesammelte Briefe*, ed. Volker Michels, co-eds. Heiner Hesse and Ursula Michels, 4 vols. (Frankfurt/M., 1973–1986), 1: 99. ["I was neither a university student nor did I ever have much sympathy with student life. Both the studious and the frivolous among the student body are aversions to me. I found university life on the whole rather silly, and I consider it a shame that such a large number of the younger generation finds attending university to be the only decent and acceptable choice of vocation."]

9. Author's italics.

having subconsciously considered himself, if not a bona fide member of the student body, at least the equal of his contemporaries at the university.[10]

The Tübingen years, of course, also saw Hesse's emergence as a writer. On 1 March 1898, just months after he began his apprenticeship, his first poem, "Madonna," was published in the Viennese *Deutsches Dichterheim*. His first collection of poetry, *Romantische Lieder*, appeared in November of 1898, and his initial volume of prose, *Eine Stunde hinter Mitternacht*, came out in June 1899. He left Heckenhauer's and Tübingen at the beginning of August 1899, spent nearly six weeks at home with the family in Calw and in Kirchheim/Teck visiting several of his student friends from the *petit cénacle*, and then assumed his new position at Reich's bookstore in Basel on 15 September. He quit Reich's the end of January 1901 and switched, after a six-month break, to a post as an antiquarian at Wattenwyl's in Basel on 1 August 1901. In March 1903, Hermann Hesse left Wattenwyl's and bookselling for good. Within weeks, he completed the manuscript of his first major novel, *Peter Camenzind*, on which he had worked for more than a year, and on 9 June 1903 he signed a contract with the prestigious S. Fischer Verlag in Berlin to publish the work. With the appearance of that novel in February 1904, as Ralph Freedman rightly notes, the bookseller "had matured and become an author."[11]

By no means, however, did this apparent success elicit a mood of self-confidence and optimism in the young author. On the contrary, he seemed tormented by the possibility of failure, even as an abbreviated *Camenzind* was being serialized in Fischer's own literary periodical, *Die neue Rundschau*, from October to December 1903. In a letter dated 25 October to his close friend and occasional mentor, Karl Ernst Knodt, Hesse noted:

> Es kommt darauf an, ob mein Roman [*Peter Camenzind*] Erfolg hat oder nicht ... Zum Buchhandel mag ich nicht zurück, er ist langweilig und man verdient Hungerlöhne dabei.[12]

10. *Briefe*, 3: 487. A similar reference can be found in another 1948 letter, to Edmund Natter, ibid., 488. See also Ralph Freedman, *Hermann Hesse: Pilgrim of Crisis*, 91: "If during the Tübingen years the ideal had been provided by the student society ..."

11. Freedman, *Hermann Hesse: Pilgrim of Crisis*, 102.

12. Unpublished letter to Karl Ernst Knodt, 25 October 1903. Copy in the Hesse Archives, Marbach.

[Everything depends on whether or not my novel *Peter Camenzind*
is successful. I don't want to go back to selling books; it is boring
and pays starvation wages.]

His aversion towards his former vocation was even more pro-
nounced in a letter, a few weeks later, to his Basel friend and fel-
low bookseller, Otto Drasdo:

Wenn der "Camenzind" ohne Erfolg bleibt, kann ich mich nicht
halten und muß wieder in irgendeine Tretmühle zurück.[13]

[If *Camenzind* achieves no success, I won't be able to support myself
and will have to get back on some treadmill.]

If Hesse's years in Tübingen represented a kind of surrogate
Studium, the nearly five years in Basel should be viewed as a
period of intense practical application of his "formal" study of lit-
erature; as in Tübingen, of course, he spent his days plying his
profession as bookseller. Although the prose works *Hermann
Lauscher* (1901) and *Peter Camenzind* (1904) were to establish his lit-
erary reputation in a broader sense, it is safe to assert that Her-
mann Hesse devoted much more of his time and creative energy
to the composition of poetry than prose during the Tübingen-
Basel years (1895–1904). In fact, as Joseph Mileck points out, these
years were by far Hesse's most fruitful period of lyric production,
in which "fully one-third" of the 1,400 poems written by the
author during his entire lifetime were composed.[14] Thus, despite
his occasional complaints in letters of this period that he was often
unable to get anything down on paper, Hesse must have com-
pleted some four hundred poems in the five years between 1898
and 1903 alone. His collection, *Gedichte*, which appeared in print
in November of 1902,[15] contains a total of 167 poems, of which 122
were finished in Basel between 1900 and 1902.[16] Before they were

13. Unpublished letter to Otto Drasdo, 20 November 1903. Original in the Hesse
Archives, Marbach.
14. Mileck, *Hermann Hesse: Biography and Bibliography*, 1: 445.
15. Both Martin Pfeifer, *Hesse-Kommentar zu sämtlichen Werken* (Munich, 1980), 19
and the Marbach exhibit catalog, *Hermann Hesse 1877–1977*, ed. by Bernhard Zeller
(Munich, 1977), 81 mistakenly report the publication date as November 1901. See
Hesse's letter of 19 October 1902 to Rudolf Wackernagel-Burckhardt, in which he
noted: "Inzwischen stellte ich eine neue Sammlung meiner Gedichte zusammen,
die nächstens erscheint" (Hesse, *Briefe*, 1: 91). ["In the meanwhile, I have put
together a new collection of my poetry which will be coming out quite soon."]
16. Of the many Hesse scholars who have perused the holdings of the Hesse
Archives in Marbach, only Joseph Mileck has made reference in print to Hesse's
own copy of the 1902 *Gedichte*, in which "almost all of the poems are individually

gathered for publication in the fall of 1902, nearly all of these Basel poems found their way into small, handwritten collections which Hesse bestowed upon family members or sold for modest sums to friends and acquaintances.

In October 1900, for example, the budding poet first offered the collection he called *Notturni* to friends and others at prices between ten and twenty marks (or Swiss francs); this seemingly modest sum can be put into perspective by noting that Hesse earned just one hundred francs a month during his sixteen months as an assistant bookseller at Reich's in Basel. From that time on and throughout his entire life, Hermann Hesse intermittently sold similar, "self-published" collections of his poetry. His sometimes handwritten, sometimes typescript collection, *Zwölf Gedichte* (first composed in 1918), was to become, in Mileck's words, Hesse's "standard sales item."[17] From time to time, Hesse included original watercolors with the *Zwölf Gedichte*, and these sets, in particular, have become quite valuable; one such collection sold for more than 20,000 francs in Basel in the late seventies.[18]

Unlike the occasional, individually composed sets of *Zwölf Gedichte* in later years, however, the *Notturni* of 1900 were copied as a "batch" of twenty-five sets in less than a month and seem to have sold quickly. In May and June 1902, Hesse put together an entirely new "edition" of *Notturni*, for which he asked fifteen marks (or francs); while no available source mentions how many sets he composed in 1902, Hesse's (and Finckh's) letters indicate that at least a dozen orders were placed for the second group. There is no evidence that the *Notturni* were ever offered for sale again after 1902.

Composed primarily for the utilitarian purpose of financing his first two journeys to Italy, Hesse's *Notturni* – and the manner in which he "produced" and distributed them – represented a quite significant, even crucial transition in the young writer's development. On the one hand, he sought to avoid "commercial uncertainty" and "journalistic nattering" by approaching only "friends and others who meant him well" with a handwritten, personalized

---

dated in pencil (presumably by Hesse himself)." (Mileck, *Hermann Hesse: Biography and Bibliography*, 1: 447). A careful comparison of these numerals with other, handwritten numbers in Hesse's letters of the time reveals, almost without doubt, that Hesse did the dating himself.

17. Mileck, *Hermann Hesse: Biography and Bibliography*, 1: 466.

18. According to auction records on file in the Hesse Archives in Marbach.

"invitation."[19] On the other hand, he quickly abandoned his initial intention of varying the original eight poems twenty-five times, ultimately composing sets of as few as five and as many as fourteen, mostly new pieces per collection. It seems clear that Hesse was, consciously and methodically, composing and accumulating poems for his next collection, *Gedichte* (1902), an assertion born out emphatically by the numbers involved: Although there are only fourteen extant sets (six from 1900, eight from 1902) of a total of some forty to fifty *Notturni* written by the poet in 1900 and 1902, they contain 116 *different* poems, eighty of which are included in *Gedichte* (1902), i.e., nearly *half* of the individual pieces that constitute that volume. Thus, there is good reason to believe that the 1902 *Gedichte* volume, to a large extent, represents the "collected" *Notturni* poems of the years 1900 to 1902. Since the fourteen extant sets contain a total of eighty poems that the author included in *Gedichte* (1902), it also seems certain that the approximately thirty *Notturni* collections yet to be located would include several more, perhaps even *most* of the remaining poems eventually published in the 1902 *Gedichte*. The 1902 *Gedichte* volume, along with Hesse's *Ausgewählte Gedichte* (1921) and *Stufen* (1961), can be fairly characterized as the author's most significant individual collection of poetry. Indeed, Hesse's own selection of 63 poems for his *Ausgewählte Gedichte* in 1921 includes eleven pieces originally contained in extant *Notturni* collections, a solid affirmation of the poet's high regard for these handwritten verses.[20]

Despite its internationally acclaimed university and seminary, Tübingen had quickly seemed provincial and confining to the young Hesse; his parents, after all, were only thirty-eight kilometers away in Calw, and he continually encountered relatives, church acquaintances, and former schoolmates, many of whom were now studying at the university in Tübingen. Little wonder

19. See, for example, the letter of "invitation" to the Wackernagel-Burckhardt family, October 1900 in *Briefe*, 1: 78.
20. As Siegfried Unseld notes, with reference to the *Ausgewählte Gedichte* (1921): "Strenge Auslese. Nur das Wertvollste sollte überdauern. Die Jugendgedichte aus der Zeit vor 1902 bestanden am besten ..." In *Hermann Hesse, Werk und Werkgeschichte* (Frankfurt/M., 1985), 87. ["Strict and careful selection. Only the most valuable should be kept. The youthful poems from the period before 1902 were best represented ..."]

that the imminent move to Basel produced a mood of excitement and optimism:

> Ich habe in Tübingen ganz abgeschlossen und werde Ende September nach Basel gehen ... Denken Sie – nach Basel! Das ist meine Lieblingsstadt, meine Stadt der Städte ... Außerdem habe ich in Basel den größten und herrlichsten Teil meiner Kindheit gelebt.[21]
>
> [I have said my farewells in Tübingen and will go to Basel the end of September ... Just think – to Basel! That is my favorite city, my city of cities ... Besides that, I spent the largest and most splendid part of my childhood in Basel.]

During his Basel years, Hesse was to achieve a sustained literary production for the first time, while experiencing important personal growth and social maturation. Largely through contacts established by his family during their earlier years there (1881–86), the youthful author was a frequent guest in the homes of several socially and culturally prominent Basel families: Rudolf Wackernagel-Burckhardt, historian and state archivist; Jakob Wackernagel, philologist and professor; Emmanuel La Roche-Stockmeyer, a prominent Basel pastor whose daughter, Elisabeth, served as the model for the Elisabeth of *Hermann Lauscher* and *Peter Camenzind*.

> In Stadt und Volk ist ein ganz köstlicher Schatz von solider Tradition, teils als Geld, teils als äußere Erscheinung, teils und vor allem als Erziehung. Dazu finde ich immer, daß in diesem fast puritanisch frommen Volk ein tüchtiger Kunstboden ist.[22]
>
> [The city and its people reflect a quite precious treasure of solid tradition, partly in the form of wealth, partly as external appearance, partly, indeed above all, in cultivation. Along with that, I am always discovering that these almost puritanically pious people have a considerable artistic foundation.]

These families appreciated and supported the young poet and were often the recipients of handwritten sets of his poetry; half of the extant *Notturni* collections were purchased by Hesse's friends and acquaintances in Basel.

In the early months of the Basel years, Hesse enjoyed a flourishing social agenda, and he thrived on the evenings with these artistic and culturally sophisticated people, savoring especially the discovery that, at least on occasion, he could charm and fascinate the young women present:

---

21. Letter of 7 August 1899 to Helene Voigt-Diederichs, *Briefe*, 1: 59.
22. Letter of 16 January 1900 to halfbrother Karl Isenburg, *Briefe*, 1: 70.

Mittwoch abend war Abendgesellschaft bei Wackernagel-Merian ... Dort in dem prachtvollen, eleganten Hause war es äußerst nett und unterhaltsam. Ich hatte meine beste Laune, und unterhielt die jungen Damen fast allein, da die jungen Herren Basler sehr zugeknöpft sind. Wir plauderten und machten Spiele etc., und ich kam die ganze Zeit bis halb ein Uhr nicht aus dem Lachen und Schwatzen.[23]

[On Wednesday evening there was a soirée at the Wackernagel-Merians ... In that magnificient and elegant house it was quite pleasant and entertaining. I was in my best mood and entertained the young ladies almost by myself, for the young men of Basel are quite reserved. We talked and played games etc., and I didn't stop laughing and chattering until half past twelve.]

With time, however, Hesse began to view his relationship with these families differently; it is probably not inaccurate to say that the young poet became increasingly aware of the social distance between himself and the Basel *Bildungsbürgertum*. As Hugo Ball noted in his 1927 biography:

Die Weltferne der schwäbischen Kleinstadt hängt ihm an, und das Autodidaktentum, das alle Zeit frißt, die man auf Tennisspielen und andere Kunststücke verwenden sollte, vermehrt noch diese Schwierigkeit. Man braucht sich nur in eine elegante Dame zu verlieben, um die verflixte Ironie solch kleinstädtischen Angebindes gewahr zu werden.[24]

[He cannot shake the aura of his Swabian, small-town upbringing, and the situation is made the more difficult by his autodidactic studies, which use up all the spare time that might be spent learning tennis and other social activities. You only need to fall in love with an elegant city lady to become aware of the frustrating irony of such provincial baggage.]

It is thus not surprising that Hesse viewed his Basel experience rather more soberly as his years there passed. He wrote to Rudolf Wackernagel-Burckhardt in October of 1902:

Denn im ganzen Basel war Ihr Haus doch das einzige, aus dem ich gelegentlich Freude und Anregung und ein gewisses Heimatgefühl mitnahm.[25]

23. Letter of 3 December 1899 to Johannes and Marie Hesse, *Kindheit und Jugend*, 2: 419.
24. Hugo Ball, *Hermann Hesse*, 80.
25. Letter of 19 October 1902 to Rudolf Wackernagel-Burckhardt, *Briefe*, 1: 91.

[For in all of Basel your home was the only one that occasionally provided me with gladness, inspiration, and a certain feeling of being at home.]

Indeed, Hesse's comments in recently discovered correspondence to Karl Ernst Knodt during the years 1900–1903 indicate with no uncertainty that the young writer's appearances at the homes of these wealthy Basel families were sometimes distasteful, even humiliating experiences for him.[26]

Still, there can be little doubt that, on balance, Hermann Hesse's Basel years, as noted above, were a time of rich, intense, and varied aesthetic experience and growth. Scarcely a week passed in which he did not attend a concert, visit a museum or go to the theater, and his circle of friends and acquaintances included – as it would throughout his life – artists, sculptors, actors, musicians, and architects. While he claimed a social aversion to writers (as well as to musicians and actors), his letters frequently revealed a genuine sympathy for painters:

Die Maler reden immer von der Natur, die andern immer von ihren Werken oder von beneideten Kollegen.[27]

[Painters always talk about nature, the others about their publications or about envied colleagues.]

Although he already maintained correspondences with dozens of writers, literary critics, editors, and publishers during the Basel years, Hesse seems to have had few direct contacts with other, more established writers in Switzerland. In fact, during this most prolific phase of verse writing, he kept up existing contacts and cultivated new literary relationships almost exclusively with German poets and writers.

In light of the solid biographical research already in print in the works of Ball, Hafner, Carlsson, Zeller, Mileck, Michels, and Freedman, to name just some of the scholar-biographers of Hesse's early literary adulthood, the present work does not attempt a completely "new" portrait of the young poet Hermann Hesse. What this study will offer, however, is a more precise delineation of Hermann Hesse's early development as a poet and writer, including, specifically, his literary self-education, his determined and systematic self-publication of autograph collections of early poetry,

26. Hesse-Knodt correspondence, 1900–1903, copies of original letters in the Hesse Archives, Marbach.
27. Hesse's first letter to Stefan Zweig, 5 February 1903, *Briefe*, 1: 94ff.

especially the *Notturni*, and his relationships with literary (and nonliterary) contemporaries around the turn of the century. In the case of the latter, most particularly, the present study offers much that is new. While Hermann Hesse's popular reputation as a novelist was established by the (Swiss) novel *Peter Camenzind* after 1904, the (German) poet Hermann Hesse had already entered the ranks of the established poets of the day in 1902. Karl Ernst Knodt's anthology, *Wir sind die Sehnsucht* (1902), contains work by fifty poets (among them, eleven women!), including Rainer Maria Rilke, Ricarda Huch, Gustav Falke, Julius Hart, Agnes Miegel, and Prince Emil von Schoenaich-Carolath. Twelve poems by Hermann Hesse also found a place in this volume, a number that exceeds the contributions of any other poet included in Knodt's collection.

PART ONE

Calw and Tübingen (1877–1899)

CHRONOLOGY

1877 – Hermann Hesse is born on 2 July in Calw/Württemberg (Marktplatz 6), to Marie Gundert Hesse (1842–1902) and Johannes Hesse (1847–1916). His mother is the daughter of the respected Indologist and missionary, Dr. Hermann Gundert, widow of Charles Isenberg, and mother of two sons (Hermann's half brothers, Theodor and Karl Isenberg) from her first marriage. His father is a Baltic-German missionary and Russian citizen. Marie and Johannes Hesse have a daughter, Adele (1875–1949); two other children, Paul and Gertrud (born in 1878 and 1879, respectively), would die in infancy. Both the Hesses and the Gunderts are steeped in the beliefs and convictions of Pietism, a seventeenth-century reform movement within the Protestant churches of western Europe and England that emphasized personal salvation and the active participation of the laity in the missionary activities of the church.

1880 – Birth of Hermann's sister Marulla, who died in 1953.

1881 – In April, the family moves to Basel where Johannes Hesse assumes the editorship of the periodical published by the Basel *Mission*; he also teaches in the *Missionsschule*.

1882 – Birth of brother Johannes (Hans), who would commit suicide in 1935.

1883 – The Hesses become Swiss citizens.

1884 – Hermann is placed in the boarding school of the Basel Mission.

1885 – Death of Marie Hesse's mother, Julie Dubois Gundert (born in 1809).

1886 – The family returns to Calw. Johannes Hesse assumes the position of assistant to his father-in-law, Dr. Hermann Gundert, and is to become his successor in the Calw *Verlagsverein*. Hesse attends the *Realgymnasium*.

1888 – Hesse's father tutors him in Latin and Greek.

1889 – Hesse's first violin lessons. He completes his third year of *Realgymnasium*. The family moves into its own apartment after more than three years of sharing Dr. Gundert's home. Hermann writes his first poems.

1890/91 From February 1890 until July 1891, Hesse lives in Göppingen (some 75 kilometers from Calw) and attends the Latin school there (under Rector Bauer) in preparation for the Württemberg state examination. So that his son will qualify for admission to the Maulbronn Seminary, Johannes Hesse acquires Württemberg citizenship for Hermann; the rest of the family retains Swiss citizenship.

1891 – Hesse passes the examination in July; in September, he enters the prestigious Lutheran Seminary in Maulbronn to begin the course of study leading to the *Tübinger Stift* and ordination as a pastor.

1892 – On 7 March, after less than six months in Maulbronn, Hesse runs away, determined "to become a poet or nothing at all." He is returned to Maulbronn but is sent home on medical orders two weeks later. He returns to Maulbronn once more on 23 April, but his mother removes him for good on 7 May and places him in the care of Christoph Blumhardt, a Pietist "healer" in Bad Boll; Hesse allegedly attempts suicide on 20 June, and on 22 June his mother brings him to the mental hospital in Stetten. In November, he is accepted to the *Gymnasium* in Cannstatt.

1893 – Hesse successfully completes the examination for the *Einjährige* (*mittlere Reife*) on 8 July and begins the fall term in Cannstatt in September. He asks his parents to take him out of school in early October, and he leaves school for good on 15 October. On 25 October, Hesse begins an apprenticeship as a bookseller in Esslingen, but quits after just three days.

1894 – Hesse begins an apprenticeship at Perrot's, a church-clock manufacturer in Calw, on 5 June.

1895 – Hesse leaves Perrot's mid-September, takes an apprenticeship as a bookseller at Heckenhauer's in Tübingen, beginning there in October.

1898 – His apprenticeship completed, Hesse accepts a salaried position at Heckenhauer's.

1899 – Hesse resigns his position at Heckenhauer's, effective 1 August 1899.

PARENTS, SON, AND SCHOOL

Ich war das Kind frommer Eltern, welche ich zärtlich liebte und
noch zärtlicher geliebt hätte, wenn man mich nicht schon früh-
zeitig mit dem vierten Gebote bekannt gemacht hätte. Gebote
aber haben leider stets eine fatale Wirkung auf mich gehabt ...
Ich brauchte nur das "Du sollst" zu hören, so wendete sich alles
in mir um, und ich wurde verstockt.[1]

[I was the child of pious parents whom I loved dearly and would
have loved even more dearly, if I had not been introduced at a
tender age to the fourth commandment. Unfortunately, com-
mandments have always had a dreadful effect on me ... I only
needed to hear the "Thou shalt," and everything inside me was
transformed, and I became intractable.]

Its subtly tongue-in-cheek tone notwithstanding, this reference to
his parents from the beginning of Hermann Hesse's *Kurzgefaßter
Lebenslauf* (1924) captures succinctly the essence of the turbulent
parent-son relationship during much of the author's childhood
and youth, while also alluding to the parents' dogmatic Pietist
faith, a primary cause of the conflict.

Almost from birth, Hesse displayed an independent streak; as
his mother noted in her diary right after his birth, Hermann "is a
very big, heavy, beautiful child who is hungry right off the bat ...
and turns his head toward the light all by himself."[2] Before he
reached the age of two, however, the child was becoming increas-
ingly stubborn and rebellious; at nineteen months, for example,
he attempted with such vehemence to free his hand from the

---

1. *Kurzgefaßter Lebenslauf*, 391–92.
2. Adele Hesse Gundert, *Marie Hesse – Ein Lebensbild in Briefen und Tagebüchern*
(Frankfurt/M., 1977), 160.

housekeeper's grip that he broke his right arm![3] While Marie
Hesse's diary and letters document vividly the preschooler's
"astonishing intellect" and his rapidly developing musical and lin-
guistic prowess – especially his affinity for rhyming[4] – there
emerges, too, a growing fear of her son's excessively strong will.

> Bete du mit mir für Hermännle, und bete für mich, daß ich Kraft
> bekomme, ihn zu erziehen … der Bursche hat ein Leben, eine Rie-
> senstärke, einen mächtigen Willen … Es zehrt mir ordentlich am
> Leben, dieses innere Kämpfen gegen seinen hohen Tyrannengeist,
> sein leidenschaftliches Stürmen und Drängen.[5]
>
> [Pray with me little Hermann, and pray for me to find the strength
> to rear him … the boy has great energy and strength, as well as a
> powerful will … It is a real drain on my own strength, this inner
> struggling against his powerfully tyrannical spirit and his impas-
> sioned ranting and raging.]

Precisely what domestic upbringing entailed in the Hesse house-
hold is not articulated in Marie Hesse's letters and diary entries,
but through the author's own frequent references to his childhood
we have a good notion of the principles which underlay the child-
rearing practices of Marie and Johannes Hesse. Probably no pas-
sage in Hermann Hesse's work more directly explains his parents
method than a paragraph from the fictional editor's foreword to
Hesse's most autobiographical work, *Der Steppenwolf*:

> Obgleich ich über das Leben des Steppenwolfes sehr wenig weiß,
> habe ich doch allen Grund zu vermuten, daß er von liebevollen,
> aber strengen und sehr frommen Eltern und Lehrern in jenem Sinne
> erzogen wurde, der das "Brechen des Willens" zur Grundlage der

3. Ibid., 164.
4. Ibid., 149. In a letter to her son Karl Isenberg on 12 March 1882, Marie Hesse
noted: "Dann kann er [Hermann] wieder so rührend nett und lieb sein, der Marulla
Bilder zeigen und sie herzen, oder mir selbstgedichtete Liedchen vorsingen, wie
zum Beispiel:

> 'Das Vöglein im Wald
> so nett ist es halt,
> und singt so schöne Liedlein
> und schlupft dann in sein Nestlein.'"

["Then, sometimes, he can be so truly sweet and nice, showing Marulla pictures
and snuggling with her or singing me little songs he has composed himself like:

> 'The little bird in the forest
> is just so nice,
> and sings such pretty little songs
> and then slips into its little nest.'"]

5. Letter of 2 August 1881 to Johannes Hesse, ibid., 172.

Erziehung macht. Dieses Vernichten der Persönlichkeit und Brechen des Willens nun war bei diesem Schüler nicht gelungen, dazu war er viel zu stark und hart, viel zu stolz und geistig.[6]
[Although I know very little of the Steppenwolf's life, I have all the same good reason to suppose that he was brought up by devoted but severe and very pious parents and teachers in accordance with that doctrine that makes the breaking of the will the corner-stone of education and upbringing. But in this case the attempt to destroy the personality and to break the will did not succeed. He was much too strong and hardy, too proud and spirited.][7]

When the six-year-old Hesse – despite reportedly being a model first-grader – became "nearly uncontrollable" at home,[8] his parents reached the undoubtedly painful decision to place the boy permanently in the Basel *Knabenhaus,* a boarding school that primarily housed children of missionary families who were abroad; from January to June 1884, Hesse, not yet six years old, was allowed to visit home only on Sundays. In her double biography, *Ninon und Hermann Hesse* (1982), Gisela Kleine reports that Ninon Hesse viewed this episode as a key experience in Hesse's psychological development. As Ninon read and transcribed letters and other family documents from those early years, in preparation for the publication of *Hermann Hesse – Kindheit und Jugend* after Hesse's death in 1962, she was frequently shocked and shaken by their contents.

Ninon erfuhr zum ersten Male, daß Hermann schon als Schulanfänger von sechseinhalb Jahren von seinen damals in Basel lebenden Eltern aus dem Hause gegeben worden war, weil er durch sein ungebärdiges Temperament den Vater zu sehr aufregte und ihn bei seinen Lehr- und Schreibpflichten für die Mission störte. Hermann muß seinen halbjährigen Aufenthalt im Knabenhaus der nur wenige Häuser entfernten Missionsschule als eine Verbannung angesehen haben, denn außer ihm waren dort nur die Kinder der im Ausland lebenden Missionare untergebracht.[9]

6. Hermann Hesse, *Der Steppenwolf, Gesammelte Werke* (Frankfurt/M., 1970) 7: 191.

7. Hermann Hesse, *Steppenwolf,* translated by Basil Creighton and updated by Joseph Mileck (New York, 1963), 12.

8. "Wir sind zu nervös, zu schwach für ihn, das ganze Hauswesen nicht genug regelmäßig und diszipliniert" wrote Hesse's father on 14 November 1883. *Marie Hesse,* 192. ["We are too high-strung, too weak for him, the whole family routine is not regular, not disciplined enough."]

9. Gisela Kleine, *Ninon und Hermann Hesse – Leben als Dialog* (Sigmaringen, 1982), 431. It is interesting that Hesse's own sons were subjected to similar treatment, though not for disciplinary reasons. When Hesse and his first wife, Maria Bernoulli, separated in 1918, Hermann Hesse put Bruno and Heiner (the two older

[Ninon learned for the first time that in Basel already, at the age of six and a half, Hermann had been sent away from home by his parents because his uncontrollable temperament disrupted his father's teaching and writing duties for the mission. Hermann must have viewed his being put up in the boys' dormitory of the mission school, just a few doors away from his parents' home, as a kind of banishment; except for him, all the children there were the offspring of missionaries who were living abroad.]

According to Kleine, Ninon Hesse believed that she had found in these documents the origins of her late husband's reluctance – indeed, inability – to involve himself emotionally with another human being "because of having once been subjected to that 'pedagogical' withholding of affection on the part of his parents."[10] In letter after letter from the 1880s and early 1890s, Ninon found evidence of the young Hermann's fear of being ostracized anew by his parents, and she repeatedly observed the various "devices" that Hermann employed in order to win, if not the love, then at least the attention of his parents and family:

> Sobald er "bös war" und "schon wieder kränkelte," kümmerte man sich – wenn auch kopfschüttelnd und in unwilliger Anteilnahme – um ihn. Als "moralisch schwach" blieb er im Mittelpunkt des familiären Rundgespräches. Durch Trotz und Eigensinn erzeugte er Gefühlsstürme – waren es auch Sorge, Tadel und Ratlosigkeit.[11]

> [As soon as he was "bad" and "once again sickly," family members concerned themselves with him, albeit with mild resignation and reluctant sympathy. As the "morally weak" one, he remained the center of family discussion; his stubborn and defiant behavior produced emotional reactions on the part of the others in the family, though mostly worry, blame, and helplessness.]

As the letters – and behavior – between son and parents through the 1890s consistently document, each side was skilled at arousing feelings of sympathy, worry, and guilt in the other. In Hesse's most angry and provocative letters, as Kleine relates, his widow Ninon recognized the deep emotional pain that the author was never to overcome completely, and she understood for the first time his tendency to regard being misunderstood and socially isolated as virtues:

---

sons) in a children's home. Both would spend much of their childhood and puberty in boarding schools and with families who were friends of the parents.

10. Ibid.

11. Ibid., 432.

Auch sein Bedürfnis, aus jeder normgebenden Gemeinschaft wieder auszubrechen, ein Thema, das in vielen Abwandlungen sein Werk bestimmte, war auf jene erpresste Anpassung zurückzuführen, der er sich nur als "Unsozialer", als Außenseiter und unverstandener Neurotiker entziehen konnte.[12]

[Even his need to break out of any normative social surroundings, a theme whose many variations were to provide the essence of his literary work, could be traced back to that forced conformity from which he was only able to flee by assuming the role of a "social misfit," an outsider, and a misunderstood neurotic.]

Another perspective on the conflict-laden relationship between Hesse and his family, and one which attempts to place it in a sociohistorical frame of reference, is put forth by Fritz Böttger, for whom the Gundert family "business," i.e., the Calw *Verlagsverein*, represents a patriarchal and authoritarian family structure more characteristic of the precapitalistic era:

In einer Periode des beschleunigten Abbaus des Patriarchalismus war eine solche altbürgerlich-idyllische Familiensituation ein Relikt der Vergangenheit, und sie mußte zu den schwersten Spannungen und Konflikten führen, sobald eine Jugend heranwuchs, die sich von den Lebensformen und Werten der älteren Generation radikal wegwandte. Der jugendliche Hermann Hesse ist an diesem Emanzipationsprozeß fast gescheitert.[13]

[In a period of accelerated decline of the established patriarchal structure, this kind of a traditional, almost idyllic bourgeois familial situation was a relic of the past. It would inevitably lead to the most difficult tensions and conflicts, as soon as a younger generation came along that diverged radically from the structures and values of the parental generation. As an adolescent, Hermann Hesse nearly perished in his attempt to emancipate himself from all of that.]

While Böttger fails to acknowledge sufficiently the role and importance of the Gundert-Hesse family's religious and moral convictions – and the effects of these on their children – there is more than ample evidence to support his notion of the family's patriarchal structure. As Marie Hesse's letters and diary entries make particularly clear, her father, Dr. Hermann Gundert, determined in

12. Ibid. It is to Gisela Kleine's great credit that she undertook such painstaking and exhaustive research of Ninon Hesse's own papers and documents. The resulting study (*Ninon und Hermann Hesse*) is the best psychological portrait of Hermann Hesse to date.

13. Fritz Böttger, *Hermann Hesse – Leben, Werk, Zeit* (Berlin, 1974), 20.

an often plainly autocratic manner the course of his extended family's destiny.[14] Although Wilhelmian Germany, to be sure, was gradually shedding some of the patriarchal societal patterns established during previous centuries, the school system – Hesse's first encounter with the institutions of that society – remained essentially patriarchal and authoritarian well into the twentieth century. It must also be remembered that Hesse spent his early school years (1883–86) in Basel at the *Missionsschule*, which was in a very real sense an extension of the Gundert-Hesse family's authority and beliefs.

Hermann Hesse's antipathy toward the school system of his day is well documented, both in fiction and nonfiction; indeed, school receives the sharpest and most consistent focus within Hesse's social criticism. When *Unterm Rad*, Hesse's devastating critique of the educational system of his time, was nearing publication in 1904, he wrote to his half brother Karl Isenberg, himself a *Gymnasium* teacher:

> Die Schule ist die einzige moderne Kulturfrage, die ich ernst nehme und die mich gelegentlich aufregt. An mir hat die Schule viel kaputtgemacht, und ich kenne wenig bedeutendere Persönlichkeiten, denen es nicht ähnlich ging. Gelernt habe ich dort nur Latein und Lügen, denn ungelogen kam man in Calw und im Gymnasium nicht durch – wie unser Hans [Hesse's younger brother] beweist, den sie ja in Calw, weil er ehrlich war, fast umbrachten. Der ist auch, seit sie ihm in der Schule das Rückgrat gebrochen haben, immer unterm Rad geblieben.[15]

> [Our school system is the only modern cultural matter that I take seriously and that occasionally gets me worked up. In my case, school did a lot of damage, and I know few important people who did not suffer similarly. All I learned was Latin and how to lie, for you couldn't get through *Gymnasium* in Calw without lying, as Hans's experience proves; his honesty at school almost cost him his life in Calw. And ever since the school system broke him, he has stayed "beneath the wheel."]

Similarly, Hesse's infamous "escape" from the theological school at Maulbronn can be viewed as his own desperate and ultimately successful attempt to break free from the stifling, conformist

14. See, for example, *Marie Hesse,* 58–61 and 196–98, as well as *Kindheit und Jugend,* 1: 15–16.
15. Letter to Karl Isenberg, 25 November 1904, *Briefe,* 1: 130–31. Hesse's remarks seem to anticipate Hans's suicide three decades later.

atmosphere that the contemporary school system seems to have meant for him.

So much has been made of Hesse's "flight" from Maulbronn in March of 1892, however, that it has tended to obscure his having initially been quite content there – or so his letters home would attest. On 14 February 1892, just three weeks before he fled the institution, Hesse wrote to his parents:

> Ich bin froh, vergnügt, zufrieden! Es herrscht im Seminar ein Ton, der mich sehr anspricht. Vor allem ist es das enge, offene Verhältnis zwischen Zögling und Lehrer, dann aber das nette Verhältnis der Zöglinge untereinander ... Dann das großartige Kloster! In einem der feierlichen Kreuzgänge mit einem Andern über Sprachliches, Religiöses, über Kunst etc. zu disputieren, hat einen besonderen Reiz.[16]

> [I am happy, cheerful, satisfied! There is an atmosphere in the seminary that really appeals to me, above all the close and open relationship between pupil and teacher, but also the good relationship among the pupils themselves ... And then there is the magnificient monastery! To stand in one of the solemn cloisters and debate with a fellow pupil matters of language, religion, art etc. has a quite special attraction.]

The exact motivation for Hesse's flight is uncertain. His mother noted in her diary that the parents were at a loss to explain their son's behavior, particularly in view of his having seemed, up to that point, to like being there, although she added:

> Ein Stuß und Ärger mit dem Musiklehrer etliche Tage vorher hatte wohl mitgewirkt.[17]

> [An argument with the music instructor a few days earlier probably had something to do with it.]

In his first letter to the family after being returned to the school, Hesse uttered the desire to drop his music (violin) instruction, "otherwise my whole life here will be without any pleasure."[18] Much later, in his retrospective *Kurzgefaßter Lebenslauf* (1924), Hesse was still unable to pinpoint the cause of his apparently quite abrupt change of attitude:

> Ein Jahr später wurde ich Zögling eines theologischen Seminars, lernte das hebräische Alphabet schreiben und war schon nahe

16. *Kindheit und Jugend*, 1: 170–71.
17. Ibid., 183. Marie Hesse likely used the word *Stuß* here in its Swabian meaning, "argument" or "fight."
18. Ibid., 187.

daran zu begreifen, was ein *Dagesch forte implicitum* ist, als plötzlich
von innen her Stürme über mich hereinbrachen, welche zu meiner
Flucht aus der Klosterschule, zu einer Bestrafung mit schwerem
Karzer und zu meinem Abschied aus dem Seminar führten.[19]
[A year later I became a pupil in a theological preparatory semi-
nary, where I was learning the Hebrew alphabet and was close to
comprehending what a *Dages-forte* implied is, when suddenly a
storm began raging within me, causing me to flee the school. This
led to punishment that included solitary detention and, eventually,
to my departure from the seminary.]

It would be inaccurate, however, to characterize Hesse's vari-
ous school experiences as exclusively negative. Already in the
Missionsschule in Basel, Hesse revered his teacher, Jakob Pfisterer,
who seems to have brought out the best in the otherwise prob-
lematic youngster. And despite the tyrannical and often sadistic
behavior of most of the instructors in the Calw *Realgymnasium*,[20]
which he attended from 1886–89, Hermann Hesse came to respect
and admire at least one of his mentors, Wilhelm Schmidt, his
fourth-grade Greek teacher. In the Latin school in Göppingen,
where Hesse was prepared for the state examination that made
possible his admission to the seminary preparatory school in
Maulbronn in September 1891, he thrived under the pedagogical
genius of the rector, Otto Bauer.[21] Ernst Kapff, who was briefly
Hesse's teacher during the latter's final year of schooling in the
Gymnasium at Cannstatt (1892–93), became one of Hesse's favorite
correspondents during his first two years in Tübingen; the two
exchanged more than a dozen letters and cards in 1895 and 1896.

It is interesting – and was perhaps more than purely coinciden-
tal – that at his own request, Hesse returned to Basel in the fall of
1892 to spend a month with his first teacher, Jakob Pfisterer. Hesse

19. *Kurzgefaßter Lebenslauf*, 395. The *Dages-forte* is a point in the "bosom" of a
Hebrew character which indicates the doubling of that letter. It is sometimes omit-
ted but still implied.

20. A good recounting of the brutality characteristic of the Calw school is con-
tained in Siegfried Greiner's *Hermann Hesse – Jugend in Calw* (Sigmaringen, 1981),
30–35.

21. Hesse himself provides a fascinating remembrance of Schmidt and Bauer in
his autobiographical description "Aus meiner Schülerzeit" (1926) in *Kleine Freuden
– Kurze Prosa aus dem Nachlaß*, ed. Volker Michels (Frankfurt/M., 1977), 187–98. In
a similar vein, Otto Mörike recounts his schooldays as Hesse's fellow pupil in Calw
and Göppingen in "Der junge Hesse – Persönliche Erinnerungen an Schul- und
Jugendzeit" in *Hermann Hesse in Augenzeugenberichten*, ed. Volker Michels (Frank-
furt/M., 1991), 17–26.

had left Maulbronn for good on 7 May 1892, and was taken by his mother to Christoph Blumhardt, a Pietist healer in Bad Boll. Initially, Hermann seemed to get along there, and he was soon allowed to leave the institution grounds to visit his brother Theo in Cannstatt. During one of his visits there, Hesse met twenty-two year old Eugenie Kolb, the daughter of Theo's landlady, and promptly fell in love with her; her subsequent rejection of the young would-be suitor was difficult for him to accept. Six weeks later, on 20 June, the tormented youth fled Blumhardt's care, leaving a suicide note behind, and purchased a revolver with money he had secretly borrowed.[22] Although he returned to Bad Boll that evening, his mother came for him the following day; on 22 June 1892, Marie Hesse had her son admitted to a treatment clinic for retarded and epileptic children (*Heilanstalt für Schwachsinnige und Epileptische*) at Stetten in the Rems Valley, just east of Stuttgart. With the exception of a two-week leave in August to visit the family, Hesse remained in Stetten until his train journey to Basel on 5 October.[23]

Whether his return to Basel was the manifestation of a subconscious desire to "start over" or merely the most expedient means by which to flee family and clinic, Hesse seems to have adjusted quickly to his former home, where he referred to Pastor Pfisterer as "Papa" and enjoyed playing with the pastor's sons, who were on fall vacation from school. As Pfisterer himself reported in his first letter to Calw after Hermann's arrival:

22. As unfathomable as it seems, given present-day Germany's extremely stringent regulation of firearms ownership, the not yet fifteen-year-old Hesse was able to purchase a weapon with no difficulty. Similarly, he sold some of his school books in January of 1893 and used the money to buy a revolver with which he threatened to kill himself. A perusal of the Württemberg law code of the time indicates that no legal obstacle would have prevented Hesse's purchase of the weapons! In the notorious letter to his father of 14 September 1892, which Hesse begins with "Sehr geehrter Herr!", addressing his father formally, he asks the elder Hesse: "[D]arf ich Sie vielleicht um 7 M oder gleich um den Revolver bitten." (*Kindheit und Jugend*, 1: 268–69). ["May I perhaps ask you for 7 marks or simply for the revolver itself."]

23. A candid remark made several years later in a letter to his parents indicates Hesse's own reaction to his surroundings in Stetten: "[U]nter dem ewigen Druck der Einförmigkeit und noch mehr unter der Umgebung von Kranken, Blöden etc., von Halbtieren, an die ich mich ohne Angst und Ekel nie erinnern kann." Letter of 16 May 1897 to Johannes and Marie Hesse, *Kindheit und Jugend*, 2: 177–78. ["Under the pressure of the monotonous everyday routine and, even more, being surrounded by sick people, crazy people, half animals – to this day I cannot think about all that without feeling afraid and disgusted."]

> Er ist nun eine Woche hier und ich kann sagen, etwas wirklich Abnormes habe ich bei ihm noch nicht bemerkt.[24]
>
> [He has been here for a week now, and I can say that I have not noticed anything really abnormal about him.]

Indeed, the month in Basel marked a kind of turning point in that phase of Hesse's life. Through his frequent, lengthy discussions with "Papa" Pfisterer, he began to focus anew on returning to school to complete the *Einjährige*,[25] even deciding to apply to the *Gymnasium* in Cannstatt (Stuttgart) where, in fact, he began school almost immediately after returning from Basel on 7 November 1892. In one of his talks with the pastor, Hesse also expressed, probably for the first time, an interest in the bookseller trade; as Pfisterer wrote to Hesse's father a week before the boy was to return to Germany:

> Ob er denn überhaupt so aufs Studium versessen sei. Er meinte, das nicht, aber er möchte doch als Deutscher den Einjährigen erlangen. (Ein Beruf wie Buchhändler würde ihm auch einleuchten, wenn es nicht gut weiterginge.)[26]
>
> [When asked if he were truly interested in going to the university, he indicated that he wasn't but as a German he would like to complete the *Einjährige*. (An occupation such as bookseller could appeal to him, he said, if things did not go well in school.)]

Pfisterer's essentially optimistic assessment of Hermann's chances for completing at least the *Einjährige* was echoed by Pastor Gottlob Adam Schall, the director of the institution in Stetten, who was instrumental in getting Hesse admitted to the Cannstatt *Gymnasium* in 1892. Although they had their differences often enough during the stormy months of what Hesse termed his "incarceration" at Stetten, Schall can justifiably be mentioned among those pedagogues who figured positively in young Hermann Hesse's life. From the outset, he was skeptical about earlier diagnoses of Hesse's "sickness," hesitating to accept that the boy suffered from *primäre Verrücktheit* (primary insanity) and opting instead for a

24. Letter from Pfisterer to Johannes Hesse, 12 October 1892, in *Kindheit und Jugend*, 1: 285.

25. The *Einjährige*, equivalent to the more prevalent *mittlere Reife*, amounted to a diploma awarded after the completion of six years of *Gymnasium*.

26. Letter from Pfisterer to Johannes Hesses, 27 October 1892, *Kindheit und Jugend*, 1: 295.

diagnosis of "moral insanity."[27] As Schall summarized in a letter to Johannes Hesse after Hermann's departure for Basel:

> Ist die Diagnose "primäre Verrücktheit" richtig, so gibt es oft allerdings zur Zeit der Pubertät einen Stillstand. Ich gebe zu, daß manche Erscheinungen bei ihm dafür sprechen. Aber auf der andern Seite spricht auch manches dagegen. Vorerst möchte ich doch an moral insanity festhalten – und diese ist heilbar.[28]

> [If the diagnosis of "primary insanity" is correct, there is nonetheless during puberty often a dormant phase. I admit that, in his case, there are symptoms that indicate this. On the other hand, though, there is evidence to the contrary. For now I would like to stick with moral insanity – and it is curable."]

The counsel of Pfisterer and Schall, along with some members of the Hesse-Gundert family, that Hermann be allowed, indeed encouraged to return to school, proved to be appropriate and beneficial. To be sure, Hesse would suffer a behavioral relapse in early 1893, a near attempt at suicide, triggered, he claimed in a letter to his mother, by the accumulated pain of the preceding months:

> Ich saß da und las im Eichendorff, da kam mit einem Mal der ganze alte böse [illegible] über mich, all das trübe Herzweh ... die Erinnerung an alles, was ich in Boll erlebte. Ich nahm rasch einige Bücher, ohne Auswahl, und kaufte in Stuttgart dafür – einen Revolver.[29]

> [I sat there, reading Eichendorff, and I was suddenly overcome by all the old evil (illegible), all the gloomy heartache ... the memory of everything that I had experienced in Boll. I grabbed some books, quite at random, and used them to purchase a revolver in Stuttgart.]

During the spring of 1893, he also discovered the pleasures of alcohol and tobacco and regularly frequented Cannstatt pubs. Nonetheless, he managed to persevere and in July 1893 passed his examinations for the *mittlere Reife*. Although his half-hearted attempt to continue in the Cannstatt *Gymnasium* in the fall of 1893

27. Schall and others involved in Hesse's treatment always employed this English designation for the affliction, and its usage at that time was apparently common in the German-speaking countries. The English term still seems to have currency in the German-speaking world, for recent editions of Wahrig's *Deutsches Wörterbuch* include the following definition under "moral insanity": "Fehlen sittlicher Urteilsfähigkeit bei normaler Intelligenz." ["The absence of moral judiciousness despite normal intelligence."]

28. Letter from Inspektor Pastor Gottlob Schall to Johannes Hesse, 10 October 1892, ibid., 1: 282.

29. Letter to Marie Hesse, 20 January 1893, ibid., 1: 324.

ended after less than a month, Hesse was beginning, in Bernhard Zeller's words, "to work on himself."[30]

Hermann Hesse was never to enjoy a truly comfortable relationship with his parents; even periods of relative calm seem to have stimulated little stress-free interaction between parents and son. Clearly, many of the difficulties in that relationship must be attributed to the young Hesse's personality and behavior. As Eugene Stelzig accurately describes him, Hermann was indeed "something of a demon child, possessed of an energy, vitality, imagination, and intelligence that in their ungovernable excesses became a source of affliction to the Hesse household."[31] For their part, of course, Johannes and Marie Hesse reacted to their gifted but often distraught offspring by attempting to eradicate (or *have* eradicated) those aspects of Hermann's personality that they construed to be character deficiencies or outright manifestations of almost diabolical insinuation.

Still, the emphasis that Hesse scholars have tended to place on many of the crises of the author's unquestionably traumatic youth seem, upon closer scrutiny, to be notably excessive. Hesse's two youthful suicide "attempts," for example, might more accurately be labeled suicide "threats," for he never actually shot himself or in any other way made a serious attempt to commit suicide during that period of his life.[32] It should be noted that in January of 1893 Hesse himself wrote to a boyhood friend, Otto Hartmann, of his attempt to shoot himself on 20 June 1892:

> Ich habe dem Tod ins Aug' gesehen und mich nicht gefürchtet. Ich habe in den Lauf des geladenen Revolvers geblickt und losgedrückt.[33]

30. Bernhard Zeller, *Hermann Hesse – mit Selbstzeugnissen und Bilddokumenten* (Hamburg, 1963), 28.

31. Eugene Stelzig, *Hermann Hesse's Fictions of the Self: Autobiography and the Confessional Imagination* (Princeton, 1988), 55.

32. Only much later, according to Volker Michels, during the days immediately preceding his marriage to Ruth Wenger, did Hermann Hesse actually attempt suicide: "Der andere – durch Aussagen seiner zweiten Frau Ruth Wenger und einen Baseler Klinikaufenthalt Hesses belegbare – Selbstmordversuch (mit Tabletten) fand … in der Steppenwolf-Zeit [statt], Anfang Januar 1924, wenige Tage vor der Trauung mit Ruth." (Personal letter to the author from Volker Michels, 10 March 1993.) ["The other suicide attempt, confirmed by the testimony of his second wife Ruth as well as by his stay in a Basel clinic, happened the beginning of January, 1924, a few days before the wedding with Ruth."]

33. Letter from Hesse to Otto Hartmann, 18 January 1893, copy in the Hermann Hesse Editor's Archive, Volker Michels, Offenbach. While this letter convinces Michels that Hesse made a serious attempt to end his life on 20 June 1892, the reaction of Christoph Blumhardt – who was present when Hesse returned later that

[I looked death in the eye and had no fear. I looked right into the barrel of a loaded revolver and pulled the trigger.]

The reaction of Christoph Blumhardt to this episode, however, fails to corroborate Hermann's claim of having made a genuine attempt to take his own life. Upon Hermann's return to Blumhardt's institution on the same day as the alleged suicide attempt, the latter wrote to Marie Hesse:

> Liebe Frau Missionar!
> Heute lief uns Ihr Sohn weg mit Hinterlassung von Selbstmorddrohungen. Er hatte sich vorher heimlich Geld geborgt und einen Revolver gekauft. Er ist wieder da. Ich nehme es als Bubenstreich, aber in so krankhafter Weise, daß ich dringend mit Ihnen beraten muß.[34]
>
> [Dear Mrs. Hesse!
> Today your son ran away from here, leaving suicide threats behind. Before he left, he secretly borrowed some money and bought a revolver. He has returned. I look at the matter as a childish prank, but one that is so abnormal that I consider it urgent to consult with you.]

The erratic behavioral patterns of the adolescent Hermann Hesse, to be sure, may be described as extreme, but if one even briefly reflects upon the oppressive family and school structures to which he was subjected, Hesse's variously anomalous phases of behavior must be characterized as well within the realm of normal adolescent rebelliousness. In his 1929 "psychograph" of Hermann Hesse, Hugo Mauerhofer characterized the teenage Hesse as "introverted" and "narcissistic," noting the youth's "self-critical stance" and commenting further:

---

day – makes a genuine suicide attempt seem less than likely. Still, Michels's contention that Hesse was not given to "Renommiererei" leaves the matter of the letter to Otto Hartmann rather unresolved; only Hermann Hesse knew for certain whether or not he had indeed pulled the trigger on 20 June 1892. In a recent book on Hesse's life, Christian Immo Schneider goes so far as to assert that the incident was indeed a suicide attempt that almost succeeded: "um ein Haar [wäre es] auch gelungen, wenn der Revolver nicht versagt hätte." In *Hermann Hesse* (Munich, 1991), p. 20. ["It came within a hair of succeeding and would have, had the revolver not malfunctioned."] Unfortunately (and annoyingly), Schneider fails to provide a reference to the source of this information.

34. Letter of 20 June 1892 from Christoph Blumhardt to Marie Hesse, in *Kindheit und Jugend* 1: 220. In Marie Hesse's own diary, she refers to this letter from Blumhardt as follows: "Am 21. Juni beim Frühstück kam von Boll ein Brief, ich möchte sofort kommen, denn gestern habe Hermann einen Selbstmordversuch gemacht." Ibid., 221. ["On 21 June, while we were at breakfast, a letter arrived from Boll, saying that I had better come right away, for Hermann had attempted to kill himself the day before."]

Diese über sich selbst Rechenschaft ablegende Haltung, die … aus
der Introversion resultiert, tritt schon beim jungen Hesse mit einer
eigensinnigen Vehemenz hervor, welche die Anpassungsschwierig-
keiten des Knaben und Schülers erklärt.[35]
[This self-critical attitude … a symptom of introversion, manifested
itself, even in Hesse's earlier years, with a stubborn intensity that
explains the difficulties he had in adapting to his surroundings as a
preschooler and grade-school pupil.]

This relatively mild evaluation, not unlike that rendered by Pastor
Schall and noted above, hardly reveals the profoundly disturbed
personality implicit in the diagnosis of "primary insanity." In fact,
one may justifiably consider that the not yet seventeen-year-old
Hesse was rather "back to normal" by the time he began his ap-
prenticeship at Perrot's clock factory in June of 1894. And by the
time he began his training as a bookseller in Tübingen the follow-
ing year, Hermann Hesse's adolescent crises were over; there is
much evidence to indicate that his life and his personality had
indeed stabilized.

That stability, however, was not achieved through any kind of
resolution of differences between Hesse and his parents, but rather
by Hesse's gradually pulling away from the family, a development
that would only partially be facilitated by his move to Tübingen in
1895. His relationship with his father, particularly, had been
severely undermined during the years of adolescent crisis. As
Ralph Freedman notes, Hesse "felt betrayed, especially by his
father … when he was needed at the time of Maulbronn, he had
been absent, and now, when he was needed even more, he exiled

35. Dr. Hugo Mauerhofer, *Die Introversion – Mit spezieller Berücksichtigung des
Dichters H. Hesse* (Bern and Leipzig, 1929), 32–33. It seems curious that this inter-
esting, if somewhat superficially researched study (unable to approach Hesse
himself, Mauerhofer relied heavily on Hugo Ball's 1927 Hesse biography), has
been almost completely ignored by Hesse scholars. Only Joseph Mileck (*Hermann
Hesse: Biography and Bibliography*) notes the existence of Mauerhofer's work, listing
also a letter written by the psychologist to Hesse that was published in the Swiss
newspaper *Der Bund* in 1937 (Mileck, 2: 961). Hesse's own reaction to Mauerhofer's
work is contained in a letter he wrote to Fritz Marti on 17 August 1929, shortly after
the latter (who was literary editor for the *Neue Zürcher Zeitung*) had sent him the
book: "Mit dem Mauerhofer kann ich wenig anfangen, doch ist er viel besser und
gewissenhafter als Schmid [Hans Rudolf Schmid, *Hermann Hesse* (Frauenfeld/
Leipzig, 1928)]. Die Feststellung, daß ein Dichter als Neurotiker einer bestimmten
Klasse zugehört, sagt über ihn so wenig aus als über Napoleon die Feststellung, er
sei Epileptiker gewesen. Und über die komplizierten Fragen, die dann entstehen,
wenn ein Dichter zeitweise seine eigene Neurose (weil sie Zeitsymptom ist) zum
Gegenstand der Dichtung macht, hat die Broschüre leider gar nichts zutage

him."[36] Johannes Hesse did, of course, strive to assure that his problematic son would be trained for some kind of trade, yet even those well-meant attempts were prompted by a rather impersonal and utilitarian motivation on the father's part. For example, just days after Hermann left the *Gymnasium* in Cannstatt on 15 October 1893, his father, through the intervention of David Gundert (Marie Hesse's youngest brother), arranged for his son to enter an apprenticeship as a bookseller in Esslingen. When Hermann fled that position on his fourth day of work, Johannes sought to commit him to yet another institution, the clinic of a certain Dr. Zeller in Winnenden near Stuttgart, noting in his appeal to the latter:

> Mein Sohn Hermann, 16 1/3 Jahr alt, scheint an "moral insanity" zu leiden.[37]
>
> [My son Hermann, sixteen and one-third years old, seems to suffer from "moral insanity."]

(The book dealer in Esslingen with whom Hesse was to complete a year-long apprenticeship, S. Mayer, noted the youth's "severe lack of firmness of will,"[38] a rather conclusive diagnosis considering that the man had known Hesse for only four days!)

As mentioned above, Hesse's relationship with his father suffered substantially during his later school years; indeed, it is probably no distortion of fact to say that father and son essentially never overcame the consequences of the emotional estrangement stemming from the experiences of those years. When Hesse and his sister Adele published recollections of their father in *Zum Gedächtnis unseres Vaters* (1930), Hesse, then fifty-three years old, noted in the epilogue that only twice in his life had he written straightforwardly and without literary intent about his father.[39] Both of those occurrences are included in that slim volume; one of them is the essay *Zum Gedächtnis*, rather documentary in tone,

---

gebracht." In *Briefe*, 2: 223. ["I don't put much stock in Mauerhofer, but he is much better and much more conscientious than Schmid. To say that a writer, as a neurotic, belongs to a certain class says as little about him as the statement that Napoleon was an epileptic. As for the complicated questions that arise when a writer at times makes his own neurosis (as a symptom of the times) the object of his writing, the little book, unfortunately, has nothing at all to say."]

36. Freedman, *Hermann Hesse: Pilgrim of Crisis*, 49.

37. Letter from Johannes Hesse to Dr. Zeller, 1 November 1893, *Kindheit und Jugend*, 1: 402.

38. Letter from S. Mayer to Johannes Hesse, 4 November 1893, *Kindheit und Jugend*, 1: 406.

39. Hermann and Adele Hesse, *Zum Gedächtnis unseres Vaters* (Tübingen, 1930), 78.

which Hesse composed shortly after his father's death in April of 1916. The other piece is a ten-page excerpt from the opening chapter of *Hermann Lauscher* (1900), entitled "Meine Kindheit," a short, utterly autobiographical recollection of the relationship between the preadolescent Hesse and his father. It is of no small significance that "Meine Kindheit" was completed already in 1896, a separately composed recounting of early school and family experiences that culminates in the school vacation before Hesse's entrance into the Maulbronn seminary in September of 1891. The final pages recall the thirteen-year-old's successful completion of the *Landexamen* in July of that year, and the author, now five years older, makes little attempt to hide his yearning for the innocence and simplicity of life before Maulbronn and for the closeness and camaraderie he felt, at least in retrospect, for his father.

> Das Examen wurde leidlich bestanden. Meine erste Schulzeit war zu Ende, und ein sommerlicher Ferienmonat lag vor dem ehrgeizig erstrebten Eingang der gelehrten Klosterpforte.
>
> In diesen Ferien las mir mein Vater zum erstenmal Lieder Goethes vor. "Über allen Gipfeln" war sein Liebling.
>
> An einem silbernen Abend, im frühen Monde, stand er mit mir auf einem bewaldeten Berge. Wir atmeten vom Steigen aus und schwiegen nach einem ernsten, herzlichen Gespräch vor der Schönheit der mondhellen, stillen Landschaft.
>
> Mein Vater setzte sich auf einen Stein, blickte rundum, zog mich zu sich nieder, schlang den Arm um mich und sprach leise und feierlich jenes unergründliche, wunderbare Lied:
>
>> Über allen Gipeln
>> Ist Ruh.
>> In allen Wipfeln
>> Spürest du
>> Kaum einen Hauch,
>> Die Vöglein schweigen im Walde,
>> Warte nur, balde
>> Ruhest du auch.
>
> Hundertmal habe ich seitdem die Worte gehört und gelesen und gesprochen, in hundert Lagen und Stimmungen – Die Vöglein schweigen im Walde –, und jedesmal befiel mich eine milde, herzerlösende Schwermut, und jedesmal senkte ich dabei das Haupt und hatte ein seltsam wehes Glücksgefühl, als kämen die Worte aus dem Munde meines an mich gelehnten Vaters, als fühlte ich seinen Arm um mich gelegt, und sähe seine große, klare Stirn, und hörte seine leise Stimme.[40]

40. Hermann Hesse, *Hermann Lauscher* (Frankfurt/M., 1976), 38–40.

[I passed the examination with decent results. Thus, the first phase of my schooling was finished, and a month of summer vacation stood between me and admission to the seminary that I had worked so hard to attain.

During this vacation, my father read some of Goethe's poems aloud to me for the first time. *Another Night Song* was his favorite.

One silver-tinged evening, with a new moon above, we stood together on a wooded mountain. We were breathing heavily from the climb and fell silent after a solemn but affectionate exchange about the beauty of the quiet countryside, now bathed in moonlight.

My father sat down on a rock and surveyed the area all around us; he pulled me down upon his knee, wrapped his arm around me, then softly and solemnly recited that unfathomably wonderful verse:

> O'er all the hill-tops
> Is quiet now,
> In all the tree-tops
> Hearest thou
> Hardly a breath;
> The birds are asleep in the trees:
> Wait, soon like these
> Thou, too, shalt rest.

I've heard, read, and recited those words a hundred times since then, in a hundred different situations and a hundred different moods: *The birds are asleep in the trees.* Every time, I was overcome by a gentle melancholy that freed my heart, and every time, I bowed my head and sensed a strangely sorrowful yet contented feeling, as if the words came from my father's mouth, as if he were leaning upon me with his arm around me, as if I were looking up at his broad, smooth forehead and were listening to his soft voice.][41]

Hermann Hesse expresses here most eloquently the genuine fondness he felt for his father in the final summer of his childhood, yet language and imagery acknowledge, with unmistakable lucidity, the irrefutable ephemerality of the experience. Indeed, the oxymorons ("milde, herzerlösende Schwermut," "wehes Glücksgefühl") hint broadly at the *Schein-Geborgenheit* and ambiguity of this remembered camaraderie, while the contrary-to-fact verb forms that dominate the passage's concluding clauses stress the irretrievability of that juvenile idyll.

Who can say to what extent Hesse reacted, at least subconsciously, with frustration and anger at the dissolution of that close,

41. Translation of "Another Night Song" by Henry Wadsworth Longfellow, included in *Johann Wolfgang Goethe: Selected Poems*, ed. Christopher Middleton (Boston, 1983), 59.

if temporary bond with his father? It seems no exaggeration to contend that the brevity of this blissful phase in the father-son relationship, not to mention the abruptness with which it undoubtedly seemed to Hermann Hesse to end as he was packed off to the seminary in Maulbronn, contributed significantly to a kind of existential crisis that effected much of the volatile and erratic behavior during Hesse's adolescent years.

In the absence of a continuing and supportive relationship with his father, Hermann Hesse often seemed to seek the friendship of older men who served as surrogate fathers. In the decade from 1892 to 1902, during which Hesse completed his formal schooling, and his apprenticeships as machinist and bookseller, and worked in the book trade in Tübingen and Basel, there were several father figures who influenced and nurtured the young man: Dr. Ernst Kapff, his teacher at the Cannstatt *Gymnasium*; the bookseller Hermes at Heckenhauer's in Tübingen; Dr. Rudolf Wackernagel-Burckhardt, the Basel historian; and the Hessian pastor and poet, Karl Ernst Knodt. Even Heinrich Perrot, in whose clock factory Hesse completed a fourteen-month apprenticeship in 1894–95, seems, at least marginally, to have set a fatherly example of industry and self-discipline.

Under Perrot's tutelage, as Bernhard Zeller has noted, Hesse became "a 'practical' person ... and did not consider the time spent in this apprenticeship as lost time . . .";[42] as a token of that experience, Hesse named a key character in *Das Glasperlenspiel*, Bastian Perrot, after his former *Meister*. It was virtually inevitable, however, that Hesse would not be fulfilled by the daily work routine at Perrot's. He began to develop a kind of *Doppelleben*, faithfully executing the increasingly monotonous tasks of filing and polishing metal clock parts by day, while in his free time savoring the quite respectable holdings in the home libraries of his parents and his grandfather Gundert. Indeed, during those fifteen months in Calw, Hermann Hesse established the balanced pattern of work, reading, and extensive correspondence that he would maintain with remarkable steadfastness for nearly a decade. In what amounted, psychologically, to an almost therapeutic kind of "backtracking," he renewed contact with some of his friends from the Maulbronn days – in particular, Wilhelm Lang and Theodor Rümelin – and also wrote to his former Cannstatt teacher, Dr. Ernst Kapff, who quickly and willingly assumed the role of teacher-critic

---

42. Zeller, *Hermann Hesse mit Selbstzeugnissen und Bilddokumenten*, 30.

in the ensuing correspondence, acting as a sounding board for the literary and philosophical views now being stimulated and informed by Hesse's extensive reading. Though Hesse's first letter to Kapff, probably written in April of 1895, has yet to be located, the latter's obviously warm response heartened his former pupil, who immediately began to compose a reply that was nearly three thousand words long and two weeks in the writing! Along with a rather detailed enumeration of his ongoing study of German, Russian, French, and English literature, Hesse also reflected in the letter on the personal changes he had experienced during the nearly two-year period since he had least seen Kapff:

> Jetzt erst habe ich allmählich wieder Ruhe und Heiterkeit gefunden, bin geistig gesund geworden – von jener Zeit voll Zorn und Haß und Selbstmordgedanken will ich nimmer sprechen ... Jetzt ist diese Zeit vorbei. Immerhin hat sie mein dichterisches Ich ausgebildet; die tollste Sturm- und Drangzeit ist glücklich überstanden.[43]
>
> [Only now have I gradually achieved some peace and serenity and have healed psychologically. I don't want to speak, ever again, of that phase filled with anger and hatred and thoughts of suicide ... That time is now past. Nonetheless, it did hone my poetic persona; I succeeded in surviving the wildest period of storm and stress.]

Lamenting the complete absence in Calw of friends with whom he could talk about anything beyond everyday, mundane matters, he then summarized quite candidly his relationship with his father, while scarcely concealing his hope that Kapff would assume the role of substitute father:

> Mein Vater ist zu einseitig mit seiner literarischen Tagesarbeit beschäftigt, um sich für mein Dichten zu interessieren; immerhin verdanke ich ihm viel: Er hat mir von Kind auf mit Sorgfalt und feinem Geschmack die beste Lektüre gegeben ... jetzt aber "wandl' ich allein". So danke ich Ihnen doppelt, daß Sie sich meiner annehmen.[44]
>
> [My father is too exclusively occupied with his everyday writing work to be interested in *my* writing. Still, I have much to thank him for: from the time I was a child, he has taken great care and exercised exquisite taste in selecting what I should read ... now, though, I am on my own. That's why I am doubly grateful to you for coming to my aid.]

43. Letter to Dr. Ernst Kapff, started on 14 May, completed on 1 June 1895, *Kindheit und Jugend*, 1: 468.
44. Ibid., 464.

During his final months in Calw and his first year in Tübingen, Hesse wrote a total of twelve letters to Ernst Kapff, many of which were accompanied by newly composed poems, and there can be no question that it was Ernst Kapff with whom Hesse discussed most openly, even effusively, his personal situation as well as his vocational hopes and plans. For example, Kapff seems to have been the only correspondent outside of the Hesse-Gundert family to whom Hesse revealed his desire to emigrate to Brazil,[45] and his mentor was also among the first to learn of Hesse's decision to pursue an apprenticeship as a bookseller. Kapff's serious, comprehensive, yet largely benevolent "reviews" of Hesse's early attempts at lyric poetry also doubtlessly encouraged the budding poet, who soon even felt secure enough in his literary judgments to critique Kapff's own authorial endeavors.[46] In view of all that, it is somewhat inexplicable that Hesse apparently did not write to Ernst Kapff again after September 1896, even though Kapff wrote him sporadically over the following two decades, for the last time in 1915! While it would be logical to assume that Hesse dutifully cultivated his end of the correspondence – he was known, after all, as a meticulously faithful respondent throughout his life – a letter penned decades later to his boyhood friend Erwin Moser seems to confirm that his own correspondence with Kapff was relatively short-lived:

Lieber Moser!
... Du nennst in Deinem Brief unter unsern Lehrern auch den Dr. Kapff.
Mit dem hatte ich noch nach seinem Tode [26 December 1944] ein merkwürdiges Erlebnis. Ich habe mit ihm von Calw und Tübingen aus, als ich etwa 17 Jahre alt war, Briefe gewechselt, und er

45. In fact, Kapff seems to have been quite seriously considering emigration himself and suggested Brazil as a possible destination for his former pupil, whose notions of emigrating were, up to that time, quite vague. (See Hesse's letter of 15 June 1895 to Kapff, *Kindheit und Jugend*, 1: 487ff.) Kapff's own reasons for emigrating were fascinating, having to do with the possibility of reestablishing "eine deutsche Kultur ... die tatsächlich früher bestanden hat (in den Reichsstädten, in Universitäten u[nd] a[nderswo])." (Ernst Kapff, letter to Hermann Hesse of 28 September 1895, quoted here from *Kindheit und Jugend*, 2: 555). ["a German culture ... which really did exist earlier (in the free cities of the *Reich*, in universities and elsewhere)."]

46. See, for example, Hesse's letters of 6 November 1895 and April 1896 to Ernst Kapff in *Kindheit und Jugend*, 2: 32ff. and 2: 96ff. Kapff did not limit his critiques to the freshly penned poems Hesse sent to him, but also wrote a lengthy personal review of Hesse's *Romantische Lieder* (1898) in an unpublished letter to the young author dated 23 January 1899 located in the Hesse Archives, Marbach.

besaß ein ganzes Bündel Briefe und Gedichte von mir aus jener Zeit. Später hatte ich keine Verbindung mehr mit ihm.[47]

[Dear Moser!

... You mentioned in your letter, among others of our former teachers, our Dr. Kapff.

I had a rather strange experience with him, even after he had died (26 December, 1944). When I was around seventeen and living in Calw and Tübingen, he and I exchanged letters, so he had a whole bundle of letters and poems I sent him back then. I had no contact with him after that.]

Nonetheless, on 1 October 1895, just days before he would accept the apprenticeship offer from Heckenhauer's in Tübingen, Hesse wrote to Ernst Kapff of the decision to look for such a position; at the same time, he left open entirely the possibility of leaving Europe for Brazil, noting that his "somewhat vague dreams and plans to go to Brazil" were beginning to take more concrete form.[48] In the next paragraph, however, Hesse described his decision to enter the apprenticeship:

[Ich] bin ... im Einverständnis mit meinen Eltern zum Entschluß gekommen ... Kaufmann zu werden. Da Buchführung etc. doch Hauptsache ist, werde ich vielleicht statt einem andern Handlungsfach mich dem Buchhandel widmen, also eine regelrechte buchhändlerische Lehrzeit durchmachen.[49]

[In agreement with my parents, I have decided to go into the retail business. Since bookkeeping etc. is the main thing to learn anyway, I may take up the bookselling trade and go through a regular apprenticeship as a bookseller.]

---

47. Letter of February, 1949 from Hesse to Erwin Moser, *Briefe*, 4: 16. Hesse describes here how the elderly Kapff, living then in Göppingen, had apparently allowed himself to be talked out of that "Bündel" of letters and early poems by a former book dealer there: "[U]nd dieser Mann kam vor einigen Monaten in die Schweiz, um aus diesen handschriftlichen Briefen Geld zu machen." ["And this man came to Switzerland a few months ago to try to turn these handwritten letters into money."] Hesse met with the man and purchased the entire packet in 1948 for the considerable sum of one thousand Swiss francs! These letters, ostensibly constituting Hesse's entire correspondence with Kapff, were housed in the Marbach Hesse Achives after the author's death in 1962. Why Hesse might have abruptly broken off the correspondence with his former teacher after writing to him in September 1896 remains a complete mystery, the more so in view of his having spent a most enjoyable Sunday visit with Kapff in Cannstatt on 16 August 1896. See Hesse's letter to his parents of 16 August 1896, *Kindheit und Jugend*, 2: 128.

48. Letter of 1 October 1895 from Hesse to Ernst Kapff, *Kindheit und Jugend*, 2: 9.

49. Ibid., 10.

A comparison of that contemporary depiction, by the way, with another contained in Hesse's retrospective *Erinnerung an Hans* (1935) provides a somewhat contradictory, but almost certainly more candid perspective on the motivation for that decision:

> Auch als ich, nach schweren Kämpfen, den Eltern nachgab und mich einem Beruf und einer Lehrzeit unterzog, als Buchhändler, hatte ich es im Blick auf mein Ziel getan, es war eine Anpassung, ein vorläufiger Kompromiß gewesen. Ich war Buchhändler geworden, um zunächst einmal von den Eltern unabhängig zu werden, auch um ihnen zu zeigen, daß ich im Notfall mich beherrschen und etwas im bürgerlichen Leben leisten könne.[50]

> [Even when, after difficult battles with my parents, I gave in to them and subjected myself to an apprenticeship as a bookseller, I did so with an eye to my eventual goal; it was nothing more than a concession to them, a temporary compromise. I became a bookseller to become independent of my parents, but also to show that, if I had to, I could exercise self-control and accomplish something in middle-class society.]

---

50. Hermann Hesse, "Erinnerung an Hans," *Werke*, 10: 223.

THE TÜBINGEN YEARS

Not Quite "Breaking Away"

Bookseller and *Privatstudent*

Tagesplan.
Aufstehen: 20 Minuten vor 7 Uhr.
Kaffee: nach 7 Uhr.
Geschäft beginnt: 1/2 8 Uhr.
Zum Essen: 12 oder 12 1/4 Uhr.
Ins Geschäft: 1 1/4 oder 1 1/2 Uhr.
Abends heim: 7 1/2 bis 7 3/4 Uhr.
Zu Bett: zwischen 9 3/4 und 10 1/4.
Gevespert wird während der Arbeit.[1]
[Daily schedule.
Rise at 6:40.
Coffee after 7:00.
Work begins at 7:30.
Go to lunch at 12:00 or 12:15.
Back to work at 1:15 or 1:30.
Leave work evenings at 7:30 to 7:45.
Go to bed between 9:45 and 10:15.
Eat supper at work.]

O n 3 October 1895, Hermann Hesse's advertisement seeking an apprenticeship position appeared in the *Schwäbischer Merkur* in Stuttgart. The next day, the owner of Heckenhauer's bookstore and antiquarian shop in Tübingen, Carl August Sonnewald, wrote to offer Hesse a three-year apprenticeship in his establishment. By mid-October, all remaining formalities had been attended to, and

---

1. Letter of 18–20 October 1895 to his parents, *Kindheit und Jugend*, 2: 23.

Hesse was ready to undertake the move to a new locale and a new life; in Ralph Freedman's words, all this "was his own."[2]

The extent to which Hermann Hesse would be allowed to become fully his own man, however, was rather strictly curtailed from the outset. Several days before Hesse's departure, Johannes Hesse presented his son with a list of ten "rules" for Tübingen, which included a precise delineation of Hermann's life and routine there: He would live in a rented room in the home of Frau Leopold, a dean's widow and Hesse family acquaintance, just outside the old city; she was to provide most of his meals, dole out his weekly pocket money (one and a half marks), as well as money for all other personal needs; the young Hesse was forbidden to charge anything or to borrow money from anyone, or to take any book from his place of employment on loan without the express permission of Sonnewald; Hermann was to reduce smoking to an absolute minimum and to avoid playing cards for money. Finally (rules number 9 and 10), the young man was instructed to send home to Calw all laundry, including items in need of mending, along with any requests for writing paper, pens, and the like: "things can always be sent along with the laundry."[3] On a symbolic level, Hesse's sending his laundry home for washing and, as it were, "inspection," invites a rather obvious Freudian interpretation. Viewed from a utilitarian perspective, however, the regular exchange of laundry bundles underlines the relative proximity of the two towns, Tübingen and Calw, which even then were little more than an hour apart by train. To be sure, Hermann Hesse had succeeded in "leaving home," but the ties to Calw remained numerous and substantial.[4]

2. Freedman, *Hermann Hesse: Pilgrim of Crisis*, 56.
3. List written by Johannes Hesse, 12 October 1895, in *Kindheit und Jugend*, 2: 18. In fairness to the parents, one must note that they obviously remembered all too clearly their son's difficulties in managing his own affairs during his Cannstatt days (1892–93). Still, Hesse is reported to have referred to the list as his "ten commandments for Tübingen."
4. Along with numerous other family friends and acquaintances, Hesse's younger sister Marulla (1880–1953) was living in Tübingen when Hermann arrived there. She spent a year, from Easter 1895 to Easter 1896, at a boarding school for girls run by a Frau von Reutern and was visited regularly by her brother, whose route home from work took him past the school. Hesse also describes regular Sunday visits to his Aunt Elisabeth Gundert, widow of his mother's brother Samuel Gundert, who had moved with her children to Tübingen a year or so before Hesse's arrival there. Her son Hermann was a student at the university during Hesse's years in Tübingen.

Those familial obligations, however, had at least one positive side, for the eighteen-year-old Hesse began immediately to exploit the epistolary "reports" he was rather expected to write home as a means of honing his own creative writing skills. Hermann Hesse assumed the role of *Lauscher*, the listener, observer, and chronicler who was to become the protagonist in his first major piece of prose, *Hinterlassene Schriften und Gedichte von Hermann Lauscher* (1901), providing his correspondents, even in his earliest letters, with comprehensive descriptions of city and surroundings, store and personnel, as well as his own living quarters.[5] As he progressed in his "private studies" during the Tübingen years, his letters increasingly contained reflections on the content of his readings, fulfilling much the same function as his ongoing correspondence with Ernst Kapff.

Hesse's daily routine at Heckenhauer's consisted of anything but intellectually challenging activity: his tasks included packing books for shipment, delivering orders in person to the homes of professors at the university or statements of delinquent accounts to fraternity students, sorting the rare book holdings, and filing bills. Despite his lowly status as apprentice, he noted frequently in his letters that he got on well with most of his younger co-workers. Among the firm's permanent employees, Hesse often mentioned the head clerk, Heinrich Hermes, describing him in an early letter to his parents as "the pride of the company" and a "bon vivant" who spoke several languages, was completely conversant on the subject of literature, yet also knowledgeable about politics.[6]

The head of the firm, Carl August Sonnewald, received less favorable treatment in Hesse's recounting; while noting that he had "tremendous respect" for Sonnewald, he also described him as "very educated, but he speaks Swabian."[7] There are also some

5. In his Hesse biography, Ralph Freedman paraphrases at length from an unpublished letter written by Hesse on 17 October 1895 and housed in the Marbach archives (Freedman, *Hermann Hesse: Pilgrim of Crisis*, 58.) In his own words, Freedman presents Hesse's fascinating depiction of his reception at Heckenhauer's, his feelings upon entering the store, Sonnewald's appearance, etc.; according to this letter, he was put right to work and did not leave the store until 7:30 that evening, the regular closing time, although he had not yet even had time to move into his room.

6. Letter of 23–27 October 1895 to Johannes and Marie Hesse, *Kindheit und Jugend*, 2: 24ff. Hermes would often provide advice and counsel to the young apprentice bookseller during his nearly four years in Tübingen.

7. Zeller, *Hermann Hesse mit Selbstzeugnissen und Bilddokumenten*, 31. In his biography of Hermann Hesse, Ralph Freedman quotes an unpublished Hesse letter in

indications in Hesse's letters of the time that Sonnewald was not the most pleasant person for whom to work. In a letter to his parents dated 14 June 1896, just a little more than half a year after beginning at Heckenhauer's, an obviously disheartened Hesse spoke plainly about his work and his relationship with the firm's proprietor:

> Es wird mich doch schlauchen, wenn Herr Sonnewald zurückkommt und sein Schimpfen wieder beginnt. Doch werde ich dann vielleicht ungestörter sein, jetzt bin ich eben Hundejunge für die Andern.[8]
> [It will be really be hard on me when Herr Sonnewald comes back and starts his nagging again. But maybe I will be left alone then, right now I am just the low man on the totem pole.]

In his Hesse biography, Ralph Freedman cites an unpublished letter in which Hesse describes Sonnewald's absolute obsession with money, noting that the word *Geld* seemed to occur in nearly every sentence the firm's proprietor spoke.[9]

As previously mentioned, it was merely coincidental that Hermann Hesse found himself in Tübingen, since his search for an apprenticeship could have taken him to almost any city or town in Swabia or beyond. Would he have pursued his *Privatstudien* with such zeal and rigor had he not found a position in a university town? He would almost certainly have continued to read voraciously, but he might well have proceeded less methodically, had his direct contact with Tübingen students, for example, not reminded him daily of the readings expected of a legitimate university student. A more important impetus, however, was likely the

which the young apprentice described Sonnewald's regular usage of rather coarse terms such as *Rindvieh* or *Saukerl*, especially in reference to delinquent customers. (Freedman, *Hermann Hesse: Pilgrim of Crisis*, 60). The original letter from Hesse to his parents, dated 31 October-2 November 1895, is in the Hesse Archives, Marbach. It should be noted here that Hermann Hesse himself did not speak a Swabian dialect as his everyday tongue, probably because neither of his parents was Swabian by birth; as he mentioned in his autobiographical fragment, *Kindheit des Zauberers*, his father spoke "Englisch und ein reines, klares, schönes, leicht baltisch gefärbtes Deutsch." (*Werke* 6: 378) ["English and a pure, clear, beautiful, slightly Baltic flavored German."] Thus, the clear implication here is that Sonnewald's Swabian speech diminished his educated status in Hesse's eyes.

8. Letter to Johannes and Marie Hesse, 14–15 June 1896. Although the letter is included in *Kindheit und Jugend* (2: 115ff.), this passage was omitted. It is quoted here, with the friendly permission of Volker Michels, from a copy in the Hermann Hesse Editor's Archive, Offenbach.

9. Freedman, *Hermann Hesse: Pilgrim of Crisis*, 60. The original letter from Hesse to his parents, dated 31 October-2 November 1895, is in the Hesse Archives, Marbach.

presence of several former schoolmates from Calw, Göppingen, Maulbronn, and Cannstatt who were now studying in Tübingen. Within a few weeks of his arrival in Tübingen, Hesse was already in contact with acquaintances from earlier years.[10] While most of them were also newcomers in Tübingen and had little time for him, Wilhelm Lang, a roommate of Hesse's back in Maulbronn, paid the young bookseller weekly visits:

> Meine Bekannten, die Studenten sind, sind zu beschäftigt mit Studieren und Kommersieren, als daß sie mich aufsuchen könnten. Nicht so mein lieber Lang, der mit rührender Aufmerksamkeit sich jede Woche einen Abend (meist freitags) im Stift losmacht und den weiten Weg zu mir kommt, um bis 10 Uhr auf meiner Bude zu bleiben.[11]

> [My acquaintances, mostly students, are too busy with studies and drinking bouts to be able to look me up. That is not the case, though, with my dear friend Lang, who is touchingly attentive to me, tearing himself away from the seminary one evening a week (usually Friday) and making the long walk to my place, where he stays until ten.]

A letter to Ernst Kapff, dated 6 December 1895, similarly confirms that Hesse suffered no lack of opportunity to engage socially with students and was occasionally even invited to fraternity gatherings, which, initially at least, seem not to have been particularly anathematic to the young bookseller:

> Ich habe das Vergnügen, fast jede Woche Gast einer Verbindung zu sein, da ich überall ein paar "Bekannte" habe und in Seminaristenkreisen für etwas Interessantes gelte … Es liegt etwas Poetisches im Studenten-, d. h. Verbindungsleben, aber lauter längst gemünztes Gold, wenig wertvolle Anregung – fahrende-gesellenliederliche Anwandlungen gestatte ich mir ungern.[12]

> [I have the pleasure of being the guest of a fraternity almost every week, since I have "acquaintances" all over the place here and am

---

10. As he noted in a letter to his parents on 31 October 1895, Hesse had already been the guest of a fraternity in which several former schoolmates from Göppingen were members.

11. Letter of 20 November 1895 to Johannes and Marie Hesse, *Kindheit und Jugend*, 2: 34f.

12. Letter of 6 December 1895 to Ernst Kapff, *Kindheit und Jugend*, 2: 39. Hesse, at least according to his own depiction, seems to have been considered "something interesting" among the seminarians because of his infamous flight from the seminary at Maulbronn. It may well have been the novelty of that adventure, especially for all the others who, for better or for worse, had persevered and eventually become students at the *Stift* in Tübingen, that lent Hermann Hesse the aura of being exotic.

considered in seminary circles to be a somewhat interesting person
... There is something poetic in student life, that is in the social life
of the fraternities, but it's really nothing original and provides little
stimulation of much value – I am not wild about playing the role of
the vagrant singer-scholar.]

This phase in Hesse's Tübingen years, however, passed quickly. In
January 1896, he mentioned to his parents that he had been suf-
fering "for weeks from a distinct, almost anxious shyness of oth-
ers, i.e., of social contact ..."[13] and by spring 1896, in a letter to
Kapff, he lamented his loneliness openly:

Seltsam, daß ich seit meiner Schulzeit immer zur Einsamkeit ver-
dammt war, die mir endlich zur Freundin geworden ist. Ich finde
keinen Freund, vielleicht weil ich stolz bin und nicht werben mag
... Seit mindestens zwei, drei Monaten bin ich Abend für Abend,
Sonntag für Sonntag allein gewesen ... wirklich ist mir der Brief-
wechsel mit Ihnen fast der einzige lebendige Umgang.[14]

[It's strange that ever since my days at school I have always been
damned to loneliness, and now it has become my girlfriend. I can't
seem to make a friend, perhaps because I am proud and don't care
to court friendship ... For at least two or three months, I have been
alone, every evening, every weekend ... my correspondence with
you is just about my only human contact.]

As the May wedding of his half brother Theo Isenberg approached,
Hesse asked his sister Adele to read a new poem he had written
for the occasion, since he planned to beg off attending, though he
greatly admired and looked up to the older Theo. Even the latter's
own plea, along with an offer to write to Sonnewald requesting
permission for Hermann to be granted a free Saturday, did not
dissuade Hesse, and his mother's last appeal was, presumably,
also unsuccessful.

Adele läßt schön grüßen und will Deinen Auftrag pünktlich erfül-
len. Aber wir alle meinen, Du sollest, wenn irgend möglich, zur
Hochzeit kommen ... Ein solches Familienfest ist ja doch etwas
Seltenes und Erhebendes.[15]

13. Undated letter (between 28 and 30 January 1896) to Johannes and Marie
Hesse, *Kindheit und Jugend,* 2: 63.

14. Letter of April 1896 to Ernst Kapff, *Kindheit und Jugend,* 2: 97.

15. Letter of 24 April 1896 from Marie Hesse to Hermann Hesse, *Kindheit und
Jugend,* 2: 100. There is no conclusive written evidence, in letters from Hesse or his
family, to indicate that Hermann indeed avoided the wedding, although all of his
statements in the weeks preceding the event make clear that he had no intention of
attending; in the spring of 1896, as has been noted, he was anything but desirous of

[Adele sends her best and intends to carry out your wishes right on time. But we are all of the opinion that you should, if at all possible, come to the wedding ... This kind of family get-together is, after all, something special and uplifting.]

Mired in introversive reflection, however, Hermann Hesse was interested in anything but a huge family affair, no matter how "rare" and "uplifting" that occasion might seem to his mother.

Both Bernhard Zeller and Ralph Freedman interpret this turn of events during Hesse's first year in Tübingen as further evidence of his inclination to assume the status of "loner" or "outsider," an assessment bolstered by the passage just quoted. Hesse must soon have sensed the distance, both social and vocational, between him and his student acquaintances; while the latter seemed to have nearly unlimited free time for drinking bouts and other "student" activities, Hesse increasingly treasured his few leisure hours, which he used almost exclusively for pursuing his autodidactic goals:

> Auch ist mir nun meine Freizeit doppelt kostbar, da ich Herrn Hermes durch einen Besuch und sonstige Liebenswürdigkeit bestochen habe, mir eine schöne Bibliothek, deren Verwalter er ist, zugänglich zu machen.[16]
> [My free time has become doubly precious to me since, by paying Hermes a visit and being nice to him, I have been able to gain access to a wonderful private library which he oversees.]

In Freedman's view, Hermann Hesse's *Privatstudien* were motivated, at least in part, by his need to compensate for the intellectual milieu in which he found himself:

---

fulfilling a major familial obligation. A photograph included in *Kindheit und Jugend* (2: 192) shows all the Hesse-Isenberg siblings, along with Theo's bride, Martha Cohen, in what distinctly appears to be a festive occasion; according to the picture's caption, that is precisely what it is: "Hermann Hesse und seine Geschwister während der Hochzeit seines Halbbruders Theo Isenberg im April 1896." ["Hermann Hesse and his siblings during the wedding of his half brother Theo Isenberg in April 1896."] This information, however, is almost certainly inaccurate, for the same photograph is also contained in *Hermann Hesse – Sein Leben in Bildern und Texten*, ed. Volker Michels (Frankfurt/M., 1979), p. 59 with the caption: "Hermann Hesse und seine Geschwister im Oktober 1893 anläßlich der Verlobung seines Halbbruders Theo Isenberg." ["Hermann Hesse and his siblings in October 1893 on the occasion of the engagement announcement of his half brother Theo Isenberg."]

16. Letter of 11–13 January 1896 to Johannes and Marie Hesse, *Kindheit und Jugend*, 2: 52.

For he was able to observe Tübingen's academic world only from a distance – as a messenger delivering books to professors' houses or as an occasional drinking companion of his former schoolmates. As a merchant's apprentice he could never be part of that world.[17]

While this assessment is largely accurate for the first twelve months or so of Hesse's nearly four-year stint at Heckenhauer's, it seems to ignore the role Hesse was to assume in the *petit cénacle* during his final two years in Tübingen, when he – the only nonstudent in the group – was often the center of attention, envied by the others for the relative freedom he seemed to enjoy to exercise his literary ambitions. It appears likely that Hesse was primarily motivated in his *Privatstudien*, aside from his own genuine intellectual interest, by the desire to please his parents (who would almost certainly have rather sent him to Tübingen as a student) and the teacher under whose tutelage he had last studied in Cannstatt, Ernst Kapff. The latter and the Hesses were, in fact, the nearly exclusive recipients of those letters from Hermann that dealt with the content of his personal *Studium*.

Nonetheless, Hesse most certainly did experience a crisis during his early months in Tübingen, and it was not merely the result of adjusting to a new place and a different type of work. He was confronted in Tübingen with the full realization of what his various adolescent escapades had ultimately wrought. Later, as he looked back over the three apprenticeship years at Heckenhauer's in a letter to his parents on 2 October 1898, he admitted that no one else was to blame for his having landed in a vocation that neither challenged nor fulfilled him, "after I had ruined my own chances for a better one."[18] To have been qualified to pursue a better career, after all, Hesse would have had to complete a university education, a path that he indeed would have preferred to follow but that he had made impossible for himself.

As Zeller and Freedman describe in detail, Hesse's longing to be a university student manifested itself in his assuming many of the habits and trappings typical of students of the day and in his even attempting to dress according to the sartorial standards of those enrolled at the university.[19] In his *Gedenkblatt* "Einzug in ein neues Haus" (1931), Hesse himself reminisced at length about the Tübingen domicile in which he spent his entire four years there,

17. Freedman, *Hermann Hesse: Pilgrim of Crisis*, 68.
18. Letter to Johannes and Marie Hesse, 2 October 1898, *Kindheit und Jugend*, 2: 285f.
19. See, for example, Freedman, *Hermann Hesse: Pilgrim of Crisis*, 67f.

recalling having decorated the otherwise austere surroundings with pictures and photographs of more than a hundred well-known men whom he admired at the time "for whatever reason," including Gerhart Hauptmann, Frédéric Chopin, and two likenesses of Friedrich Nietzsche.[20]

> Außerdem war eine halbe Stubenwand, über dem Sofa, auf studentische Art mit einer Anordnung symmetrisch aufgehängter Tabakspfeifen dekoriert.[21]
>
> [Besides that, above the sofa, half of one wall was decorated with a symmetrically displayed collection of tobacco pipes, quite in student style.]

In addition, Hesse sprinkled his letters liberally with Latin quotes, a feature of his correspondence that was missing in his pre-Tübingen letters and can also likely be traced to a desire, albeit subconscious, to write more in the student style of his time.

On the other hand, Hesse did not arrive in Tübingen without having already begun to question the value of a university *Studium*, a skepticism that may well be ascribed to a kind of "sour grapes" attitude in the face of the now distinctly improbable likelihood of his ever being permitted to study himself. More significant, however, is the fact that Hesse was almost certainly influenced in his opinions regarding university study by Ernst Kapff, whose counsel the young man valued most highly. Even the earliest letters written by Kapff to Hermann Hesse, during the summer of 1895 (well before the position in Tübingen materialized), stressed the former mentor's doubts about the necessity of acquiring a university education.

> Man muß einem vernünftigen Menschen ... heutzutage entschieden vom Studium abraten. Eine höhere Bildung läßt sich ohne Universität sehr wohl erreichen, das Wissen liegt ja heutzutage auf dem Markt, man muß nur richtig einzukaufen verstehen.[22]
>
> [These days, one should most decidedly advise a reasonable human being not to go to university. Higher education is quite attainable without university study, knowledge is out there on the market, you just have know how to shop for it.]

Considering the social status of a *Gymnasium* teacher at the time and the careful propriety one would expect to characterize an exchange

20. Hermann Hesse, "Einzug in ein neues Haus" (1931), *Werke*, 10: 136ff.
21. Ibid., 138.
22. Unpublished letter of 10 (13?) June 1895 from Ernst Kapff to Hermann Hesse, original in the Hesse Archives, Marbach, quoted here from *Kindheit und Jugend*, 2: 555f.

of letters between a teacher and a seventeen-year-old former pupil, Kapff's remarks here – and elsewhere – are astonishingly candid; they must also have been most welcome sentiments to the young Hermann Hesse, for he seems to have taken them quite to heart!

After his initial fascination with student life and his rather extensive contact with fraternities and their activities, Hesse became increasingly critical of the entire university spectrum. In a letter written to his parents just weeks after he settled in Tübingen, his first reactions to university life bear an unmistakable touch of cynicism, while reflecting, at the same time, both Kapff's influence and his own reading of Goethe:

> So sehr es mich manchmal nach den Quellen des Wissens zieht, so gern ich zuweilen mit dem bunten Schwarm in die Aula wanderte, – im ganzen erscheint mir das akademische Treiben doch nicht ganz ideal, sondern eng und lückenhaft wie alles Irdische ... Es muß doch jeder selber sorgen, daß er lernt und wird, daß er frei wird und das Auge bewahrt für's Wahre und Edle. "Sehe jeder, wie er's treibe!"[23]
>
> [As much as I am sometimes pulled toward the fountains of knowledge, as much as I would occasionally like to traipse along with the colorful crowd into the lecture hall, the whole academic endeavor seems to me to be less than ideal, indeed rather narrow and incomplete like all else in this earthly existence ... Everyone must put forth his own effort to learn and develop, to become free and to keep an eye out for truth and beauty. "Let each discover for himself how he would best achieve it!"]

The social life of his student cohorts had also begun to lose any attraction for Hermann Hesse; indeed he came increasingly to despise many of the activities associated with the student life of the time. In various letters to parents and other family members, Hesse complained of disturbances on his own street. For the serious *Privatstudent* Hermann Hesse, who had only the few evening hours at his disposal for reading and writing, the commotion caused by carousing students was doubly annoying, distracting him from his work and robbing him of desperately needed sleep. Reporting on such an evening incident, he described a student in the street below, singing at the top of his lungs and yelling for a compatriot to join him: "This kind of noise goes on almost every

23. Letter of 27 November 1895 to Johannes and Marie Hesse, *Kindheit und Jugend*, 2: 38f. The quoted line is from the final strophe of the young Goethe's poem "Beherzigung" (1789).

night."[24] Throughout that spring, the evening activities of student fraternities were particularly rowdy:

> Die hiesigen Studenten tollen diese Zeit ärger als je. Zwei hiesige Corps haben solchen Unfug getrieben, daß einzelne strafrechtlich belangt werden ... Auch ich leide darunter, indem viele Nächte vor Lärm nicht zu schlafen ist.[25]

> [The students here are acting crazier than ever now. Two of the local fraternities were involved in such serious mischief that some of them were charged by the police ... And I suffer from it, too, for I am often unable to sleep because of the noise.]

Despite occasionally having to forego an evening of reading and study, Hesse stuck resolutely to his regular perusal of literature and literary history. The truly enormous spectrum of his reading, during the first two Tübingen years in particular, is chronicled precisely in the letters to (and from) his parents, relatives, and friends that can be referenced in the second volume of *Kindheit und Jugend*; many of his own letters, in fact, were loosely structured literary-historical essays, some reaching a length of 2,000 words or more! The following, chronologically arranged enumeration of Hermann Hesse's own references to his respective current readings, extracted from his correspondence between October 1895 and June 1897, reveals the breadth of the literary inquiry he referred to as his *Privatstudium*.[26]

* Bible [26 October 1895, p. 27–28]
* Moses Mendelsohn: *Phaedon* [6 November 1895, p. 32]
* J. W. von Goethe: *Werther, Wahlverwandtschaften, Faust* [10 December 1895, p. 44]
* Horace; Goethe: *Wilhelm Meister, Dichtung und Wahrheit, Reineke Fuchs*; Socrates [11–13 January 1896, p. 53, 56]

24. Letter of 29 May 1896 to Johannes and Marie Hesse, *Kindheit und Jugend*, 2: 108.
25. Undated letter (early June 1896) to Johannes and Marie Hesse, *Kindheit und Jugend*, 2: 114.
26. All information is culled from letters found in *Kindheit und Jugend*, vol. 2; page numbers cited refer to that source. I have attempted here to ascertain and include only authors and works that Hesse was currently reading, studying or analyzing when he mentioned them in a given letter. It must be remembered that Hermann Hesse had begun his serious and methodical reading of literature in his father's library during his nearly two-year stay in Calw, from November 1893 until leaving for Tübingen in October 1895. Beginning roughly in the spring of 1897, his time was increasingly devoted to his own creative writing endeavors, signalling a kind of *Abschluß* to the most serious phase of his *Privatstudium*. Still, he can be said to have continued these "studies" sporadically through his entire life.

* Rudolf von Gottschall [undated, between 28 and 30 January 1896, p. 64]
* Horace: *Epodon Liber*; Boccaccio; Cervantes; Fielding; *The Thousand and One Nights*; Heine; Franz von Gaudy [7 February 1896, p. 65, 66, 69]
* Virgil [16 February 1896, p. 71]
* Virgil; Ossian; Christoph Martin Wieland; Bible [21 February 1896, p. 75]
* Virgil; J. W. von Goethe: *Götz von Berlichingen*; Friedrich Schiller [27 February 1896, p. 79, 81]
* Virgil; Isocrates; Xenophon [7 March 1896, pp. 84–85]
* Homer: *The Iliad*; Virgil: *Aeneid* [14 March 1896, p. 88]
* L. Preller: *Griechische Mythologie*; Johannes Scherr: *Allgemeine Geschichte der Literatur* [between 22 and 25 March 1896, p. 90]
* Johann H. A. Ebrard: *Cheirisiphos' Reise durch Böotien*; Heyse; Gustav Freytag [29 March 1896, pp. 92–93]
* Greek mythology (Hephaestus, Artemis, Hermes); J. W. von Goethe: *Briefe, Torquato Tasso, Iphigenie* [undated, early May 1896, pp. 102–3]
* Ossian; Hermann Sudermann: *Frau Sorge, Im Zwielicht*; William Shakespeare: *Hamlet*; J. M. Miller: *Siegwart, Eine Klostergeschichte* [May 1896]
* Emanuel Geibel; Paul Heyse; Hermann Sudermann [29 May 1896, p. 109]
* Gotthold Ephraim Lessing: *Laocoon*; Karl Heinemann: *Goethe*; I. S. Turgenev; Vladimir Korolenko [June 1896, pp. 113–14]
* Henrik Ibsen; Alexandre Dumas, fils; Friedrich Nietzsche: *Also sprach Zarathustra, Menschliches, Allzumenschliches* [15 June 1896, pp. 115–17]
* Ennius Quintus; Ovid; Horace; August von Platen; Joseph von Eichendorff; Martin Greif; Stephan Born; Emanuel Geibel [1 September 1896, pp. 133–34]
* Ossian; Hieronymus Lorm; Gustav Falke; Oskar von Redwitz; Emanuel Geibel; Paul Heyse; Theodor Storm [undated, probably September 1896, pp. 135–36]
* Gottfried Keller; Gustav Falke; Richard Dehmel; Franz Evers; Hermann Sudermann; Gerhart Hauptmann: *Die versunkene Glocke*; Ludwig Fulda [24 January 1897, pp. 157–58]
* Richard Dehmel: *Aber die Liebe, Weib und Welt, Lebensblätter* [January 1897, pp. 161–63][27]
* Paul Verlaine; Nikolaus Lenau; Heinrich Heine [undated, February 1897, pp. 166–67]

27. These references are contained in a letter Hesse wrote to Dehmel personally. When the older man answered him, Hesse wrote again during the same month (January 1897). Unfortunately, Dehmel's early letters to Hesse have never been found.

* Recent Baltic literature; Hermann Bahr: *Studien zur Moderne*;
  Jens Peter Jacobsen [2 April 1897, pp. 172–73]
* Hermann Bahr; J. W. von Goethe; Ludwig Tieck; Ludwig
  Uhland; Hermann Sudermann: *Morituri* [9 May 1897,
  p. 175]
* Cornelius Nepos [16 May 1897, p. 178]
* Gustav Falke [11 June 1897, p. 189]
* H. Höffding; *Rousseau und seine Philosophie*; Friedrich Nietzsche
  [12 and 13 June 1897, p. 191]

A comparison of this list of authors and works with Hermann
Hesse's intended plan of reading for the same period reveals an
interesting disparity. By November 1895, after settling somewhat
into his new life in Tübingen, Hesse had begun what he planned
as a systematic study of the past hundred years of literature, and
he noted that his work at Heckenhauer's essentially sustained
this endeavor:

> Daß mein Privatstudium der Ästhetik and Literatur im Einklang
> mit meinem Beruf steht, erfrischt mich natürlich sehr. Ich treibe
> noch immer Geschichte der deutschen Literatur von 1790 bis 1890
> und hoffe verhältnismäßig bald dies Stück Geistesgeschichte wirk-
> lich innezuhaben.[28]
>
> [It is very refreshing to me that my private study of aesthetics and lit-
> erature fits together so well with my occupation. I am still working
> on the history of German literature from 1790 to 1890 and hope to
> have really mastered this piece of intellectual history relatively soon.]

It is obvious that Hesse was unable to restrict himself to a chron-
ological study of nineteenth-century German literature, for he
regularly left both German literature *and* the nineteenth century
to conduct "forays" into the literature of other countries (Russia,
France, Scandinavia, England) and earlier ages (classical antiq-
uity). Ironically, his lack of adherence to a systematic, chronolog-
ical approach may have resulted, to a substantial extent, from
his purely random exposure to works of literature and intellec-
tual history at Heckenhauer's, where his fascination with the
printed word was regularly aroused by chance conversations
with students and the inevitable perusal of incoming shipments
of books.

---

28. Letter of 11–13 January 1896 to Johannes and Marie Hesse, *Kindheit und
Jugend*, 2: 53.

A Poet Emerges

As Hermann Hesse's *Privatstudien* progressed, he gradually began to concern himself quite exactingly with matters of poetic form, especially metrics. His interest in the latter was at once theoretical and pragmatic, for he now proceeded to apply his newly acquired knowledge to his own lyrical endeavors. As his first three published poems appeared in the Viennese *Deutsches Dichterheim*[29] between late winter and summer 1896, Hesse was engrossed in his study of metrics and versification, brandishing in his letters a quite academic arsenal of prosodic terminology. On several occasions during the summer and autumn of 1896, he wrote detailed descriptions of his experimentation with meter, referring on 16 August, for example, to two poems he had submitted to the *Deutsches Dichterheim* in early July:

> In dem einen der Gedichte habe ich zum erstenmal fünffüßige Trochäen mit männlichem Reim in Zweizeilern versucht, einen der einfachsten, aber schwer wirksam zu machenden Rhythmen.[30]
> [In one of the poems I tried, for the first time, to use trochees of five feet, with masculine rhyme scheme, in couplets; it is one of simplest, yet difficult rhythms to achieve.]

Shortly thereafter, Hesse offered his friend Eberhard Goes a brief treatise on entering the world of rhyme and meter, from learning to discern between an iamb and a spondee, a Nibelungian strophe and an Italian *ottava rima*, to unlocking "a world of enticing secrets whose scope is infinitely broad, the music of language." In the lengthy passage that follows, Hesse provided convincing evidence of his own genuine fascination with the historical and substantive study of prosody:

> Es kann ebenso lehrreich und packend sein, den keuschen Reizen südlicher Ottaverime und Sonaten nachzugehen, als dem Wind und den Bäumen zu lauschen, um die wildwachsenden Rhythmen Ossians begreifen zu lernen.[31]

---

29. "Madonna," presumably Hesse's first published poem, appeared in vol. 16, no. 5 of the *Deutsches Dichterheim – Organ für Dichtkunst und Kritik*, 1 March 1896. In April of the same year, his poems "Makuschka. Lieder eines Verbannten I/II," written about a year earlier, also appeared in that journal (no. 8); "Wenn man alt wird" was published there in December 1896 (no. 23).

30. Letter of 10 August 1896 to Johannes and Marie Hesse, *Kindheit und Jugend*, 2: 129.

31. Undated letter, September 1896 to Eberhard Goes, in *Kindheit und Jugend*, 2: 135ff. Goes, whom Hesse had met during his first month in Tübingen through his

[It can be just as informative and fascinating to pursue the chaste enticements of southern *ottava rima* and sonnets as to listen to the wind and trees, in order to learn to comprehend the wildly growing rhythms of Ossian.]

The notion of the "music of language" had permeated Hesse's emerging personal conception of poetry and became a kind of measuring stick for his evaluation of other poets. Even August Graf von Platen, a nineteenth-century master of German poetry and a favorite of the young lyricist, rarely achieved what Hesse would have considered *Musik der Sprache*:

> Bei uns Deutschen hat z. B. der Held der Poetik, Graf Platen, doch nur sehr selten sich über die Poetik zu den feineren, dem Leser unsichtbaren Gesetzen sprachlicher Musik erhoben ... Von Früheren hat fast nur Heine mit Bewußtsein die Ecken der steifen Form abgeschliffen, daher sind die bessern seiner Gedichte sämtlich auch singbar.[32]

> [Among us Germans, to cite one example, the hero of poetics, Count Platen, only quite rarely transcended mere poetics and mastered those laws of spoken music that are invisible to the reader ... Among earlier poets, Heine was almost the only one to consciously file away the edges of stiff poetic form; for that reason, all his better poems are singable.]

Although Hesse apparently never formulated a very refined aesthetics of the musicality of poetic language, he demonstrated an affinity for traditional prosodic form, especially in his early creative phase. In addition, of course, his enduring love of music contributed substantially to an aesthetic expectation of balance, symmetry, and semantic clarity that would also characterize his own verse. Throughout his life, Hesse sought repeatedly to articulate his conception of the essence of music, and an extensive selection of his many utterances is contained in *Hermann Hesse – Musik*.[33] Among the essays, reviews, letter passages, and verse in that anthology is Hesse's poem "Flötenspiel" (1940), the closing

---

former Maulbronn roommate Wilhelm Lang, maintained an intermittent correspondence with the author until shortly before his death in 1958. His son is the novelist Albrecht Goes (*Unruhige Nacht, Das Brandopfer*), born in 1908.

32. Letter of 1 September 1896 to Johannes and Marie Hesse, *Kindheit und Jugend*, 2: 132ff.

33. Volker Michels, ed. *Hermann Hesse – Musik* (Frankfurt/M., 1986). Another important source of information about Hesse's relationship to music is the lengthy discussion included in vol. 6 of *Die Musik in Geschichte und Gegenwart* (Kassel, 1957). The essay is printed in its entirety in *Kindheit und Jugend*, 2: 571ff.

strophe of which holds what is likely the poet's most succinct statement on the essence of music:

> Es war der Welt geheimer Sinn
> In seinem Atem offenbart,
> Und willig gab das Herz sich hin
> Und alle Zeit ward Gegenwart."[34]
> [The secret essence of the world
> Was revealed in his breaths,
> And willingly the heart succumbed
> And all of time became the present.]

Hesse himself said of this verse:

> "Die Schlußzeile des Gedichts ist übrigens das Endergebnis vieljähriger Spekulationen über das Wesen der Musik. Sie ist, so scheint mir, philosophisch formuliert: ästhetisch wahrnehmbar gemachte Zeit.[35]
> [The final line of the poem, by the way, is the result of many years of contemplation about the essence of music. To state it philosophically, music is, it seems to me, time made aesthetically perceivable.]

(Ironically, therefore, it was by means of a *poem* that Hermann Hesse, by his own evaluation, most precisely articulated his notion of the true nature of music!)

The musicality of much of Hesse's early poetry, of course, is legitimately attributable to his extensive reading of the German Romantics, many of whom assigned to works of music a status superior to that of literary works and whose poetic form Hermann Hesse often enough seemed to emulate. As Hermann Kasack emphasized in his insightful essay on Hesse's relationship to music:

> Natürlich ist der Zauber der Musik, dem der junge Hesse erliegt, vorwiegend romantisch gefärbt. Man braucht nur an Zeilen und Überschriften vieler Gedichte zu denken: Spielmann, Der Geiger, Melodie, Gavotte, Marienlieder, Nocturne und Chopinwalzer ... Motive aus der deutschen Romantik, aus *Des Knaben Wunderhorn* bestimmen als Liedergruß, Traum, Nacht und Dichtersang Hesses frühe lyrische Welt. Dichten heißt ihm: singen. Gedicht gilt lange Zeit als Text, als Lied.[36]

---

34. Hermann Hesse, *Die Gedichte*, 2 vols. (Frankfurt/M., 1977), 2: 673.

35. Letter of April, 1940 to Otto Korradi, in *Hermann Hesse – Musik*, 177.

36. Hermann Kasack, "Hermann Hesse's Verhältnis zur Musik," in *Hermann Hesse – Musik*, 9ff. Kasack first presented the essay as a lecture at the University of Frankfurt on 23 September 1950, on the occasion of the German premiere of Richard Strauss's "Vier letzte Lieder" – four Hesse poems set to music. It might

[Naturally the musical magic to which the young Hesse succumbed is primarily romantic in coloration. One only needs to consider lines and titles of many of his poems: Musician, The Violinist, Melody, Gavotte, Songs of Mary, Nocturne, Chopin's Waltzes ... The lyrical world of Hesse's youth is shaped by motifs from German Romanticism, from *Des Knaben Wunderhorn*: a greeting sung, a dream, night, a poet's song. Writing means singing to him. For a long time, poetry was song for him.]

One should not overlook, however, Hermann Hesse's rather quick "recovery" from the fawning adulation toward the Romantics that characterized him in the mid-1890s. By 1900, as his essay "Romantik und Neuromantik"[37] makes clear, he had attained an objectively critical attitude vis-à-vis German Romanticism, while by no means rejecting the movement nor its writers. Indeed, as early as fall 1896, his increasingly discriminating analysis of individual Romantic poets prompted comments of near "Heinean" irony!

> Freund Eichendorff z. B ... . schwimmt häufig in seinen Gedichten auf gar zu trüben Wellen, man merkt, wie ihm mit dem Bewußtsein der Taktsicherheit fast immer auch die Reinheit der Sprache verloren geht.[38]
>
> [Our friend Eichendorff, for example ... often swims in all too murky waters, and one notices how the purity of his language gets lost as he becomes too conscious of securely measured time.]

Hesse's own meticulous, analytical, indeed almost academic study of prosodic form reflects a significant divergence from the visceral and emotional characteristics usually associated with the "romantic soul," and his strident opposition to the *Moderne* (at least as he understood the latter at age nineteen) was a rather logical consequence of his adherence to a really quite traditional spectrum of prosodic types.[39] It is also interesting to speculate on the

---

also be mentioned here that Hesse's *Notturni* (1900 and 1902) offer another example of Hesse's fascination with musical form and theme.

37. Hermann Hesse, "Romantik und Neuromantik," in *Werke* 10: 105ff.

38. Letter of 1 September 1896, to Johannes and Marie Hesse, *Kindheit und Jugend*, 2: 134.

39. In a letter to Ernst Kapff written on 6 November 1895, Hesse summed up his analysis of "modern" art and literature: "Dies Verschwimmen und Verschwinden der scharf gegrenzten künstlerischen Form ist es vor allem, was mich fast mit Leidenschaft der 'modernen' Kunst opponieren heißt" (*Kindheit und Jugend*, 2: 33). ["This blurring and disappearing of sharply artistic form, more than anything else, is what makes me passionately opposed to 'modern' art."] It seems little wonder that Hermann Hesse never really warmed up to Expressionism when it emerged some fifteen years later!

extent to which Hermann Hesse's apprentice training at Perrot's shaped his work habits and honed his analytical skills; reading those Tübingen letters that contain details of Hesse's evaluation of poetic form and of the content of individual literary works, one is struck by what sometimes seems to be a quite technical interest in the manner in which poems, in particular, were composed.

Hesse's preoccupation with literary form and style and the subsequent emergence of a personal literary credo during 1896 and 1897, however, corresponded not only with the beginning of his own serious writing and his first publications. Strikingly often, in letters to his parents from that period, Hermann Hesse tied his discussion of literary form, indeed, of aesthetic principles generally, to what was a provocative declaration of his gradual shedding of the religious beliefs with which he had grown up and to which his parents still held with dogmatic steadfastness. As early as the second week after his arrival in Tübingen, Hesse touched upon his changing attitudes about church attendance;[40] it is significant that this topic was among the very first to be discussed – by letter – with his parents.

> [E]s kostet mich viel Überwindung, in die Kirche zu gehen. Der Gottesdienst macht mir immer den etwas peinlichen Eindruck eines Erzwungenen, Berechneten … ich vermag eben etwas Festes, Einheitliches, eine Kirche, in der protestantischen "Kirche" nicht zu finden und bin noch zu sehr Kunstenthusiast, um nicht zu bedauern, daß die Protestanten sich wie vom Papst, so auch von Raphael getrennt haben.[41]

> [I have to force myself to go to church. The service always gives the somewhat awkward impression of something contrived and calculated … I am not able to find anything solid and consistent in the Protestant church, and I am too much of an art enthusiast to keep from regretting that in breaking with the Pope, the Protestants also broke with Raphael.]

Hesse's allusion here to a feeling of alienation caused by the absence of art in the Protestant church was but the first expression

40. During most of his life up to this point, Hermann Hesse had attended church services with almost rigid regularity, especially during the nearly two years (November 1893 to October 1895) when he again lived at home with the family in Calw. It must be remembered, too, that the Hesse-Gundert family "lived" its beliefs, quite literally, on a day-to-day basis, so that Hesse may well have yearned to escape the totally pervasive religious atmosphere of his parents' home.

41. Letter of 26 October 1895 to Johannes and Marie Hesse, *Kindheit und Jugend*, 2: 27.

of the realization that his own notion of art was ultimately incompatible with his parents' church. Nonetheless, he seems to have attempted to present his incipient system of aesthetic values to his parents as a kind of *Ersatzreligion*, subconsciously hoping, perhaps, that they would view his intellectual and creative maturation as an acceptable substitute for those beliefs with which they had always striven to imbue their children. Thus, as he gradually asserted his religious independence, Hermann Hesse was also, in effect, insisting that his parents validate his literary aspirations.

In his epistolary treatises, however, Hesse's tone was sometimes neither conciliatory nor even tolerant, as a letter written in September 1896 demonstrates only all too emphatically:

> Und immer wieder sehe ich den Sonntagsgott der Kirchenchristen und sehe, wie er des Werktags nicht helfen kann. Solche Christen sind doch wohl viele auch unter unsern Bekannten. Ich gestehe, mein eigenes Lebensideal, meine Poesie, mein bißchen Goethekult sogar, sind bessere und treuere Götter als jener Sonntagsgott ... Ich suche wieder die Sterne meiner bisherigen Ideale und will wieder versuchen, durch den poetischen Pantheismus zum Geheimnis des Friedens und der Gesundheit zu dringen. Mir ist wieder, als seien meine Augen mehr dazu geeignet, in den Offenbarungen der Dichter als der Bibel zu lesen.[42]

> [Again and again, I observe how little the Sunday deity of churchgoing Christians helps people through their work week. A good number of this type of Christian can likely be found among our acquaintances too. I confess that my personal ideals, my writing, even my modest, cultish affection for Goethe, are better and more faithful gods than that Sunday deity ... I am seeking again the stars of my previous ideals, and I intend to try once more to discover the secret of peace and health through poetic pantheism. It seems to me once again that my eyes are better suited for reading the revelations of poets than those of the Bible.]

It is understandable that Johannes and Marie Hesse did not at all welcome this new path their son had chosen to follow, given the scarcely inadvertent allusions to pre-Christian (or *non*-Christian) belief systems ("Sterne," "Götter"), worldly idolatry ("Goethekult"), or the rejection of an anthropomorphic conception of God ("poetischen Pantheismus") contained in this letter. Marie Hesse responded within days to her son's lengthy epistle:

42. Letter of 13–19 September 1896 to Johannes and Marie Hesse, *Kindheit und Jugend*, 2: 138f.

Mein lieber Hermann!
Herzlichen Dank für Deinen lieben Brief, schreibe nur immer ganz offen, wir leben mit dir weiter, und unsre Gebete begleiten dich überall hin.[43]

[My dear Hermann!
Our hearty thanks for your nice letter; you should always be open and honest in your letters, we continue to be with you in your life, and our prayers accompany you everywhere you go.]

In the context of her son's inchoate, if only implicit critique of her beliefs, Marie Hesse reacted with the weapons she knew best how to employ – parental "love" and prayer for his endangered soul. Although this is certainly not to assert that her convictions, quaint as they must have begun to appear to her rapidly maturing son, were not deeply held and sincere, Marie Hesse's reaction here serves to exemplify the almost exclusively religious manner in which she related to her son. Just a few months earlier, she had also asked Elias Schrenk, one of the elders of the Pietist faith known throughout Swabia and northwesten Switzerland for his powerful sermons, to pray for her son, as she wrote to the latter, "that you might become a happy person."[44] Schrenk even composed a short, terse letter to Hermann, telling him what he needed to do to save his soul:

Was hast Du also zu tun? Du hast Dich dem Heiland einfach zu übergeben mit Leib und Seele; gerade wie Du bist. Er hat Dich erkauft mit Seinem Blute, Du gehörest Ihm.[45]

[What must you do, then? You must give yourself to the Savior with body and soul, just as you are. He has purchased you with His own blood, you belong to Him.]

Hesse himself found the letter somewhat strange and requested of his parents that they deal directly with him in the future:

Ich bitte nur, laßt uns selber zusammenhalten und herzlich verkehren – weshalb durch Dritte?[46]

[I ask you, please let us stick together and deal with each other cordially – why do we need outsiders?]

43. Letter of 23 September 1896 from Marie Hesse to Hermann Hesse, *Kindheit und Jugend*, 2: 140.
44. Letter of 22 February 1896 from Marie Hesse to Hermann Hesse, *Kindheit und Jugend*, 2: 77.
45. Letter of 20 February 1896 from Elias Schrenk to Hermann Hesse, *Kindheit und Jugend*, 2: 77f.
46. Letter of 27 February 1896 to Johannes and Marie Hesse, *Kindheit und Jugend*, 2: 79.

Although the youthful poet was never to delineate his notion of "poetic pantheism" more extensively by name, his scattered letter references to the analogy between belief in a god and faith in the power of pure beauty were regularly accompanied by pronouncements of his own allegiance to the latter.[47] Perhaps his most articulate discourse on the subject is provided in a nearly essay-length letter to his half brother, Karl Isenberg, in the summer of 1897, in which he stated:

> Meine "Centrale" habe ich im Glauben an das Schöne gefunden, der mit dem Glauben an die Kunst annähernd zusammenfällt ... Das Schöne in der Natur und das Schöne in der Kunst (auch Dichtung) stehen mir ziemlich auf einer Stufe, obwohl ich für das letztere fast empfänglicher bin ... Da mir als Ende und Ziel jeder Weltanschauung eine persönliche Religion erscheint, war das einzige Resultat, das ich fand, die Bestätigung meiner Ansicht, daß eine Moral das Ergebnis einer Religion sein kann, daß aber nie, gar nie aus einer Moral eine Religion erbaut werden kann.[48]

> [My "center" is my belief in that which is beautiful, and it is almost identical to my belief in art itself ... Beauty in nature and beauty in art (including poetry) are about on the same level, as far as I am concerned, although I am perhaps more receptive to the latter ... Since I believe that the end and goal of every personal creed is a personal religion, the only result that I have found confirmed my belief that a moral system can result from a religion, but that never, absolutely never can a religion be built upon a moral system.]

A few months later, in a letter to his parents, Hesse synopsized his aesthetic creed as based on the firm belief "that aesthetics take the place of morality for the artist ... and that art, especially poetic art, is not intended to serve the purpose of propagating that which is morally good."[49]

Hermann Hesse's exchange of the religious doctrines with which he had been reared for a surrogate belief system anchored

---

47. Bernhard Zeller interprets Hermann Hesse's youthful cult of beauty as "gefährlich und gefährdend, zunächst auch noch reichlich unausgegoren. . ." (Zeller, *Hermann Hesse mit Selbstzeugnissen und Bilddokumenten*, 35). ["dangerous and perilous, and from the outset quite immature. . ."] Hesse would probably have defined his "poetic pantheism" as the expression of a supreme spirit through works of (literary) art, a concept that ineluctably implies the artist's assumption of a kind of prophetic role. The mature Hesse, of course, eschewed such thoughts, perhaps an indication that his earlier *Schönheitsglaube* was indeed intended to facilitate, on one level at least, his separation from the Pietist dogma of parents and family.

48. Letter of 12–13 June 1897 to Karl Isenberg, *Kindheit und Jugend*, 2: 189ff.

49. Letter of 4 October 1897 to Johannes and Marie Hesse, *Kindheit und Jugend*, 2: 209.

in a vague but obviously compelling aesthetics was at least partially motivated by his desire to break free from the influences of the family's all-pervading Pietist faith. For their part, Johannes and Marie Hesse found it impossible to accept their son's departure from the family religion in favor of an aestheticism that smacked distinctly of "worldliness," and Hermann's first successes as a publishing poet incurred their skepticism from the outset. As they read the first pieces that appeared in print and discovered that their young offspring had no intention of effecting "moral good" through his poetry and prose, they reacted with silence. Neither father nor mother responded to Hesse's mention of the first of his poems to be published in the *Deutsches Dichterheim*;[50] in fact, neither parent, it seems, responded to *any* of his first three or four published pieces of verse, though Hesse regularly apprised the family in Calw of those modest successes.

When Hesse heard that two of his poems had been accepted for simultaneous publication in the *Dichterheim*, he even quoted to his parents the mild praise he had received from the journal's editor: "Both submissions will be printed; it is clear that you write with diligence and with love."[51] Still, there was apparently no reaction by his parents to his publications, although a month later his mother would praise in detail an epic poem (*Der Mönch von Hirsau*) by a young woman from Calw who had requested the Hesses' assistance in finding a publisher for her work. (The fact that Hesse answered his mother's letter immediately is but one indication of the frustration and hurt he must have felt, and his caustic cynicism

50. In an undated letter of late March 1896 to his parents, Hesse noted: "Das *Deutsche Dichterheim* in Wien beginnt nun einige Gedichte von mir zu drucken." (*Kindheit und Jugend*, 2: 90.) ["The *Deutsche Dichterheim* in Vienna is starting to publish a few of my poems."] Sister Adele, on the other hand, quickly wrote to ask him to send a copy: "[V]on dem *Deutschen Dichterheim*, ich möchte so gern mal eine Nummer sehen, wo was von dir kommt ... schick mir doch mal eine." (Letter of 1 April 1896 from Adele Hesse, *Kindheit und Jugend*, 2: 95.) ["I would so like to see an issue of the *Deutsche Dichterheim* that has something of yours in it ... do send me one."]

51. Letter of 10–16 August 1896 to Johannes and Marie Hesse, *Kindheit und Jugend*, 2: 129. The praise that the young poet quoted to his parents here was not contained in a letter, but in a quite original kind of editor-contributor "mailbox" that appeared in each issue of the journal! Hence, Hesse referred in this letter to the editor's having put the message in the "mailbox" of a recent issue.

took as its target not only *Der Mönch von Hirsau* but extended also to women poets of the day in general.)[52]

For nearly a year thereafter, Hermann Hesse refrained almost completely from mentioning his "lyrical attempts" in letters home, and when, in September 1897, he again called the family's attention to another poem that was about to appear in the *Deutsches Dichterheim*, he arranged at the same time to have that issue sent to Calw. If Hermann Hesse expected even a modestly tolerant reception of his verse (*Chopins grande valse, eine Phantasie*), he was to be sorely disappointed. His mother, in the opening section of the parental response a few days later, ignored the poem completely, mentioning instead the recent arrival of a book of Swiss poetry entitled *Von Gott – zu Gott, Lieder einer Volksdichterin im Schweizerland*. Johannes Hesse, on the other hand, did acknowledge receipt of the *Dichterheim* issue, but noted:

> Auch von mir herzlichen Dank für deinen Brief, sowie die unter Kreuzband gesandte Nummer vom Dichterheim, die freilich nichts enthält, was ich zu würdigen in der Lage wäre.[53]
>
> [My thanks, too, for you letter as well as for the issue of the *Dichterheim* sent separately, though it contains nothing that I would be capable of appreciating.]

As he had done almost a year to the day earlier, Hermann Hesse again suppressed the pain and anger he must have felt toward his parents, lashing out instead at "Schweizer Volksdichterinnen" and, more pointedly, at "religious poetry":

> Gott sei mit der Kunst, wenn sogar die Schweizer beginnen, Volksdichterinnen zu entdecken! Und gar religiöse Lyrik! Das heikelste und im ganzen trostloseste Gebiet, das ich kenne.[54]

---

52. "[D]enn über die 'schreibende Frauenwelt,' d. h. über die Werke dieser Frauen, besonders über poetische, denke ich sehr pessimistisch … Wenn die süddeutsche Dichtung neben den Herren Ostpreußens und Berlins wieder aufkommen will, so darf sie, wie ich glaube, ja nicht ins liebe alte Waldhorn der burschikos-sentimentalen Romantik blasen." (Letter of 23 September 1896 to Johannes and Marie Hesse, *Kindheit und Jugend*, 2:142f.) ["As far as the world of writing women is concerned, that is the works of these women, particularly their poetic writings, I am very pessimistic … If south German writing is to attain the level of the gentlemen writers of East Prussia and Berlin again, then it cannot afford to toot the dear old trumpet of the naive, fraternity style of Romanticism."]

53. Letter from Johannes and Marie Hesse, 21 September 1897, *Kindheit und Jugend*, 2: 204.

54. Letter to Johannes and Marie Hesse, 25–27 September 1897, *Kindheit und Jugend*, 2: 205.

[God be with art, when even the Swiss start discovering popular women writers! And religious poetry, at that! That is the most touchy and, overall, most dreary area that I know.]

Of course, Hesse was attacking his parents here by assailing a poetic genre that was popular in his parents' religious community and especially cherished by his mother, who defended the poetry vigorously, emphasizing that such verse was not intended for worldly tastes:

[D]ie gottgeweihten Klänge sind für die, die als Pilger und Fremdlinge hier weilen und an dem, was die Welt von Kunst und Weisheit hat, einmal eben durchaus nicht satt werden können, Melodien aus der Heimat ... Wenn man einmal droben das Lied Mosis und des Lammes singt, dann hoffe auch ich mit neuer Zunge einzustimmen. O was wird das herrlich sein![55]

[Such divinely consecrated tones are melodies from our heavenly home, intended for those who are passing through this life as pilgrims and strangers, and who do not receive sufficient sustenance from the art and wisdom of this world ... When we all join together in that life beyond to sing the song of Moses and the lamb, I hope to chime in with a new voice. Oh, how splendid that will be!]

For Bernhard Zeller, the Hesses' implicitly deprecatory reaction to their son's poem was "understandable,"[56] and a quick perusal of *Chopins grande valse, eine Phantasie* tends to bear out that assessment.

> Ein kerzenheller Saal
> Und Sporengeläute und Tressengold!
> In meinen Pulsen klingt das Blut.
> Mein Mädchen, gib mir den Pokal, –
> Und nun zum Tanz! Der Walzer tollt.
> Erhitzt vom Wein mein Brausemut
> Nach aller ungenoss'nen Lust begehrt.

---

55. Letter of 3 October 1897 from Marie Hesse, *Kindheit und Jugend*, 2: 207. Again and again in their letters to Hermann, his parents alluded to the dangers of following "worldly" ways. An excellent illustration of Pietist renunciation of the "things of this world" is reproduced in Volker Michels's splendid pictorial history of Hesse and his times, *Hermann Hesse – Sein Leben in Bildern und Texten*, 24. The caption refers to the picture as a *Pietistisches Erbauungsbild*, and the illustration itself bears the title *Der breite und der schmale Weg*, a reference to Matthew 7:13–14, and depicts in intricate detail the "stations" along each of the two paths: The "broad" path includes such sinful venues as a gambling hall (*Spielhalle*), a lottery booth, a theater, and a dance hall featuring a *Maskenball* (masked ball). (Might the latter have been the model for Hesse's *Maskenball* in *Steppenwolf*?)

56. Zeller, *Hermann Hesse – mit Selbstzeugnissen und Bilddokumenten*, 35.

Vor den Fenstern wiehert mein Pferd.

Und vor den Fenstern hüllt die Nacht
Das dunkle Feld. Es trägt der Wind
Von fern Geschützebrüllen her,
Noch eine Stunde bis zur Schlacht!
Es wiegt der Sturm die Binsen hin und her,
Die nächste Nacht mein Bette sind.

Mein Totenbett vielleicht! Juchhe, Musik!
In durstigen Zügen trinkt mein heißer Blick
Das junge, schöne Leben ein;
Und trinkt sich nimmer satt an seinem Licht.
Noch einen Tanz! Wie bald, – und Kerzenschein
Und Klang und Lust zerrinnt – der Mondschein flicht
Schwermütig seinen Kranz in Tod und Graus.
Juchhe, Musik! Vom Tanz erbebt das Haus,
Erregt am Pfosten klirrt mein hängend Schwert.

Vor den Fenstern wiehert mein Pferd.[57]

[A hall by candles brightly lit
And sounds of spurs and golden jacket trim!
My blood beats audibly within my veins.
My maiden, pass me the drinking cup,
And now to dance! The waltz rolls on.
And warmed from wine my effervescent spirit
Hungers now to savor what I've long desired.

And I hear my horse before the windows neighing.

Before the windows night enshrouds
The darkened field. And with the wind
Comes from afar the roar of cannon over,
One hour only more until the battle!
But gently sway the rushes from the storm,
On which tomorrow night I'll lay my head.

Perhaps as my death bed! Hurra, more music!
In thirsty gulps my heated glance
Drinks in this youthful, lovely life;
Yet never drinks its fill out of life's light.
But one more dance! How soon this all will pass,

---

57. Hermann Hesse, *Chopins grande valse, eine Phantasie,* in *Deutsches Dichterheim – Organ für Dichtkunst und Kritik* (Vienna) 17 (1897), 394. A good discussion of this poem and its origin can be found in Peter Spycher's comprehensive study of Hesse's poetry, *Eine Wanderung durch Hermann Hesses Lyrik* (Bern/Frankfurt/M./ New York/Paris, 1990), 89ff.

The candle's glow, the song, and the desire -
Of death and dread the moonlight sadly weaves
Its wreath. Hurra, music! Dancing shakes the house,
And my hanging sword clanks ready on its post.

And I hear my horse before the windows neighing.]

For Johannes and Marie Hesse, unswervingly committed to the "narrow way," their son was already well along the "broad way" that, according to St. Matthew, can only lead to sin and destruction. The unmistakable sexual imagery particularly (from *Pokal* to *Erregt ... mein hängend Schwert*, with *Tanz* as a by no means unskilled metaphor for sexual union) must have seemed to Hesse's parents to reflect an almost carnal existential orientation.

This exchange of letters, coming at almost precisely the midpoint of Hermann Hesse's period of residence in Tübingen, marked the beginning of a kind of withdrawal vis-à-vis his parents – especially, his mother – which was reflected in two ways: First, he became, once again, quite taciturn in his correspondence with the family about his own creative authorial endeavors; second, he wrote noticeably less often to his parents. The second volume of *Kindheit und Jugend* contains nearly sixty letters and cards from Hermann to Johannes and Marie Hesse during the former's first two years in Tübingen, but only thirty-four in the final two years, i.e., scarcely more than one letter per month. If the Maulbronn experience (and the subsequent traipsing from one "healer" to another) had sown the seeds of an eventual alienation between Hesse and his parents, a nearly tangible estrangement now took root. It seems no exaggeration to assert that the strained relationship between Hermann Hesse and his mother, which would culminate in a crisis that, for a brief period at least, nearly divided them permanently when Hesse's *Eine Stunde hinter Mitternacht* was published in the summer of 1899, was never to right itself before her untimely death in April 1902.

SOCIAL LIFE AND FIRST SUCCESSES

Although the publication of *Chopins grande valse, eine Phantasie* precipitated a critical phase in Hesse's relations with his family, it also led, ironically, to what was probably the young poet's first adult friendship with a woman – even though the two were never to meet in person. Helene Voigt, a fledgling writer from Schleswig-Holstein who was two years older than Hermann Hesse, requested his address from the *Dichterheim* upon reading the Chopin poem, and subsequently wrote to him, on 22 November 1897, his first "fan" letter. While his parents had been offended by the tone of his verse, Helene Voigt was deeply touched by it, asking "what does one say, when, with just a few words, another strikes a chord within us that resonates long thereafter." Obviously mistaking Hesse for a considerably older man, she continued:

> Wird der Dichter unwirsch die Achseln zucken, wenn ein junges Mädchen kommt und ihm die Hand gibt und – schweigt? Nein, denn er muß fühlen, daß dies der schlichte Ausdruck ist für ein großes innerliches Ergriffensein.[1]
> [Will the poet casually shrug his shoulders, if a young woman comes and shakes his hand and nonetheless stays silent? No, for he has to sense that this is the unadorned external expression of having been truly moved within.]

Though his initial reply to Helene Voigt was cautious, indeed almost coy ("I am so unaccustomed to friendship and friendliness!"),[2] the twenty-year-old Hesse was clearly buoyed by this

1. Letter of 22 November 1897 from Helene Voigt to Hermann Hesse, *Kindheit und Jugend*, 2: 225.
2. Letter of 27 November 1897 to Helene Voigt, *Kindheit und Jugend*, 2: 226. Hesse would also wait nearly ten months before revealing his occupation to his correspondent in the north, although he did initiate an exchange of portrait pho-

warm and unexpected praise, and the close *Brieffreundschaft* that developed would endure for more than six decades, during which the two exchanged dozens of letters. Their early correspondence can be said to reflect a passion for more than each other's writing (they often addressed each other as "my lady friend" and "dear friend"), since they found numerous points of common interest – for example, in their appreciation of the poetry of Maurice Maeterlinck, Jens Peter Jacobsen, and Prinz Emil von Schoenaich-Carolath.

Shortly after first writing to Hesse, Helene Voigt departed for Italy as travel companion and cultural guide for a wealthy Hamburg woman, and Hesse lamented, some weeks later, that it had been impossible for him to meet her in person, "in Straßburg perhaps,"[3] during her journey south. As she returned to Germany in February 1898, she again passed through the capital of Alsace-Lorraine, just 135 kilometers west of Tübingen; Hermann Hesse apparently knew nothing of the details of her return journey, a journey that took her to Leipzig, where she met and quickly fell in love with Eugen Diederichs:

> Ihr Brief ist mit dem 12. Februar gezeichnet, dem Tage, an dem ich meine junge Freiheit verlor. Ich bin Braut, eine lachende und eine weinende zugleich.
>
> Von Straßburg fuhr ich (nicht ohne auf der Karte Tübingen noch einmal aufgesucht zu haben) nach Leipzig. Dort lernte ich im Hause meines Verlegers den Verlagsbuchhändler Eugen Diederichs kennen. In wenigen Tagen hatten wir uns gefunden. Das ist die äußere Handlung. Wenn je der Himmel zwei Menschen füreinander bestimmt hat, so sind wir es.[4]
>
> [Your letter is dated 12 February, the day on which I gave up my youthful freedom. I am engaged and am laughing and crying about it at the same time.
>
> From Strasbourg, I traveled to Leipzig (but not without checking on the map again to see where Tübingen is). At my publisher's in

tographs in the spring of 1898, but *only* after Voigt had announced her impending marriage to the Leipzig publisher Eugen Diederichs.

3. Letter of 12 February 1898 to Helene Voigt, *Kindheit und Jugend*, 2: 236f.

4. Letter of 1 March 1898 from Helene Voigt, *Kindheit und Jugend*, 2: 241. Ralph Freedman notes that the two did not meet at this time, "because she had just fallen in love with the young publisher Eugen Diederichs." (Freedman, *Hermann Hesse: Pilgrim of Crisis*, 79.) As this letter from Helene Voigt makes quite clear, however, she did not even meet Diederichs until her trip to Leipzig in February 1898. Helene Voigt and Eugen Diederichs divorced in 1911. He married poet Lulu von Strauß und Torney in 1916, but Helene never remarried.

Helene Voigt (Diederichs)

Leipzig, I met Eugen Diederichs, a publisher. In but a few days, we
found that we were meant for each other. That is the external plot
of the story. If ever Heaven intended two human beings for each
other, we are they.]

In his response to the news of Helene's engagement, Hesse was
unable to avoid revealing his emotions through a particularly
poignant bit of poetic imagery:

Für den schönen, ehrlichen Brief viel Dank. . . Mich traf er an einem
schlechten Tage. Eben als ich ihn zu Ende gelesen hatte, klang von

der Straße der Trauermarsch zu mir herein, der einen meiner Bekannten, einen Selbstmörder, zum Kirchhof begleitete.[5]

[Many thanks for your good, honest letter. . . It reached me on a bad day. Just as I finished reading it, I heard the music of a funeral procession out on the street, accompanying an acquaintance who committed suicide.]

Two paragraphs down in the same letter, however, Hesse expressed his disappointment quite directly, while at the same time politely revealing the hope that the correspondence might continue:

Beim ersten Lesen Ihres Briefes habe ich sogar etwas von Eifersucht gespürt, so lieb und gegenwärtig ist mir die Gewißheit Ihrer Kameradschaft. Aber ich denke, diese soll weiter bestehen, weil sie aus dem Zusammenwandern nach Einem Heimwehland erwuchs und aus dem Beten zu gemeinsamen Göttern.[6]

[When I first read your letter, I sensed some jealousy, so dear and so present is the certainty of your companionship. But I think that the latter will continue to exist, because it has grown out of a common journey to a land of yearning, out of our praying to common gods.]

Still, this turn of events caused scarcely an interruption in the exchange of letters and writings between the two, and Hermann Hesse would recollect much later, that this unusual friendship "at a distance" was "the only dear and true friendship that I experienced during those years."[7]

By no means, however, was Helene Voigt-Diederichs Hesse's only "friend" during his final two years in Tübingen. Indeed, the

5. Letter of 8 March 1898 to Helene Voigt, *Kindheit und Jugend*, 2: 243f. Hesse's reference here is to the shooting suicide of a student acquaintance in early March 1898, upon which he later based the episode "Eine Novembernacht" in his *Hinterlassene Schriften und Gedichte von Hermann Lauscher* (1901). The student, Paul Eberhardt, had even been a fellow pupil of Hesse's in Maulbronn. See Martin Pfeifer, *Hesse Kommentar zu sämtlichen Werken* (Munich, 1980), 70.

6. Ibid., 244. In her answer, Helene Voigt revealed how touched she was by Hesse's poetic, indeed almost spiritual reference to their friendship: "Wie schön das klingt, wenn Sie sagen, daß unsere Freundschaft erwuchs aus dem Zusammenwandern nach Einem Heimwehland und aus dem Beten zu gemeinsamen Göttern. Und wir wandern weiter, nicht wahr?" (Letter of 26 April 1898 from Helene Voigt, *Kindheit und Jugend*, 2: 252). ["How beautiful it sounds when you say that our friendship grew out of a common journey to to a land of yearning and out of our praying to common gods. And we shall continue our journey, shall we not?"] The sincerity of Helene Voigt's affection for Hermann Hesse is borne out by her letter of 27 November 1898, in which she notes the first anniversary of her initial letter to him, *Kindheit und Jugend*, 2: 303.

7. Letter of 2 October 1898 to Helene Voigt-Diederichs, in *Hermann Hesse, Helene Voigt-Diederichs. Zwei Autorenportraits in Briefen 1897–1900* (Köln, 1971), 74.

years 1897 and 1898 can justifiably be said to mark his first significant social maturation and adaptation, a kind of "coming out" that culminated in his participation in an informal group of students who called themselves the *petit cénacle*. Hesse biographies customarily trace the founding of this "club" to the beginning of the important friendship between Hesse and Ludwig Finckh, based, presumably, on Finckh's assertion that he first met Hesse at Heckenhauer's:

> In Tübingen traf ich in einem Buchladen, bei Heckenhauer, einen jungen Stift, der mir auf den ersten Blick merkwürdig auffiel. Sein Rock war unscheinbar, seine Gestalt hager, – aber sein Gesicht leuchtete. Wir sprachen ein paar Worte miteinander; es stellte sich heraus, daß er ungemein belesen war, und daß er auch dichtete. Da war eine Freundschaft geschlossen.[8]

> [In Tübingen, I met a young officeboy in Heckenhauer's bookstore who immediately caught my attention in a strange sort of way. His attire was plain, and he was almost gaunt in appearance – but his face shone brightly. We exchanged a few words; it turned out that he was unusually well read, and that he also wrote poetry. From that moment on, our friendship was sealed.]

Considering that Finckh's words were written more than six decades later, when he was eighty-five years old, there can be some question as to the accuracy of this tidy depiction, although as a Tübingen student Finckh would certainly have had occasion to see Hesse often in the store. In his much earlier and heavily autobiographical first novel, *Der Rosendoktor* (1906), Ludwig Finckh may well have recounted the beginning of his friendship with Hesse more correctly:

> Seit kurzem begegnete ich in einer Gasse oft einem jungen Menschen in abgerissenem Kittel, der merkwürdig leuchtende Augen hatte. Ich kannte ihn nicht, aber als ich ihm zum zweitenmal begegnete, mußte ich ihn grüßen. So gingen wir einige Tage aneinander vorbei, bis ich ihn eines Abends bei Gustav traf. Wir sahen uns an und lächelten. Und als wir uns die Hand gaben, wußten wir, daß wir Freunde waren. Er war Buchhändler und lud mich ein, ihn zu besuchen. . . Er gab mir einen zerrissenen Zettel in die Hand … darauf stand eine kurze Strophe. "Das ist hinreißend schön," sagte ich. "Wer hat das gemacht?" Da sah ich ihm ins Gesicht und wußte

---

8. Ludwig Finckh, *Himmel und Erde* (Stuttgart, 1961), 7–8.

es. "Sie sind ein Dichter," sagte ich leise. Er sah mich traurig an. "Ich glaube, daß ich's bin."[9]

[Several times recently, while passing through a side street, I had run into a young person in a shabby smock who had strangely radiant eyes. I didn't know him, but the second time I saw him, something made me say hello. Thus we passed by each other on several different occasions, until one evening I ran into him at Gustav's. We looked at each other and smiled. He was a bookseller and invited me to pay him a visit at work. . . He put a torn scrap of paper in my hand, upon which there was a short verse. "This is enchantingly lovely," I said. "Who wrote it?" I looked at him and knew the answer. "You are a poet," I said softly. He looked at me sadly. "Yes, I believe that I am."]

It seems more likely that Hermann Hesse met Ludwig Finckh through Karl (Carl) Hammelehle, an aquaintance from the Maulbronn days and a fellow law student of Finckh's in Tübingen. Hesse's first mention of the two occurs in the same letter to his parents on 7 August 1897 and indicates that his first visit to Finckh's family in Reutlingen (thirteen kilometers east of Tübingen) may have been in the company of Hammelehle, in whom Hesse had already rediscovered an old friend:

Neulich war ich einen Augenblick bei Finckh's in Reutlingen. . . Ich hatte im Sinn, etwa morgen nach Calw zu kommen. Nun ist aber mein Freund Hammelehle (früher in Maulbronn) mir zulieb noch diesen Sonntag (er hat schon Vakanz) hier geblieben, so daß ich bleiben muß. . . Hier wird die Vakanz etwas Ruhe bringen. Die letzte Zeit war auch durch allerlei Verkehr gesellschaftlich anstrengend. Doch freut es mich, in Hammelehle einen fast vergessenen Mitseminaristen wieder lieb gewonnen zu haben.[10]

[Recently, I stopped by the Finckhs in Reutlingen. . . I thought about coming up to Calw tomorrow, but my friend Hammelehle (formerly in Maulbronn) agreed to stay this Sunday on my account (he is already on vacation), so that I have to stay. . . Still, I am quite pleased to have gotten to know and like this fellow seminarian again, whom I had almost forgotten.]

9. Ludwig Finckh, *Der Rosendoktor* (Munich, 1943), 64–68. In a very late recollection of their first meeting (*Briefe*, 4: 394), Hesse himself recalled meeting Finckh at the *Seegerei*, apparently a pub or restaurant that is no longer in existence in Tübingen. (Information obtained by Prof. Thomas Rommel of the University of Tübingen.)

10. Letter of 7 August 1897 to Johannes and Marie Hesse, *Kindheit und Jugend*, 2: 198f. After this weekend, Hammelehle began his vacation, apparently traveling to his parents' home in the Swabian Alb, some fifty kilometers to the east of Tübingen.

Petit Cénacle (Faber, Rupp, Finckh, Hammelehle, Hesse)

There is no doubt, on the other hand, that Ludwig Finckh was to become and would remain Hesse's closest friend for the next fifteen years, and Hesse's parents seemed also to appreciate the young student of jurisprudence; despite the fact that he, too, wrote poetry (some of which, in Hesse's words, had "unusual tenderness, taste, and mood") he was, as their son hastened to assure them, "very stable."[11] Though they began to drift apart during World War I, they maintained intermittent contact until the beginning of the Nazi era, when Finckh's unflinching allegiance to National Socialism and the *Führer* provoked an estrangement that would never be overcome.

In 1897, however, after emerging from a period of social withdrawal that, paradoxically, saw him achieve an admirable degree of personal independence, Hermann Hesse relished the attention

11. Letter of 10 September 1897 to Johannes and Marie Hesse, *Kindheit und Jugend*, 2: 202f. After Hesse married Maria Bernoulli on 2 August 1904 and settled in Gaienhofen on the Untersee at the western end of Lake Constance, Finckh wasted no time in moving there himself in 1905. He thus gave up his medical career in order to pursue his own literary aspirations, which were given a substantial boost with the appearance in 1906 of his first novel, *Der Rosendoktor*. When Finckh also married, in 1907, he settled permanently in Gaienhofen, where he would spend the rest of his life, while Hermann Hesse moved to Bern in 1912 and rarely returned to Gaienhofen.

and acceptance he now began to experience in the company of Finckh, Hammelehle, and Oskar Rupp (the third "original" member of the group); by spring 1898, two more students had joined the *petit cénacle*, Otto Erich Faber and Wilhelm Schönig. Over the following two years, in letters to family and friends, Hesse repeatedly and enthusiastically recorded the activities of the clique, which included hikes in the gently mountainous countryside around Tübingen, regular evenings of beer and banter (with occasional rounds of billiards or cards) in local taverns, or quiet hours with one or the other in Hesse's room. All in all, the effect of this *Kameradschaft* was quite positive on Hesse, as he openly admitted:

> Ich bin sehr froh, diesen harmlosen, aber doch anregenden und erwärmenden Umgang gefunden zu haben.[12]
>
> [I am really happy to have found this harmless, yet inspiring and cheery camaraderie.]

As noted above in some detail, Hesse often assumed the role of the "outsider," although that trait was causally related to his having always been overly sensitive, indeed nearly paranoid about being excluded from his family or from groups of his peers. His initial anxiety in Tübingen, where he quite legitimately saw himself as a nonstudent "outsider," had gradually diminished during his first two years. Among the various factors effecting that adaptation was the young bookseller's gradual awareness of the fact that he was in no way intellectually inferior to most of the students he met. In fact, he came to realize that, compared with them, he was equally well read and even possessed a superior knowledge of many periods and genres of literature. It is of considerable significance that Hermann Hesse successfully integrated himself into a group of five advanced students, was welcomed by them, and, by all accounts, was considered to be their full peer. There is ample evidence to indicate that the others (Finckh and Hammelehle, in particular) admired and even envied Hesse, who was, after all, persevering in his literary endeavors with demonstrable, if still modest success.

His self-esteem enhanced by his acceptance into the *petit cénacle*, Hermann Hesse now entered a fruitful period of creative activity during the winter, spring, and summer of 1898, finishing the

---

12. Letter of 10 November 1897 to Johannes and Marie Hesse, *Kindheit und Jugend*, 2: 221. A good depiction of a typical *petit cénacle* evening at Hesse's abode is contained in a letter to his parents dated only April 1898, in *Kindheit und Jugend*, 2: 250.

fifty-six poems that would appear in October 1898 in the collection entitled *Romantische Lieder*. As his writing began to flourish, his Tübingen friends (and his correspondence with Helene Voigt-Diederichs) would also provide a kind of buffer against his parents' cool reception of the *Romantische Lieder*. The first to receive the slim volume was Ludwig Finckh, who wrote immediately to lavish effusive praise upon his friend:

> Lieber! Lach mich nicht aus: ich hab' geweint um Dich vor Glück; es ist wunderbar, jedes einzelne Stück ein Schatz. Ich jauchze darüber, daß Du endlich hervortrittst. . . Du bist jetzt berühmt.[13]
>
> [Dear Friend! Don't laugh at me: I cried with happiness for you; it is wonderful, every single poem a treasure. I'm shouting with joy at your having finally made a public appearance with your work. . . You are now famous.]

Similarly, Helene Voigt-Diederichs wrote:

> Es ist wunderlich, was Ihre Gedichte für eine innerliche Musik haben, es ist wunderlich was für Stimmung sie bringen. Ein wenig Rokoko, ein wenig Lavendel, schlafende Zeit, schlafende Außenwelt, ein feines Flüstern und Verstecken hinter Tönen, Mondschein und Mitternacht.[14]
>
> [It is strange what an inner music your poems have, what a mood they create. A bit of rococo, a bit of lavender, time and the external world in sleep, a delicate whispering and hiding behind tonal hues, moonlight, and midnight.]

Undoubtedly recalling the crisis generated by his Chopin poem a year earlier, however, Hesse waited nearly a month after receiving copies of the *Lieder* before sending the family his new book. Although his sister Adele wrote promptly from Calw to pass along Marie Hesse's own thanks for the book, his mother's first reaction – several days later – was pointedly reserved and focused on the few poems that she found wanting:

> [Ich] hab ... gleich am Samstag jeden freien Moment in Dein Büchlein hineingesehen und wohl manches Schöne gefunden. Die Form und Sprache gelingt dir fein – nur möchte ich dir für deine Dichtung höheren Inhalt wünschen ... die Kunst muß rein und durchaus edel sein; Gott hat dir Talent gegeben, wenn du einmal Ihn gefunden hast und Ihm diese schöne Gabe weihst, dann erst wird

---

13. Letter of 6 November 1898 from Ludwig Finckh, original in the Hesse Archives, Schweizerische Landesbibliothek, Bern.
14. Letter of 27 November 1898 from Helen Voigt-Diederichs, *Hermann Hesse, Helene Voigt-Diederichs. Zwei Autorenportraits in Briefen 1897–1900* (Köln, 1971), 88.

dein altes Mutterle über dir [sic] glückselig sein, einstweilen bete ich für mein "Königskind."[15]

[I looked through your little book right away Saturday, every free moment I had, and did find some nice things. You are doing quite well with form and language – it's just that I would hope you could achieve a more exalted content with your poetry. . . Art must be pure and completely noble; God has given you talent, when you one day find Him and dedicate this lovely gift to Him, only then will your little old Mama have a blissful feeling about you, meanwhile I will pray for my "King's Child."]

No sooner had Hesse composed a "justification" for his work along with a rather forced assurance that his mother's criticisms were well taken, than he received a similarly disapproving letter from his half brother Karl:

Ich habe sie alle mit teilnehmendem Herzen gelesen u. mich an manchen herzlich erfreut. . . Die fast allezeit düstere traurige Grundstimmung läßt ja freilich eine Freude am Stoff nicht aufkommen.[16]

[I read them all with a sympathetic heart and took pleasure in some of them. . . Still, the almost pervasive, gloomy basic mood does not allow the reader much joy.]

While others wrote to praise and congratulate the poet,[17] Hesse – who viewed the *Lieder* as a "finale of a now concluded phase" – was quite uncomfortable with the diverse reactions to his work. As he confided to Helene Voigt-Diederichs:

Ich bin noch verwirrt durch allerlei schwer zu beantwortende Briefe über die *Lieder*, und einige Kopfwehtage. Diese Lieder waren mir fast alle schon halb fremd geworden. . . Nun kommen allerlei Briefschreiber, böse und gute, denen diese Lieder neu und viel wichtiger als mir sind, und wollen Aufschlüsse und Rechenschaften über Dinge, die mich zum Teil kaum noch berühren.[18]

15. Letter of 1 December 1898 from Marie Hesse, *Kindheit und Jugend*, 2: 304f. "Königskind" is the title of a poem in the *Romantische Lieder*. Karl Isenberg, an accomplished musician, would set the poem to music in early 1899.

16. Letter of 3 December 1898 from Karl Isenberg, *Kindheit und Jugend*, 2: 307.

17. See, for example, the letters in *Kindheit und Jugend* from Eberhard Goes (15 January 1899, 315), Ernst Kapff (23 January 1899, 317f.), and Adele Hesse's close friend, Gertrud Fischer, who lived in Ben Avon, Pennsylvania and noted: "Seien Sie nicht böse, wenn ein Gruß aus dem poesielosen Amerika Sie einen Augenblick in den Dichterträumen gestört hat" (31 January 1899, 319). ["Don't be angry if greetings from America, this unpoetic land, take you away from your poetic musings for a moment."]

18. Letter of 4 December 1898 to Helene Voigt-Diederichs, *Kindheit und Jugend*, 2: 309.

[I am still confused by all kinds of letters about the *Lieder*, letters that are difficult to answer, along with days on which I have headaches the whole day. Almost all these poems had already become half foreign to me. . . Now there are all kinds of letter writers, bad ones and good ones, to whom these verses are new and much more important than they are to me, and these people want explanations and answers for things that, to some extent, don't even have anything more to do with me.]

This desire for a transition into a new phase of writing was also a reflection of Hesse's need for a change of milieu in his personal life, for by spring of 1899, even the activities of the *petit cénacle* were becoming somewhat monotonous. There can be little doubt that Hermann Hesse was also much encouraged in his hopes of becoming a self-supporting writer as a result of the publication of the *Romantische Lieder*. In February 1899, he selected nine short prose pieces he had composed during the preceding two years and presented them for consideration to Eugen Diederichs, the publisher husband of his *Brieffreundin* Helene Voigt-Diederichs. *Eine Stunde hinter Mitternacht* was accepted, and at Hesse's bidding, Diederichs agreed to have the volume in print in time for Johannes Hesse's birthday on 14 June 1899. This first prose publication can fairly be characterized as a paean to aestheticism, comprising as it does the narrations of a traveler who moves along the boundary between the real world and a realm of fantasy, mystery, and beauty. In the first tale, "Der Inseltraum," the narrator sets an appropriate tone for the entire collection by referring to himself as a "shipwrecked dreamer."[19]

Eugen Diederichs honored Hesse's request to publish *Eine Stunde hinter Mitternacht* in time for Johannes Hesse's birthday, although the elder Hesse was bedridden and unable to look at the volume until several days later. Marie Hesse, however, quickly skimmed the book's contents and, not surprisingly, was appalled by what she found:

Papa hat also dein Buch nicht ansehen können. Ich habe es schnell durchgehastet und dann nachts nicht schlafen können. Die "Fiebermuse" meide als eine Schlange, sie ist dieselbe, die ins Paradies schlich und noch heute jedes Liebes- und Poesie-Paradies gründlich vergiften möchte. . . Gott helfe dir und segne dich und rette dich heraus![20]

19. Hermann Hesse, *Eine Stunde hinter Mitternacht* (1899), *Werke*, 1: 159.
20. Letter of 15 June 1899 from Marie Hesse, *Kindheit und Jugend*, 2: 357f.

[Papa wasn't able to look at your book. I leafed through quickly and was not able to sleep that night. Avoid your "fever muse" like a snake; it was she who slithered into paradise and still today would poison completely any paradise of love and poetry. . . May God help you, bless you, and save you from her!]

Before the day was out, Hesse's mother wrote a second letter,[21] in which she similarly deplored other passages in *Eine Stunde hinter Mitternacht*, some of which she found so indecent as to be unsuitable reading for any girl. Hesse's initial response to the mildly hysterical tone of his mother's letters betrayed all too distinctly the bitterness and deep disappointment he felt; as he noted in a second, somewhat more gentle letter, he stood in front of the public mailbox for a good while before deciding not to send it. Nonetheless, that never-dispatched letter (which was found among Hesse's correspondence after his death in 1962) is quite instructive regarding Hermann Hesse's near exasperation at his parents' intolerance:

Wollt Ihr mir einen Gefallen tun, so schickt mir das zum 14. gesandte Exemplar meines Buches wieder zu, denn ich habe wenig Freiexemplare, bedaure auch sehr, es irgendwo gelesen zu wissen, wo jedes Wort mir zum Üblen gewendet wird. . . Ihr kennt wohl das Wort: "Den Reinen ist alles rein" und habt mich sonach zu den Unreinen gestellt.[22]

[If you want to do me a favor, then please send back the copy of my book that I sent you on the 14th, for I don't have many free copies and also regret very much now that it is being read with each word in it turned against me. . . You all know well the words: "To the pure all is pure," and therewith you have dispatched me to the impure.]

In his second missive, Hesse did repeat his request for the book to be returned to him, which it presumably was; there is no indication in the correspondence of the time that Johannes Hesse ever did read the book. Referring to the incident years later, in a 1920 letter to his sister Marulla, Hesse noted:

[F]ür mich war eines der deprimierendsten und schädlichsten Erlebnisse der Jünglingsjahre ein Brief von ihr, in dem sie meine ersten Dichtungen mit Prüderie und Moralpredigt besprach.[23]

21. Letter of 15 or 16 June 1899 from Marie Hesse, *Kindheit und Jugend*, 2: 358f.
22. Letter of 16 June 1899 to Marie Hesse (never sent), *Kindheit und Jugend*, 2: 361.
23. Letter of 4 July 1920 to Marulla Hesse, *Briefe*, 1: 453f.

[One of the most depressing and damaging experiences of my young years was a letter from her, in which she referred to my first poetic attempts with prudery and moral chastizing.]

"Lulu," the Summer of 1899, and Leaving Tübingen

Since the fall of 1898, as his letters made increasingly evident, Hermann Hesse had been tiring of the bookselling trade – if, indeed, he had ever been more than mildly enthusiastic about it. Though he had been hired as a permanent employee at Heckenhauer's upon completion of his apprenticeship on 30 September 1898, he quickly realized that this "career" was becoming little more than a mundane retail sales position. Try as he might, there was scant encouragement for him to exert much mental energy in familiarizing himself with the finer points of the profession, and by the time he arrived home evenings, his work was "dead and forgotten until the next morning."[24] His friends in the *petit cénacle*, whose company he had come to depend upon as the nearly sole basis of his *Privatleben* in Tübingen, were all advancing in their studies, facing examinations, and also regularly absent from Tübingen for months at a time during their lengthy vacations between semesters. At times, Hesse must have felt a bit of the loneliness and isolation he had known during much of his first two years there, yet he was also quite probably starting to sense that the time was nearing when he would leave Tübingen. In a letter to Helene Voigt-Diederichs in October 1898, while lamenting his loneliness ("all my friends have been gone for two months now"), the complete absence of women in his life, and the feeling that even his friends no longer provided the stimulation that he fancied needing, he mentioned for the first time the possibility of leaving Tübingen.[25] By late spring 1899, Hesse

24. Letter of 2 October 1898 to Johannes and Marie Hesse, *Kindheit und Jugend*, 2: 285f. In a similar vein, Hesse wrote to Helene Voigt-Diederichs – even after accepting a position at Reich's in Basel – concerning his vocation: "Er ist interessant, aber ich liebe ihn nicht. Daran ist vor allem die Kollegenschaft schuldig, welche zu zwei Dritteln überaus ungebildet und roh ist. Auch bin ich zwar ein guter Bücherkenner, aber ein schlechter Kaufmann." Letter of 29 August 1899 to Helene Voigt-Diederichs, *Kindheit und Jugend*, 2: 380. ["It is interesting, but I am not enamored of it. That has mostly to do with colleagues, two-thirds of whom are quite uneducated and coarse. Also, while I am good connoisseur of books, I am a bad salesman."]
25. Letter of 2 October 1898 to Helene Voigt-Diederichs, *Kindheit und Jugend*, 2: 287f.

began to consider seriously taking another position, and, most likely assisted by his uncle David Gundert, he secured a position at Reich's bookstore in Basel, a post he would assume in September 1899.[26]

His decision to leave Tübingen and his plans to take several weeks off before beginning the new job in Basel were undoubtedly stepped up by his pressing physical need for rest and recuperation. In June of 1899, after many weeks of worsening headaches and eye strain, he was ordered by his doctor to forego all reading and writing, at least aside from his work at Heckenhauer's; around mid-June, he submitted his resignation from Heckenhauer's, effective 31 July. (The necessity of writing letters, occasioned by the publication of *Eine Stunde hinter Mitternacht*, made it difficult for Hesse to follow his physician's orders very strictly.)

After the traumatic exchange of letters with his parents following their rejection of *Eine Stunde hinter Mitternacht*, Hesse was probably less than eager to spend his six weeks of vacation in Calw, yet he sensed that his parents would expect him to share much of that time with the family and it would appear that he vowed to make the best of his stay there. Nonetheless, it was likely with a feeling of relief that he received the counsel of his "medicine men" in Tübingen to spend the month of August on the Alb rather than in Calw. When Ludwig Finckh encouraged Hesse to join him in Kirchheim unter Teck (at the western edge of the Alb), where he was undergoing a so-called *Wasserkur*, the latter joyfully agreed and asked his friend to arrange for a room. Apparently, however, Finckh was unable to obtain accommodations for his fellow *cénacler*, for Hesse informed his parents on 17 July that he would be in Calw in early August. On 14 or 15 August 1899, Hermann Hesse left Calw for what, as he later recounted, was to be a two-day visit to Kirchheim.

According to the tale entitled "Lulu," in Hesse's heavily autobiographical *Hermann Lauscher* (1901), the *petit cénacle* was fully represented in Kirchheim in August 1899: Karl Hammelehle (Karl Hamelt in "Lulu"), Otto Erich Faber (Erich Tänzer), Oskar Rupp (Oskar Ripplein), Ludwig Finckh (Ludwig Ugel), and Hesse himself (Hermann Lauscher). Although none of the poet's own

26. See the letter of 15 July 1899 from Marie Hesse, *Kindheit und Jugend*, 2: 368. It seems likely that David Gundert learned of the opening at Reich's and assisted his nephew in obtaining the position.

correspondence from the period provides conclusive proof that, in reality, all were present, a lengthy missive written eight months later by Erich Otto Faber recounts the August episode and notes:

> Wie Du fort warst, da waren wir ja noch zu Vieren am Cénacletisch, dann im Herbst ging Ugel [Finckh], nachdem Carlo [Hammelehle] schon vorher nach Tübingen entschwunden war, Oskar [Rupp] und ich blieben.[27]
>
> [After you were gone, there were just four of us at the *cénacle* table, then, after Carlo had already departed for Tübingen, Ugel left in the fall. Only Oskar and I remained.]

Biographical accounts of the episode, however, are uniformly inconsistent in many details pertinent to this important and, in some respects, seminal event in the early phase of Hermann Hesse's creative development. In the account of Hesse's Kirchheim stay, for example, contained in his concise biography of Julie Hellmann, Martin Pfeifer states firmly that Hesse arrived there, "with violin case and bags," on 7 August 1899.[28] This date conflicts, however, with the arrival date determined by Gerhard Kirchhoff, editor of the second volume of *Kindheit und Jugend*, and noted above (14 or 15 August 1899). It is certain that Hermann Hesse was still in Calw on 7 August 1899, for he wrote a lengthy letter to Helene Voigt-Diederichs on that date, appending two more pages the same evening, in which he described having been surprised by an unexpected storm while hiking late that afternoon. His letter concludes with the request that she write him soon at his parents' address in Calw,[29] an indication that he may still have been undecided about making the journey to Kirchheim at all.

Upon his return from Kirchheim to Calw – probably the day after his arrival – the lovestruck young poet wrote his first letter to Julie Hellmann on 26 August, proclaiming his "sweet, tortuous

---

27. Letter of 13 April 1900 from Erich Otto Faber, *Kindheit und Jugend*, 2: 459ff. The nickname "Ugel," according to Ludwig Finckh himself, was conferred upon him as a child by his siblings: "Ugel wurde ich von meinen Geschwistern gerufen, Ugele, denn ich war der Jüngste und wohl etwas rundlich, – Ugele, Kugele." Ludwig Finckh, *Verschiedenes – Materialien zu einem Buch über Hermann Hesse*, handwritten manuscript dated 6 June 1949, in the Hesse Archives, Marbach. ["I was called Ugel by my brothers and sisters, Ugele, since I was the youngest and apparently somewhat chubby, – Ugele, Kugele."] The word *Kugele* is a Swabian diminutive form of the noun *Kugel*, meaning ball or sphere.

28. Martin Pfeifer, *Julie Hellmann – Hermann Hesses Lulu* (Kirchheim, 1991), 32.

29. Letter of 7 August 1899 to Helene Voigt-Diederichs, *Kindheit und Jugend*, 2: 373f.

Julie Hellmann ("Lulu")

love" for her, while at the same time lamenting the "feverish con-
dition" that was making it impossible for him to work:

> Ich möchte immer wieder zu Ihnen sagen, wie wunderbar Ihre
> Schönheit mich besiegt und ergriffen hat, Sie Wunderkind, und
> wie weh es mir tut, daß Sie so viel dulden und sich plagen müs-
> sen, statt Ihren gebührenden Platz als Fürstin und Liebesherrin
> einzunehmen.[30]

30. Letter of 26 August 1899 to Julie Hellmann, *Kindheit und Jugend*, 2: 377ff.

[I would like to say to you again and again how wonderfully your beauty has conquered and taken control of me, you wonderful child, and how it hurts me to hear that you have to put up with so much and to work so hard, instead of assuming your deserved position as Princess and Mistress of Love.]

Who was this beautiful young woman with whom Hermann Hesse had almost instantly fallen in love in Kirchheim?

Julie Hellmann was born in Heilbronn on 8 May 1878. Orphaned at an early age, she earned her keep as a maid and nanny and came to Kirchheim to work for a much older cousin (or, possibly, second cousin), Carl Müllerschön, proprietor of the *Gasthof zur Krone* there. More than half a century later, in two separate, written recollections of her original encounter with Hermann Hesse and the other members of the *petit cénacle*, Hellmann reports of having arrived in Kirchheim in the summer of 1899, joining her sister, Sophie, who was two years older and already working in the kitchen of the *Krone*. The earlier of these two accounts, loosely composed as a kind of tale in which she employs the fictional names Hesse had invented for the "Lulu" episode in *Hermann Lauscher*, is contained in the second volume of *Kindheit und Jugend* (pp. 612–14). This text was written at Ludwig Finckh's request – Hellmann addresses him directly toward the end of the piece – sometime after World War II, but before the death of Sophie Hellmann in 1954. The second recollection, composed shortly after Hesse's death in 1962, exists only in handwritten and typescript form; it was apparently solicited by Erna Jauer-Herholz, a journalist from the Heilbronn area, who included it in her manuscript entitled *Briefe und Abschriften aus der Freundschaft mit Hermann Hesse's 'Lulu'.*[31]

In both documents, as noted, Julie Hellmann recounts having arrived in Kirchheim in 1899, but evidence indicates that she actually arrived a year earlier.[32] In the later recollection, she states that

31. Copy in the Hesse Archives, Marbach. In the handwritten title of this manuscript, Hellmann is listed as *Julianne* Hellmann, apparently by Erna Jauer-Herholz herself. However, there is no other documentation of that longer form, and even Hellmann's gravestone in Möckmühl bears the name Julie.

32. Given Julie Hellmann's advanced age – she was around seventy when she wrote the first account, well over eighty when she narrated the second – such inconsistencies are not surprising. There are actually very few discrepancies, and except for this obvious mistake with regard to the date of her arrival, the others are minor. (She reports in the later version, for example, that Hesse and Finckh often serenaded her "by moonlight" with violin duets. The earlier *Erzählung*, on the other hand, notes, probably more accurately, that Hesse played his violin only in his room.)

she spent two years working for her relatives in the *Krone*, and Martin Pfeifer has documented her departure from Kirchheim on 12 March 1900. Similarly, a letter from Erich Otto Faber to Hermann Hesse, written in Kirchheim and dated 13 April 1900, also refers to Julie's having recently moved away from the town.[33] The most conclusive proof, however, that Hesse's "Lulu" was in Kirchheim, at the latest, by the fall of 1898 are two postcards written by Erich Otto Faber and sent to Hesse from Kirchheim. The first card, signed by two other *cénacle* members, Oskar Rupp and Wilhelm (Schönig), opens as follows:

> L[ieber] H[ermann]! 10. Oct. 98.
> Sie saßen zu viert in der Krone, eigentlich zu fünft denn Julie gehörte auch dazu ja vielmehr sie war die Seele von das ganze [sic].[34]
> [Dear Hermann! Oct. 10, 98
> Four of them sat in the Krone, actually there were five, since Julie also belonged to the group – indeeed, she was the soul of it.]

The second card, written a week later, leaves absolutely no doubt as to Julie Hellmann's presence in Kirchheim, for she signed the card herself with "Best Greetings, Julie Hellmann."[35] Had Hermann Hesse perhaps already met Julie Hellmann? Had one of his occasional trips to the Stuttgart region taken him through Kirchheim, perhaps to visit briefly one or the other member of the *petit cénacle*? Faber's first-name reference to Hellmann on the first card, to say nothing of her own, handwritten greeting to Hermann Hesse at the bottom of the second, might well lead one to suppose that. As enticing as this speculation is, however, it is not likely that Hesse met Julie Hellmann before the summer of 1899, although given the warm description of her in Faber's cards to Hesse, it is clear beyond doubt that the latter knew *of* her by fall 1898.

As his letters to Helene Voigt-Diederichs during the fall of 1898 make abundantly clear,[36] it was precisely during the first half of October 1898 that Hesse again complained of being lonely and at least mildly depressed. The regular reports of the festive activities

33. See footnote 27 above.
34. Unpublished postcard of 10 October 1898 from Erich Otto Faber (in Kirchheim) to Hermann Hesse (in Tübingen), original in the Hesse Archives, Marbach. Only Gerhard Kirchhoff, editor of the second volume of *Kindheit und Jugend*, has previously made mention of this card. See *Kindheit und Jugend*, 2: 539.
35. Unpublished postcard of 17 October 1898 from Erich Otto Faber (in Kirchheim) to Hermann Hesse (in Tübingen), original in the Hesse Archives, Marbach.
36. See Hesse's letters of 2 October and 8 October 1898 to Helene Voigt-Diederichs, *Kindheit und Jugend*, 2: 287ff.

of several of his *cénacle* fellows in Kirchheim hardly effected a positive mood in the young bookseller, who still had only Sundays free and was thus scarcely able to join them, yet their accounts may well have sparked a curiosity on Hesse's part for the idyllic little town, its rustic *Gasthof zur Krone*, and the intriguing Julie Hellmann. It is quite likely, though, that he was there before his August vacation. As he wrote to his parents, on 8 June 1899, he had spent the previous Sunday hiking:

> Letzten Sonntag war ich den ganzen Tag im Freien und habe sogar die Teck erstiegen, wo ich zum erstenmale war.[37]
>
> [Last Sunday I was outside all day and even climbed the Teck, where I was for the very first time.]

It is almost certain that Hesse was hiking with friends from the *cénacle*, and it is quite likely that they met and started their day's journey from Kirchheim.[38] Thus, the probability is considerable that Hermann Hesse met Julie Hellmann or at least saw her for the first time on that Sunday in June 1899.

It is commonly acknowledged that Hermann Hesse's early prose works are closely autobiographical. As Joseph Mileck notes, Hans Giebenrath and Hermann Heilner, the main characters of *Unterm Rad* (1904), "tell Hesse's story of 1891 to 1895, just as Peter Camenzind [in the 1903 novel of the same name] and his close friend Richard together tell Hesse's story of 1901 to 1903."[39] It seems accurate to add that Hesse's *Hinterlassene Schriften und Gedichte von Hermann Lauscher, herausgegeben von Hermann Hesse*, published by Reich's (his new employer in Basel) at the end of 1900, represents Hesse's own "story" of the Tübingen years, at least the tales "Die Novembernacht," "Tagebuch 1900," and the nine poems that constitute "Letzte Gedichte." It is significant that Hesse wrote "Lulu" separately during the early months of 1900, and that the piece was not included in the original edition of *Lauscher*. He sent the manuscript, under the title of *Prinzessin Lilia*, to Eugen Diederichs in August of 1900, but there is no indication

37. Letter of 8 June 1899 to Johannes and Marie Hesse, *Kindheit und Jugend*, 2: 354.

38. See Gerhard Kirchhoff's note in his *Chronik* of the years 1895–1900 in *Kindheit und Jugend*, 2: 673: "4. Juni: Ausflug H. Hs. auf den [sic] Teck (Berg der Schwäbischen Alb), wohl auch nach Kirchheim unter Teck." [4 June: Hesse takes a hike up the Teck (mountain in the Swabian Alb area), and probably on to Kirchheim below Teck.] Though variations of the town's name seem to be common even among inhabitants of the area, Kirchhoff uses the correct designation here, according to *Der Große ADAC Reiseführer* (1991 edition): Kirchheim unter Teck.

39. Mileck, *Hermann Hesse: Life and Art*, 36.

that the latter expressed any interest in publishing the piece despite Hesse's subsequent inquiries about it.[40] "Lulu" did not appear in print at all until 1906, when its author allowed publication in *Die Schweiz*;[41] a year later it would appear along with "Schlaflose Nächte" in the second edition of *Lauscher*.

Hesse's reasons for not publishing "Lulu" earlier may have had to do with his disappointment at Diederichs's apparent rejection of the story. But it is also possible that the tale was primarily intended as a kind of cathartic articulation of the Julie Hellmann episode and the impending dissolution of the *petit cénacle*, and that its publication was not a pressing matter. In the author's preface to the third edition of *Hermann Lauscher* in 1933, he indicates rather pointedly that the latter was the case:

> *Hinterlassene Schriften und Gedichte von Hermann Lauscher* war der Titel einer kleinen Schrift, die ich Ende 1900 in Basel erscheinen ließ und in der ich pseudonym über meine damals zu einer Krise gediehenen Jünglingsträume abrechnete. Ich dachte damals, mit dem von mir erfundenen und totgesagten Lauscher meine eigenen Träume, soweit sie mir abgetan schienen, einzusargen und zu begraben. . . Im übrigen soll der Lauscher, der jetzige [1907] wie der alte, eben nichts als ein Bekenntnisbuch für mich und meine Freunde sein.[42]

> [*Hermann Lauscher* was the title of a small work that I had published in Basel the end of 1900, in which, under a pseudonym, I settled accounts with my own adolescent fantasies, which had grown to crisis proportion. Through the character of the late Lauscher, whom I invented, I intended to bury those of my fantasies that I had outlived. . . Otherwise, this Lauscher, the new one (1907) as well as the original was to be nothing more than a confessional for me and my friends.]

There is no doubt that Hesse meant "Lulu" as a kind of monument to his friendship with the members of the *cénacle*, for, as he wrote in his calendar diary less than a month later, he sensed quite acutely both the uniqueness of the "Lulu" interlude and the finality of this *cénacle* adventure:

40. See Hesse's letters of 27 August 1900 (to Helene Voigt-Diederichs) and 9 October 1900 (to publisher Eugen Diederichs), *Kindheit und Jugend*, 2: 486 and 2: 500, respectively.

41. "Lulu. Ein Jugenderlebnis, dem Gedächtnis E. T. A. Hoffmanns gewidmet," *Die Schweiz* 19 (1906), 1–8, 29–36, 53–57.

42. Quoted in: Hermann Hesse, *Hermann Lauscher* (Frankfurt/M., 1976), 156–58.

Dann, nach schwerem Entschluß, kurzer Abschied von Lulumä-
dele und den Freunden, von denen ich bloß Finckhs sicher zu
sein glaube.[43]
[Then, after making that difficult decision, a brief farewell from lit-
tle Lulu and my friends, of whom I only feel certain of Finckh's con-
tinuing friendship.]

Nonetheless, this short tale must also be viewed on its literary
merits. In Joseph Mileck's assessment, "Lulu" is "undoubtedly the
most significant" of Hesse's early prose works, foreshadowing the
"characteristic pendulating rhythm" of the author's life and subse-
quent prose works, even that of his masterpiece, *Der Steppenwolf*:

Harry Haller's crisis, his emergence from a lonely retreat, his
renewed contact with life, and his subsequent return to his ascetic
dedication to things of the spirit is in its essence prefigured in
Lauscher's brief encounter with life in Kirchheim and his return to
a lonely retreat, to his art and to the more ideal world of his imagi-
nation. Both protagonists swing from isolation to contact, from the
ideal to the real.[44]

The tale's structure, too, shows a surprising virtuosity, in Mileck's
view, for Hesse successfully portrays a setting in which the "com-
monplace visible world and a wondrous fairy-tale realm are not
merely juxtaposed but adroitly fused."[45] It does indeed seem that
Lauscher, in the "Lulu" story, finds himself in a world at once
made up of real and fairy-tale elements and figures. It is almost as
if the standard romantic notion of a "barrier" between the real and
otherworldly has been completely removed here for the fictional
poet; his is a "real" world in which the wondrous has been seam-
lessly assimilated. It is hardly surprising that Hesse dedicated this
little story to the memory of E. T. A. Hoffmann.

Despite the temptation to treat Hermann Hesse's fictional
recounting of those magical ten days in Kirchheim as a hyperbol-
ically tainted variant of the actual episode, accounts of other *céna-
cle* members lend substantial credence to Hesse's fiction. In her
two written recollections of the episode, Julie Hellmann (dubbed
the "crown princess" by the group) describes at some length the
playful and romantic aura of those days, particularly the farewell
party for Hesse on the evening before his departure:

43. Entry of 20 September 1899 in *Bagels Geschäftskalender*, *Kindheit und Jugend*, 2:
384. He would also pen a short, light poem about this time in honor of the *cénacle*.
See "Dem 'petit cénacle'" (1899), in *Die Gedichte*, 2: 740.
44. Mileck, *Hermann Hesse: Life and Art*, 29.
45. Ibid.

In knabenhafter Reine hat Hermann Hesse mich verehrt, er war von vornehmer Zurückhaltung, so daß ich von dieser Verehrung kaum etwas merkte... Ein wenig zutraulicher wurde unser Benehmen zu einander an dem Abend vor Hesses Abreise, an dem wir im Kreis der Cenacler Hesses Abschied feierten. Wir hatten das Zimmer, in dem uns die Verwandten erlaubten zu feiern, mit Blumen und Girlanden geschmückt, wir lachten, sangen und waren harmlos fröhlich, denn wehe, wenn nicht alles in der damaligen Zeit der engherzigen Auffassung im Rahmen des Erlaubten geblieben wäre.

Bei mir wurde dieses schöne Jugenderlebnis mit Hesse und seinem Freundeskreis durch nichts verwischt. Bei Hesse ... zeugten manche Verse und auch die Niederschrift des Kirchheimer Jugenderlebnisses im Lauscherbuch davon, daß er diese Zeit mit dem Herzen erlebt hat. Nach Kirchheim gekommen ist er nie mehr, er schrieb einmal, er hätte den Zauber nicht verwischen wollen.[46]

[Hermann Hesse idolized me with a boyish purity that was nobly restrained, so much so that I scarcely took note of his adoration... Our behavior toward each other became somewhat bolder on the eve of his departure, when the whole cénacle celebrated his impending farewell. The room in which my relatives permitted us to celebrate had been decorated with flowers and garlands, and we laughed, sang, and had a harmlessly merry time; woe to any of us, if we had exceeded the narrow-minded notions of the time.

Nothing has erased this beautiful teenage experience with Hesse and his circle of friends. As for Hesse ... many a poem, as well as the recording of the Kirchheim experience in his Lauscher book, bears witness to his heartfelt experiences at that time. He never returned to Kirchheim, and he once wrote that he did not want to risk destroying the magic of that experience.]

The other members of the *cénacle* were also quite enamored of Julie Hellmann, though not so completely smitten as Hesse. Ludwig Finckh would write to Hellmann much later:

Liebe Kronprinzeß, wir sind alle froh, daß Du für uns auf der Welt warst und wir Dich kennen durften und lieben, Du hast uns Reinheit geschenkt und Deine hellen Jugendtage. Hab Dank Lulu![47]

[Dear Crown Princess, we are all happy that you were in this world for us and that we were permitted to know and love you, for you gave us innocence and your bright days of youth. Accept my thanks, Lulu!]

---

46. *Briefe und Abschriften aus der Freundschaft mit Hermann Hesse's "Lulu"*, copy in the Hesse Archives, Marbach.
47. Ibid.

Similarly, another *cénacler* (almost certainly Oskar Rupp) wrote to her of the Kirchheim days, "when you scorched all our hearts with your beauty."[48] It was Erich Otto Faber, however, who was apparently to become most closely involved with Julie Hellmann. Faber was already in Kirchheim by fall of 1899, as his postcards to Hesse in October 1898 make clear, having been sent there for his practical law training after completing the state examination. He was undoubtedly one of the *Referendare* (attorneys in training) mentioned by Julie Hellmann as among the first acquaintances she made in the *Gasthof zur Krone*:

> Unter anderen Gästen kamen ziemlich regelmäßig nach Schluß ihrer Dienstzeit beim Amtsgericht und Oberamt in Kirchheim einige Referendare in die Krone, wo sich zwischen diesen und Lulu eine nette Freundschaft herausbildete.[49]

> [Among the guests, there were some law interns who came by pretty regularly after finishing work at the local civil court in Kirchheim, and a nice relationship developed between Lulu and those young men.]

Hesse may well have envied Faber this advantage with Julie Hellmann, and the brief sixth episode in "Lulu," in which Erich Tänzer (Faber) awkwardly attempts to articulate his love for Lulu (Julie), can likely be viewed as an intentionally unflattering portrayal of his fellow *cénacler*:

> "Wo ist der Vorrat sämtlicher Paragraphen des Bürgerlichen Gesetzbuches, den ich mir ... so mühselig in den Kopf getrichtert hatte? Und das Strafrecht und der Zivilprozeß? Ja, wo sind sie? In meinem Kopf steht nur noch ein einziger Paragraph, der heißt Lulu! Und die Fußnote heißt: O du Schönste, o du Allerschönste!"
> Erichs Augen standen weit hervor ... seine Rechte umklammerte Lulus kühle Hand. Diese spähte ängstlich nach einer Gelegenheit zu entrinnen.[50]

> ["Where is that stock of memorized paragraphs from the civil code that I so painstakingly crammed into my head? And criminal law, and civil lawsuits? Yes, where are they? In my head there is but a single paragraph, the one entitled Lulu! And the footnote says: Oh, you most beautiful woman, you most beautiful of all!"
> Erich's eyes were bulging ... his right hand clung to Lulu's cool hand, as she anxiously sought an opportunity to make her escape.]

48. Ibid. Hellmann refers only to "ein anderer" ("another young man").
49. Ibid.
50. *Hermann Lauscher*, 83–84.

Hesse's admission of jealousy in his first letter to Julie Hellmann ("You have no idea how I am continuously tormented by thoughts of love and jealousy")[51] might, similarly, have been based on the friendship between Faber and Hellmann. As already noted, Faber provided Hesse with an update of the *cénacle*'s activities after Hesse's departure, detailing his own relationship to Julie, as well as the problems in the *Gasthof zur Krone* that led to her leaving in March 1900:

> Also die Geschichte vom reizenden kleinen Lulumädchen, damit hast Du dann auch meine Geschichte, wie's mir gegangen die ganze lange Zeit, seit wir nichts mehr von einander hörten.
>
> Ach die Zeiten, die Tage, wie Du sie noch in Erinnerung haben wirst von der Krone, von Lulu und dem Schwesterlein der Prinzessin.
>
> Dieses zarte, feine Geschöpf, das sich mir wie eine aufbrechende Blüte zart, schmeichelnd, duftend zuneigte und vertrauend offenbarte, warum habe ich nicht die Mittel, die Macht – oder vielleicht ehrlicher – den Mut, sie herauszuheben und in ein freies schönes Land zu heben und zu pflegen.[52]
>
> [Now to the situation with our charming little Lulu, whose story actually parallels my own story during this whole time since we last heard anything from each other.
>
> Oh, those times back then, the days in the *Krone*, the way you remember them and Lulu and her little sister.
>
> This fine and delicate creature, who came to me like a blossoming bud, tender, fawning, so sweetly scented, so trustingly open, why don't I have the means, the power, or, perhaps more honestly, the courage to rescue her, to bring her to a land of beauty and freedom where I could take care of her.]

(When Hesse received this news, he had already begun writing the Lulu episode as a separate tale, and it is not at all unlikely that Faber's informative letter prompted Hermann Hesse to complete the story quickly; it was finished by early June 1900.)

It is interesting that, decades later, Faber looked back upon the Kirchheim period and Hesse's portrayal of it with a skepticism tinged with unmistakable disregard. In a letter to Martin Pfeifer in 1951, he proclaimed:

> Von den Cénaclern und einer sogenannten "Kirchheimer Zeit" gibt es überhaupt nichts zu berichten. – Die Personen sind gänzlich nebensächlich und spielen für die ganze Erzählung keine Rolle.

51. Letter of 26 August 1899 to Julie Hellmann, *Kindheit und Jugend*, 2: 377.
52. Letter of 13 April 1900 from Erich Otto Faber, *Kindheit und Jugend*, 2: 459f.

Kurz gesagt: es ist alles Fantasie und Dichtung – im Sinn etwa E. Th. A. Hoffmanns.[53]

[I have absolutely nothing to report about any so-called "Kirchheim period" that the *cénacle* went through. The characters are quite secondary and play no role at all in the whole of the story. To put it bluntly: this is all fantasy and fiction, rather in the style of E. Th. A. Hofmann.]

Even more intriguing is the fact that Julie Hellmann did not mention Faber's name at all in her 1962 portrayal of the Kirchheim days, and her earlier account mentions Faber only once:

Eine spätere Begegnung mit O. E. Tänzer [Faber], dem ich einmal näher stand, möchte ich aber nicht erwähnt wissen, denn er hat mich damals schwer in meiner Frauenehre gekränkt.[54]

[I would rather not have you mention my later encounter with O. E. Tänzer (Faber) here. Though I was once quite close to him, he offended my sense of feminine honor deeply back then.]

To judge solely from Hesse's dozen or so letters to Julie Hellmann, which often included poems and were even accompanied by flowers, during the months following the Kirchheim visit, the young poet was indeed deeply moved by the experience. There is evidence, though, that Hermann Hesse never desired any deeper involvement with the object of his adoration, that having witnessed Julie's youthful beauty and having joyously immersed himself in the sensation of an almost feverish love for her, he had already achieved a kind of satisfaction. Upon his return to Calw, he began to internalize and "aestheticize" the entire experience. In a letter to Helene Voigt-Diederichs written just three days after his first missive to Julie Hellmann, Hesse noted having just returned "from a ten-day tourist sojourn in the Swabian hill country."[55] As Ralph Freedman astutely observes:

Julie ... may have existed only as a highly literary figure in a symbolist universe ... The love letters Hesse sent to Julie from Calw and

53. Pfeifer, *Julie Hellmann – Hermann Hesses Lulu*, 21.

54. Julie Hellmann: *Erzählung aus der Hessezeit – Kirchheim Teck 1899*, location of original unknown, reprinted in *Kindheit und Jugend*, 2: 612ff.

55. Letter of 29 August 1899 to Helene Voigt-Diederichs, *Kindheit und Jugend*, 2: 380. It is interesting that this letter also includes the poem "Ich will mich tief verneigen," which Hesse sent to Julie Hellmann somewhat later (according to Martin Pfeifer, *Julie Hellmann*, 25f.) but which was not published until it appeared in *Lulu* in 1906. Indeed, Hesse refers to the poem in this same letter as "the only poem that I wrote here [in Calw]."

Basel during the next few months were flowery and sometimes urgent, but it is striking how much they remain essentially nostalgic. They seemed to focus almost entirely on that particular "enchanted" vacation and the final gathering of the *cénacle*.[56]

It turned out, as Hesse predicted in his diary entry of 20 September 1899, that Ludwig Finckh was indeed the only *cénacle* member to maintain his friendship with Hesse. The closeness of the two at that time is also attested to by their mutual inclusion of a poem written by the other in their early works: Hesse included "Ugel's" poem "Die Fürstin heißt Elisabeth" in *Hermann Lauscher*, and Finckh's first collection of poems, *Fraue, du Süße* (1900), contained a short poem by Hermann Hesse entitled "Bild der Geliebten."[57]

Hesse's literary direction at the turn of the century, as "Lulu" and the other tales in *Hermann Lauscher* demonstrate with little ambiguity, may definitely be characterized as "neo-Romantic." The separation of life from art, so typical of German Romanticism of the nineteenth century, had become the norm for Hermann Hesse in his Tübingen years. Indeed, he lived that romantic notion fully, in a literally "day-night" dualistic existence, working in the mundane world of commercial bookselling during the day and devoting himself, first to his development as a writer, and then to writing itself during the hours of evening and night. Nothing he wrote at that time so completely captures his view of literature and the direction in which he would continue to create than his essay "Romantik und Neuromantik," which was written in 1900 and revised in 1902.[58] In a passage devoted to one of his contemporary literary idols, Maurice Maeterlinck, Hermann Hesse rather transparently describes a kind of "wish projection" of himself:

> Betrachten wir uns zum Schluß noch einen Romantiker von heute, einen lebenden, noch jungen, der schon abseits vom naturalistischen Bekenntnis aufwuchs und zur Zeit als Typus des Neuromantikers gelten kann. Ich rede von M. Maeterlinck. Bei ihm finden wir scheinbar keine Spur von Naturalismus mehr. Er stilisiert, er komponiert, er schmückt seine Dichtungen scheinbar mit der freien Willkür eines Brentano oder Hoffmann. Doch nur scheinbar. Auch er hat realistisch sehen und darstellen gelernt, man bemerkt das

---

56. Freedman, *Hermann Hesse: Pilgrim of Crisis*, 86.

57. There is no evidence that Hesse ever admitted to having written the poem, although Finckh acknowledged Hesse's authorship in a later edition of the collection. (See Mileck, *Hermann Hesse: Biography and Bibliography*, 1: 667.) The opening line of this poem goes as follows: "Wenn mich dein Bild im Traum besucht . . ."

58. Hermann Hesse, "Romantik und Neuromantik," *Werke*, 2: 105ff.

nur nicht sofort, weil er fast nur von unsichtbaren Dingen spricht. Im Eifer des Neuerers begann er seine Bahn als weltabgewandter Träumer und Einsiedler. Seither aber ist er mitten in seine Zeit und ihr Leben getreten. . . Er sieht in jedem Menschen verborgen und verschüchtert die Seele wohnen, und er lockt sie mit zarten, schonenden Worten hervor, spricht ihr Mut ein und versucht ihr die verlorene Herrschaft zurückzugeben.[59]

[In conclusion, let's take a look at another contemporary Romantic, one who is still living and still young, who grew up quite outside of the naturalistic sphere of influence and who today can be viewed as an example of the neo-Romantic. I am talking about M. Maeterlinck, in whose work we seem to find no trace of naturalism. He seems to stylize, to compose decoratively *ad libitum*, much in the spirit of Brentano or Hoffmann. But it only seems so. He, too, learned to look at the world realistically and to present it that way, it's just that you don't notice it right off, since he speaks almost exclusively of invisible things. With the zeal of an innovator, he began his journey as a dreamer, as a recluse removed from the world. Since then, however, he has stepped into our own age, our own lives. . . He sees the soul of each of us living hidden and frightened within us, and he draws it forth, inspires it, and tries to return it to its former dominance.]

---

59. Ibid., 111–12.

PART TWO

Basel (1899–1903)

CHRONOLOGY

1899 –   Hermann Hesse resigns his position at Heckenhauer's
in Tübingen, effective 1 August 1899. From 3 August
until 10 September, he vacations in Calw and Kirch-
heim unter Teck.

On 10 September, Hesse takes a short trip through
central Switzerland, accompanied by his brother Hans,
before beginning work at Reich's bookstore in Basel on
15 September. He moves into a rooming house at Euler-
straße 18, the first of seven abodes he will inhabit dur-
ing his four years in Basel. He begins learning French.

On 24 September, Hesse pays his first visit to friends
of his parents, the family of the noted historian and
Basel city archivist, Dr. Rudolf Wackernagel. That
evening, he meets Elisabeth and Marie La Roche,
daughters of Pastor Emmanuel La Roche, also friends
of his parents. During his first year in Basel, he will
visit these families often.

Around the middle of October, he moves to new
quarters (Holbeinstraße 21), next door to two young
architects, Jennen and Drach. (In January 1900, Hesse
moves in with Jennen in the latter's larger apartment.)

On 12 November, Ludwig Finckh visits Hesse in
Basel. That evening, Hesse is invited for the first time to
the family of Jakob Wackernagel, brother of Rudolf and
professor of language at the University of Basel.

In December, he publishes his first newspaper piece
("Kleine Freuden") in the *Allgemeine Schweizer
Zeitung*. He spends Christmas eve with the Rudolf
Wackernagels.

1899/00   During winter and spring, Hesse begins to write occasional reviews and short literary pieces for the *Allgemeine Schweizer Zeitung* and becomes friends with the paper's editor, Dr. Hans Trog. Through the Wackernagel and La Roche families, he quickly comes into contact with a variety of people in the Basel academic and art world.

Ludwig Finckh comes from Freiburg on 12 February and again in April, when he and Hesse make a trip to Lake Vierwaldstätter. Hesse travels to Freiburg a week later; the two friends exchange several more visits during 1900.

On 17 April, he moves into his own room in the Baeschlin home (Mostackerstraße 10). As often as possible, he goes on lengthy walks in the vicinity of Basel or makes short excursions to the mountains, where he hikes, swims, and rows. (Throughout the year 1900, Hesse is composing *Lauscher*, which appears in print in December 1900 in Reich's publishing house.)

On 8 July, he reports for his military physical in Lörrach (Baden). Due to severe nearsightedness, he is judged to be unfit for military service.

After ten days in Calw during the second half of August, he takes a vacation in Vitznau on Lake Vierwaldstätter until 11 September. Upon his return to Basel, he gives Reich's notice that he will leave at the beginning of 1901.

In October, Hesse completes twenty-five handwritten copies of his *Notturni*, which he sells to friends and acquaintances in Basel and Germany.

As in the previous year, he spends the evening of 24 December with the Wackernagels. Hesse initiates contact with Karl Ernst Knodt, sending him the freshly published *Hermann Lauscher*, and in return receives Christmas greetings from Knodt.

1901   –   Hesse quits his position in Reich's new-book department the end of January and begins to plan his first trip to Italy.

He returns to Calw the end of February and spends nearly a month with the family before leaving for Italy.

25 March to 19 May: Journey through Italy (Milan, Genoa, Florence, Bologna, Ravenna, Padua, Venice).

After a post-Italy visit in Calw, Hesse returns to Basel around mid-June and moves into a new room at Burgfelderstraße 10.

In mid-July, Hesse pays his first visit to Karl Ernst Knodt in Ober-Klingen (Odenwald).

On 1 August, Hesse begins work for the antiquarian Wattenwyl in Basel, where he will be employed until March 1903, when he will leave the bookselling trade for good. During August, he again spends several days vacation in Vitznau.

In October, Hesse's correspondence with Prince Emil von Schoenaich-Carolath begins with a card from Carolath praising *Lauscher*.

At the end of November, Hesse moves once again to new quarters (Stiftsgasse 5).

Hesse spends ten days with the Knodt family in Ober-Klingen at Christmas.

1902 – January, beginning of Hesse's correspondence with Cesco Como, a friend and protégé of Knodt. Near the end of January, publisher Eugen Diederichs (husband of Helene Voigt-Diederichs) offers to assist Hesse in applying for a position in the Leipzig Museum of Books and Publishing.

In March, Hesse decides against pursuing the position in Leipzig.

On 24 April, Hesse's mother dies in Calw; he does not attend the funeral.

In early May, Hesse begins composing his second set of *Notturni* and again enlists the help of Ludwig Finckh in finding "subscribers" for the small collection of poems.

Beginning of correspondence with Kurt Piper.

Hesse completes the compilation of his new work of poetry (*Die Gedichte*) and sends a first draft to Carl Busse on 5 June.

On the last day of July, Hesse changes addresses again, now moving to St. Albanvorstadt 7.

Toward the end of August, Hesse leaves Basel for Calw, where he stays until the end of October.

On 3 November, Hesse's *Gedichte* appear in print in the Grote publishing house in Berlin as volume 3 of the Neue Deutsche Lyriker series, edited by Carl Busse.

In early December, Knodt's anthology of poetry, *Wir sind die Sehnsucht*, appears in print. Hesse is represented in the volume by twelve of his poems.

Hesse spends Christmas again with the Knodt family in Ober-Klingen, where he also meets Cesco Como for the first time in person.

1903 — Hesse moves into new quarters at Feierabendstraße 37, which will be his address until he leaves Basel for good at the end of September.

On 5 February, Hesse writes his first letter to Stefan Zweig, beginning a correspondence that will endure for nearly four decades.

On 1 April, Hesse leaves Basel on his second journey to Italy, accompanied by Maria Bernoulli. They visit Milan, Florence, Pisa, and Genoa, before she returns to Basel on the 14th. Hesse continues to Venice and returns to Switzerland on 24 April.

Hesse and Maria Bernoulli become engaged on 31 May, though he waits several days before informing his father in Calw.

On 10 June, Hesse signs a contract with Samuel Fischer to publish his nearly completed *Peter Camenzind*. Hesse submits the finished novel on 5 September, and it is serialized in issues of the *Neue Rundschau* during October, November, and December 1903.

During the first week of October, Hesse gives up his apartment in Basel to live with his family in Calw until shortly before his wedding on 2 August 1904.

ADJUSTING TO BASEL AND NEW FREEDOM

Übrigens ward ich in Basel bald geselliger und nahm am Leben teil. Dankbarst muß ich das Wackernagel'sche Haus nennen, wo nicht nur eine liebe Familie, sondern ein Kreis von interessanten, tüchtigen Männern mich aufnahm.

Trost und Heilung brachte mir in all dieser rasch aber kühl und gottlos gelebten Zeit die schöne Natur der Schweiz.[1]

[In Basel, by the way, I soon became more convivial. I must mention the home of the Wackernagels with utmost gratitude, where not only a dear family took me in but also a circle of interesting and intelligent men. . . Throughout this fast-paced phase, though I was living a rather dispassionate and impious life, the natural beauty of Switzerland served to console and to heal me.]

Hermann Hesse must have sensed acutely that his move to Basel signified the beginning of a transition in his life that was infinitely more fraught with existential risk than had been his departure from Calw for Tübingen nearly four years earlier. In almost every respect, Hesse now removed himself by an additional and substantial distance from the proximity of parents and siblings, the rustic familiarity of the Swabian countryside in which he had spent most of his life, and the friendship and often adulatory support of his comrades in the *petit cénacle*. More disquieting, though, was likely the young poet's realization that he was on the threshold of an ineluctable and final commitment to his poetic art. Thus, it is not surprising that, almost from the outset at Reich's in Basel, Hermann Hesse increasingly viewed his career in the book

---

1. Entry of 5 February 1901 in *Bagels Geschäftskalender*, in *Kindheit und Jugend*, 2: 525.

trade as an annoying necessity that was nearing its end.[2] Sustained by his love of books, he had endured the peripheral inanity of retail bookselling through his Tübingen years of apprenticeship and novice clerk status. Now confronted with the reality of full-time employment in the trade, however, he opted after little more than a year at Reich's for the antiquarian branch:

> Ich blieb dem Beruf jedoch nur so lang treu, als ich ihn brauchte, um das Leben zu fristen. Im Alter von sechsundzwanzig Jahren, auf Grund eines ersten literarischen Erfolges [*Peter Camenzind*, 1903] gab ich auch diesen Beruf wieder auf.[3]
>
> [I only stuck with this trade as long as I needed the income to get by. At the age of twenty-six, on the strength of my first literary success (*Peter Camenzind*, 1903), I gave it up.]

His arrival in Basel, however, was a return to the site of an important phase of his childhood. Having lived there from the age of four until nine, Hesse knew and remembered many of the city's landmarks as well as the more significant of the area's natural features. Basel was also the seat of the religious missionary service to which many members of the Hesse and Gundert families had, for generations, committed their own lives, although from the beginning the young bookseller seems to have resolutely avoided all but the most passing contact with that institution and its community. As Ralph Freedman notes, Basel appears to have been for Hesse "less a homecoming than a fresh beginning" with Hesse "entering Basel as a new cultural home."[4] In the original version of

2. In a letter to Eugen Diederichs written just six weeks after he took his post in Basel, Hesse referred with little ambiguity to his position: "Aber bei allem Provisorischen dieses jetzigen Lebens fühle ich mit doch sehr gesundet und erneuert und habe einen Kopf voll fröhlicher Lebens- und Dichtungspläne." Letter of 5 November 1899 to Eugen Diederichs, *Kindheit und Jugend*, 2: 399. ["But despite the largely temporary nature of my present situation here, I do feel much healthier and renewed, and my head is full of positive plans for my life and for my writing."]

3. *Kurzgefaßter Lebenslauf* (1924), *Werke* 6: 396. It was probably the encouragement of publisher Eugen Diederichs that helped Hesse make the decision to change branches. Diederichs, who had published *Eine Stunde hinter Mitternacht* in April 1899, wrote on 1 September 1899, upon learning that Hesse, too, was trained in the book business: "Unser Beruf bietet in abhängiger Stellung fast nie Gelegenheit sich auszuleben, man ist Buchsklave, und deswegen möchte ich Ihnen raten, daß Sie, falls Sie es noch nicht sind, Antiquar werden." (*Kindheit und Jugend*, 2: 382). ["As a regular employee in our business, one almost never has the opportunity to be creative; one is simply a slave of the books. Therefore, I would advise you to become an antiquarian, in case you are not one already."]

4. Freedman, *Hermann Hesse: Pilgrim of Crisis*, 87.

his "Basler Erinnerungen" (1937), Hermann Hesse pondered his reasons for having decided on Basel nearly four decades earlier:

> Wie stark Basel in der Kinderzeit auf mich gewirkt hatte, zeigte sich, als ich am Ende meiner Lehrzeit als Buchhändler und Antiquar zum erstenmal frei und nach eigener Wahl in die Welt hinauszog. Ich hatte keinen anderen Wunsch, als wieder nach Basel zu kommen... Basel war für mich jetzt vor allem die Stadt Nietzsches, Jacob Burckhardts und Böcklins.[5]
>
> [The extent to which Basel had affected me during my childhood days there became apparent when I set out on my own for the first time after my apprenticeship as a bookseller and antiquarian. I had no other desire than to return to Basel... To me, Basel meant the city of Nietzsche, Jacob Burckhardt, and Böcklin.]

Almost immediately, he would be accepted into the very circle of Basel *Bildungsbürger* in which Burckhardt (1818–1897) and Nietzsche (1844–1900) were known and cherished. Ironically, it was through his parents' acquaintance with the Wackernagel brothers, Rudolf (a noted historian and the Basel city archivist at that time) and Jakob (professor of philology at the university), that the young writer first made contact with these and other families, many of whom had affiliations with the local university. Among the younger scholars whom Hesse regularly encountered during soirées at one or the other Wackernagel home were the German historian Johannes Haller (1865–1947),[6] author of *Epochen der deutschen Geschichte* (1923) and *Geschichte des Papsttums* (1934–45); the Silesian-born philosopher Karl Joel (1864–1934), best known for his *Wandlungen der Weltanschauungen* (1928); and the renowned Swiss art historian Heinrich Wölfflin (1864–1945), whose *Kunstgeschichtliche Grundbegriffe* (*Principles of Art History*, 1915) remains to this day a masterpiece of scholarship on art and cultural history. All of this was a rich and heady, indeed sometimes overwhelming, experience for the young man from Swabia, and only in retrospect was he able to convey the distinctive tone of his first months in Basel

5. Hermann Hesse, "Ein paar Basler Erinnerungen," *Basler Nachrichten*, Basel, 4 July 1937, Sunday supplement. Reprinted in its entirety in *Kindheit und Jugend*, 2: 614ff. As regards Hesse's indisputable fascination with Friedrich Nietzsche and his works, it is surprising that the philosopher's death on 25 August 1900 appears to have elicited no reaction at all on Hesse's part.

6. Haller, or von Haller, belonged to a German family whom Johannes Hesse's family had known already in Estonia. Presumably, as with so many other Basel "connections," Hermann Hesse initially met the young historian through his family.

and the considerable fervor of his own enthusiasm for the famed historian Burckhardt:

> [E]s wurde mir erst später klar, daß es ein einziger Mann war, der diesem Geist die charakteristische Prägung gegeben hatte. Eine schöne Stadt mit alter Tradition und einer gebildeten höheren Bürgerschaft, einer kleinen Universität, einem schönen Museum usw. mochte es auch anderswo geben. Hier aber war alles getränkt vom Geist, vom Einfluß und Vorbild eines Mannes. . . Er hieß Jacob Burckhardt.[7]
>
> [Only later did I realize that it was a single individual who characterized the spirit of this city. There may well be another beautiful city of old traditions, with an educated upper class, a small university, a fine museum etc. But here everything was saturated with the spirit, the influence, and the example of one man. . . His name was Jacob Burckhardt.]

Hesse had begun to read and appreciate Burckhardt's works in Tübingen, notably *Die Kultur der Renaissance in Italien* (*The Civilization of the Renaissance in Italy*) (1860) and the historian's *Cicerone* (*Cicerone: A Guide to the Works of Art in Italy*, 1855) served as Hesse's own "guide" to the cultural treasures of the country when he made his first journey to Italy in the spring of 1901.

On 24 September 1899, just nine days after arriving in Basel, Hermann Hesse paid his first visit to the Rudolf Wackernagel family. As he reported in a letter to his parents later that day, he found Dr. Wackernagel to be a friendly and interesting man who spoke, as Hesse noted with unmistakable approval, flawless High German without a trace of Swiss accent.[8] Hesse became a regular Sunday evening guest at the Rudolf Wackernagels and was quite soon also welcomed at the home of Jakob Wackernagel. During his first month on the job in Basel, he was also invited to the home of his employer, Herr Reich, and he had already paid a visit to the von Huene-Hoiningen family, friends of his father's going back to their common Estonian ties. As an early letter to his parents indicates,

---

7. Ibid. As Ralph Freedman rightly notes, however, Burckhardt's influence on Hesse is rarely found in the author's works: "A significant exception is the character of Father Jakobus in *The Glass Bead Game*, that Goethean magnum opus of his old age, where he conveys Burckhardt's philosophy of history rather than his specific judgments of art." Freedman, *Herman Hesse: Pilgrim of Crisis*, 89–90.

8. Letter of 24 September 1899 to Johannes and Marie Hesse, *Kindheit und Jugend*, 2: 386f. (This remark, by the way, provides another example of Hermann Hesse's decided appreciation of those around him who spoke High German rather than Swiss or Swabian dialect.)

the young bookseller had a full social calendar: "Tomorrow, Sunday, I am invited to the Huenes for dinner and to Mr. Reich's house for tea."[9]

Ralph Freedman has rightly noted that Hermann Hesse, who had striven in Tübingen to emulate the life style of his student contemporaries there, now took the artist "type" as his model:

> The artistic temperament, as he was to write again and again, became an essential ingredient of his life and work, and the artist of whatever medium (painter, musician, or poet) became an ideal embodiment of human vision and creativity. Artists were also associated with freedom from social restriction, a state he thought essential to creation.[10]

Among the many regular visitors to the Wackernagel home were two young architects, Heinrich Jennen and Hans Drach, with whom Hesse quickly became friends, moving into a room adjoining the three-room quarters occupied by the two other men (Holbeinstraße 21) on 14 October 1899. Jennen, a German from the Rhineland, had been awarded first prize for his plans for the expansion of the old Basel city hall, and he was rapidly establishing a reputation for his neo-Gothic architectural designs. Both men were also apparently quite artistically inclined – Hesse referred to Jennen as "artistic and sensitive," albeit "absolutely unliterary" – and, as a letter written to his parents shortly after he moved in with Jennen and Drach reveals, Hesse was quite pleased to be part of this threesome of "devoted art apostles."[11] Indeed, this was a situation that suited the young bookseller perfectly, for his early months in Basel witnessed an almost frenzied immersion into the visual arts:

> [W]ährend meine Tübinger Zeit, soweit sie mir gehörte, ausschließlich literarischen und intellektuellen Eroberungen gewidmet gewesen war ... ging mir in Basel auch das Auge auf, ich wurde ein aufmerksamer und bald auch ein wissender Betrachter von Architekturen und Kunstwerken.[12]
>
> [While I had devoted what free time I had in Tübingen exclusively to literary and intellectual conquests ... I began to develop a visual sense in Basel, and I became an attentive and soon also a knowledgeable student of architectural style and works of art.]

9. Letter of 14 October 1899 to Johannes and Marie Hesse, *Kindheit und Jugend*, 2: 393.

10. Freedman, *Hermann Hesse: Pilgrim of Crisis*, 91.

11. Letter of 22 October 1899 to Johannes and Marie Hesse, *Kindheit und Jugend*, 2: 395.

12. Hermann Hesse, "Beim Einzug in ein neues Haus" (1931), *Werke*, 10: 138.

No artist aroused Hesse's interest and passion more than Arnold Böcklin (1827–1901), the Basel-born landscape painter who died while Hermann was living in Basel. While his early works are characterized by a more classical landscape style, Böcklin developed into a significant precursor of twentieth-century surrealism during the second half of the nineteenth century. It may well have been the allegorical-surrealistic element in Böcklin's nature paintings that most appealed to the young author of *Eine Stunde hinter Mitternacht*. As Hesse wrote to his parents immediately after his first viewing of the works on 24 September 1899:

> Der Aufenthalt in diesem Böcklin-Zimmer ist überaus köstlich – Ihr wißt, wie sehr ich Böcklin schon verehrte, ehe ich Originale von ihm kannte – jetzt geht mir das Herz auf vor dieser unerhörten Pracht.[13]
>
> [A visit to this Böcklin room is thoroughly delightful – you know how I revered Böcklin before I ever saw originals of his – now my heart swells in the face of this inimitable splendor.]

Twelve of Böcklin's works were displayed in their own room of the *Kunsthalle*, and Hesse's Basel letters reveal that he visited this small collection almost weekly during his first year in Basel. He was particularly taken by the artist's allegorical *Vita Somnium Breve* (*Life is A Short Dream*), and he described it in almost excessive detail in a letter to his parents on 1 October 1899, summarizing the painting's theme as follows:

> Kinderlust, Liebeszeit, Tatenlust und Greisenalter sind auf kleinem Raum in ganz wunderbaren Gestalten dargestellt.[14]
>
> [Childhood desire, the romance of adulthood, the urge to accomplish, and old age are presented in quite wonderful figures within a small space.]

A Basel *Cénacle*

After his departure from Tübingen, Hesse's contact with most of the members of the *petit cénacle* in Germany was minimal. While an occasional letter or card was exchanged with one or the other of the now scattered *cénaclers*, the young bookseller in Basel heard

---

13. Letter of 24 September 1899, *Kindheit und Jugend*, 2: 387. As completely fascinated as Hesse was at the time with Böcklin's work, it is interesting that he seems to have made no mention anywhere of the artist's death on 16 January 1901.

14. Letter of 1 October 1899 to Johannes and Marie Hesse, *Kindheit und Jugend*, 2: 389f.

only from his closest friend, Ludwig "Ugel" Finckh, on a continuing basis. Even as he took leave of his friends (and Julie Hellmann) in Kirchheim on 25 August 1899, Hesse had sensed that he could really count only on Finckh's friendship.[15] As he noted in his provisional diary nearly sixteen months later, that feeling had proven true, for all his former friends in the *cénacle*, except Finckh, had indeed grown silent. Despite his quite active social life in Basel, Hermann Hesse missed the camaraderie of the Tübingen group and found solace only in the fact that his beloved "Ugel," having abandoned law for the study of medicine, had moved to Freiburg, just a short hour's train ride north of Basel.

Hermann Hesse was successful, however, in establishing rather quickly a circle of young, male friends in Basel which approximated the *cénacle*, but also included young fellow booksellers along with Jennen, Drach, and others. In fact, one can discern the emergence in Basel of a pattern of relationships strikingly similar to Hesse's circle of friends and acquaintances in Tübingen. At Reich's, his superior was Karl Lichtenhahn, who assumed quite the same mentor role as Heinrich Hermes had at Heckenhauer's in Tübingen. At Christmas 1901, Hesse presented Lichtenhahn with one of four handwritten copies of poetry entitled *Zehn schoene neue Lieder* that contained the dedication: "To the person, the teacher, the man of letters, and benefactor K. Lichtenhahn with many greetings of the season, H. Hesse."[16] Hesse maintained contact with Lichtenhahn, who later assumed proprietorship of the Reich firm, for several years after he had left Reich's, and even after leaving Basel for good, Hesse was sometimes an overnight guest at Lichtenhahn's home when he had occasion to return to Basel.[17] At Wattenwyl's antiquarian bookstore, he would also enjoy a quite pleasant and professionally instructive relationship with his older colleague, Julius Baur, to whom he referred as one of the "most genuine and dearest human beings" he had ever known.[18]

Unlike his employment situation in Tübingen, where by all accounts he rarely socialized with other apprentices or clerks in the book trade, Hesse made fast friends with at least two fellow

15. Entry in his provisional diary, *Bagels Geschäftskalender*, 20 September 1899, in *Kindheit und Jugend*, 2: 384.

16. Unpublished manuscript in the Hesse Archives, Marbach.

17. According to information provided by Volker Michels, Hermann Hesse Editor's Archive, Offenbach.

18. Quoted without a source in Zeller, *Hermann Hesse in Selbstzeugnissen und Bildokumenten*, 45.

booksellers, one of whom was Theodor Baeschlin, in whose mother's home (Mostackerstraße 10) Hesse lived from April 1900 until May 1901. "Theo" Baeschlin, nearly eight years younger than Hermann Hesse, had just started his own bookseller's apprenticeship when Hesse arrived in Basel in the fall of 1899. Almost from the day he met Hermann Hesse, Theo was an "enthusiastic fan" of Hesse's writing,[19] and he would soon try his own hand at poetry and short prose. After he left Basel in the fall of 1900 to assume a clerk's position in Munich, Hesse visited him in the summer of 1901. Upon Baeschlin's return to Basel in 1902, the two were the heart of the pseudoliterary "club" called *Die Entgleisten,*[20] which Hesse had been instrumental in forming and which, according to Baeschlin, considered itself a kind of literary "cabaret" along the lines of Munich shows they had seen. In a handwritten "poetic club book" composed during 1901 and 1902 and edited by Hesse, the group's pseudonymous members are introduced:

> Die Kameraden stellen sich vor:
> 1. Hermann Lauscher, verstorbener Dichter.
> 2. Il Maestro, lebender Musikant.
> 3. Canis Finus, ein bescheidener Jüngling.
> 4. Ego, ein gemeiner Feld-, Wald- and Flurphilosoph.
> 5. Friedrich, früherer Mime und entgleister Selbstmörder.
> 6. H. Hesse, Antiquar und Wanderer.[21]

> [The members present themselves:
> 1. Hermann Lauscher, deceased poet.
> 2. Il Maestro, living musician.
> 3. Canis Finus, a modest youth.
> 4. Ego, a common philosopher of the field, forest, and meadow.
> 5. Friedrich, former mime and failed suicide.
> 6. H. Hesse, antiquarian and hiker.]

19. Theo Baeschlin, "Hermann Hesse in Basel," in *Hermann Hesse in Augenzeugenberichten*, ed. Volker Michels (Frankfurt/M., 1991), 39. (Originally published in *Das Bücherblatt – Zeitschrift für den Bücherfreund und den internationalen Buchhandel*, Zürich, 20 June 1947.)

20. The title, literally, means "the derailed ones"; good contemporary English equivalents might be "the failures" or "the losers." Hesse had also composed a poem with the title "Die Entgleisten" about this time, and it was included in *Die Gedichte* (1902). Mileck dates the poem as 1902 (*Biography and Bibliography*, 1: 578), but in Hesse's own copy of the first edition (Hesse Archives, Marbach), in which the author himself penciled in the dates of origin for each of the 167 poems, he wrote the date 1900 next to the title "Die Entgleisten." See Theo Baeschlin, *Hermann Hesse in Basel* in *Hermann Hesse in Augenzeugenberichten*, ed. Volker Michels (Frankfurt/M., 1991), 39ff.

21. Unpublished, handwritten manuscript in the Hesse Archives, Marbach.

The thirty-two page manuscript contains thirty-five poems, the majority obviously composed by Hesse himself, even though several are attributed to others of the "Kameraden."[22] In an autobiographical short story first published in 1905, *Der Städtebauer*, the author made reference to the "club" by name, characterizing the group's members as follows:

> Da gab es noch den Klub der "Entgleisten," der obdachlos und von Gläubigern verfolgt von einem Wirtshaus ins andere flüchtete. . . Wir waren Lumpen und Zigeuner, aber wir waren keine *bohémiens*, wir lagen nicht mit langen Locken in den Kaffeehäusern herum und spielten nicht im Interesse kleiner Anpumpereien die verkannten Genies.[23]

> [And then there was the "failures" club which, without a fixed meeting place, fled from one pub to the other, pursued by bill collectors. . . We were ne'er-do-wells and drifters, but were not Bohemian types with long hair lying around in coffee houses and playing the role of the misunderstood genius for the sake of putting the touch on other patrons.]

While little evidence is available today regarding the identities of others in the group, it is certain that Hermann Baeschlin, Theo's older brother and a student of art and architecture, was a regular participant in the group's activities as were, at least occasionally, Hesse's former roommates, Jennen and Drach. Hermann "Alfredo" Baeschlin, who would live abroad for many years, wrote a fond commemoration of those early Basel days more than half a century later:

> Vor etwas mehr als 50 Jahren begannen in den *Basler Nachrichten* anmutige literarische Skizzen zu erscheinen, welche allgemeines Aufsehen erregten. . .
> Selten hat ein Mensch in meinem Leben einen solch tiefen Eindruck auf mich gemacht, wie Hermann Hesse. So hieß nämlich unser damaliger Hausgenosse und ich fühlte mich außerordentlich

22. Some of the poems in this manuscript also appear in Hesse's 1902 collection of *Notturni*, while others were included in his *Gedichte* (1902). Only eight pieces, however, are contained in the two-volume, 1977 Suhrkamp edition of the collected poems. In his definitive bibliography, Joseph Mileck lists all individual titles of the poems in this collection. See *Hermann Hesse: Biography and Bibliography*, 2: 1072. Mileck, too, is of the opinion that Hesse probably wrote most, if not all, of the poems.

23. Hermann Hesse, *Der Städtebauer*, first published in the Viennese *Neue Freie Presse*, 31 March 1905. Quoted here from *Gesammelte Erzählungen* (Frankfurt/ M., 1977 and 1993), 6: 207ff. The figure of the "city builder" in this *novella* is yet another character based on Hesse's good friend, the architect Heinrich Jennen.

geschmeichelt, daß ein Mann, der in der Zeitung so schöne Sachen schrieb, sich mit mir abgab, mir das Billardspiel beibrachte, das er sehr gut beherrschte und mich den Wein – nicht das Trinken – lieben lehrte. . . Ganz schön wurde es, wenn Hesse seine Geige nahm und zu improvisieren begann. Jene inhaltsvollen Stunden mit ihm haben mich die Musik und die Dichtkunst kennen und lieben gelehrt.[24]

[More than fifty years ago, the *Basel Nachrichten* started carrying delightful literary sketches that caught most everyone's attention. Rarely in my life has someone made such a deep impression on me as Hermann Hesse did. That was the name of our boarder back then, and I felt exceptionally flattered to receive the personal attention of a man who wrote such beautiful things in the paper; he taught me to play billiards (which he knew well) and to love wine (though not drinking as such). . .

It was especially nice when Hesse picked up his violin and began to improvise. Those delightful hours spent with him taught me to love music and literature.]

While Hesse had maintained intermittent correspondence with Theo, he had lost contact with Hermann Baeschlin, yet he responded warmly after reading the latter's touching recollection:

Lieber Jugendfreund [Hermann] Baeschlin!
Wir haben uns nicht wiedergesehen, seit ich als Jüngling in Basel bei Deiner Mutter wohnte und mit Dir und Theo so manche halbe Nacht verbrachte, bald bei Wein und Billardspiel, bald bei kleinen Festen auf meiner Bude, zu deren Schmuck Theo und ich die Verse lieferten, Du die Zeichnungen beitrugst.[25]

[Dear Baeschlin, friend of my youth!
We haven't seen each other since I was a young man living at your mother's place in Basel, where I spent many a long evening with you and Theo, sometimes drinking wine and playing billiards, sometimes getting together in my apartment. Theo and I used to provide the poems, and you contributed the drawings to decorate that place.]

Hermann Hesse actually seems to have filled a kind of "big brother" role for the two Baeschlins,[26] a circumstance not without

24. Alfredo Baeschlin, "Begegnung mit Hermann Hesse," in *Hermann Hesse in Augenzeugenberichten*, ed. Volker Michels (Frankfurt/M., 1991), 492f.
25. Hermann Hesse, letter dated spring, 1953 to Alfredo Baeschlin, *Briefe*, 4: 174f. The Hesse Archives in Marbach contain two of Hesse's handwritten collections of poetry from the time that are embellished with drawings by Hermann "Alfredo" Baeschlin.
26. In a letter he wrote to Theo Baeschlin on 17 November 1903, just after he left Basel for good, Hesse waxed almost parental in chiding his young friend about

a certain irony in view of his irregular contact with his own younger brother, Hans. When the pressures of school in Calw became too great, the younger Hesse brother, at the family's urging, came to Basel in December 1900, where he worked in the *Missionshaus* until early in 1902. There is little evidence that Hermann went out of his way to involve his younger sibling in his own life, although Hermann's desire to avoid contact with the people at the mission may partially explain his maintaining a discernible distance from Hans. There is a good probability that Johannes and Marie Hesse had hoped Hans's presence in Basel would help to provide them with more regular news of Hermann's various activities; indeed, the parents also may well have aspired to nudge the older sibling into closer contact with the *Missionshaus* community. Some of Marie Hesse's letters written during the first year of Hermann's stay in Basel reveal a renewed effort on her part to dispense, if not spiritual, then at least moral guidance to her son. Hermann's relationship with Heinrich Jennen, for example, inspired a stern, albeit apparently completely unfounded reprimand from his mother:

> Seit du mit Herrn Jennen zusammenwohnst, kommen wir zu kurz, du schriebst früher viel mehr an uns. Je weniger du schreibst, desto mehr beschäftigst du mich in schlaflosen Nächten. . . Liebes Kind! O strebe nach wahrhaft Gutem und Hohem und fliehe die Sünde! Die Welt liegt im Argen, die Versuchung zum Bösen ist mächtig: da muß ein *ganzer Wille* da sein, sich nicht hinabziehen zu lassen und ein Schreien zu Gott um Kraft zum Sieg.[27]

> [Since you have been living with Jennen, you have neglected us; you used to write us much more often. The less you write, the more you occupy my thoughts in sleepless nights. . . Dear child! Do strive for that which is truly good and valuable and avoid sin! The world is in desperate shape, the temptation to do evil is mighty: One must maintain a strong will in order to keep from being pulled down into degradation, and one must cry out to God for the strength to conquer evil.]

---

having fallen victim to a kind of melancholic lethargy: "Dennoch kann ich nicht anders, als etwa die Hälfte Deiner Schwermut Deinem Alter zuzuschreiben. . . Die Zeit, in der man anfängt, zum Verständnis seiner Persönlichkeit zu kommen, aber noch nicht Raum und Luft zur Betätigung und noch keine Anerkennung findet, ist immer heikel. Aber das geht vorüber." (*Briefe*, 1: 112.) ["Still I cannot help but attribute about half of your melancholy to your age. . . The phase is a particularly difficult one in which one starts coming to grips with his own personality, while not yet having enough space to grow and not yet having achieved any recognition. But it does pass."]

27. Letter of 9 March 1900 from Marie Hesse, *Kindheit und Jugend*, 2: 453f.

Hesse seems to have been genuinely surprised by the tone and severity of his mother's admonition, which undoubtedly reminded him all too vividly of similar harangues on her part during the previous two years. Still, he rather dutifully, if sarcastically, related to them his intention to leave Jennen's apartment and to move into a room of his own at the Baeschlins:

> Ihr Lieben!
> Danke für Mamas Brief, dessen erzählender Teil ja leider auch nicht viel erfreulicher ist, als der moralische. ... Daß ich Ende März von dem Ungeheuer Jennen wegziehe, wird Euch mit Freude erfüllen. Da Mama glaubt, er sei mir gefährlich oder raube Euch mein Interesse, muß ich doch berichten, daß ich seit unserm Zusammenwohnen, also seit Neujahr, einen Sonntag und drei Abende mit ihm verbrachte.[28]

> [My dear ones!
> Thank you for Mama's letter, the narrative section of which is unfortunately not much more joyous than the moralizing part. . . That I will be moving away from that monster Jennen the end of March will fill you with joy. Since Mama believes that he is dangerous to me or deprives you of my attention, I have to report that since we moved in together at the start of the year, I have spent one Sunday and three evenings with him.]

As one result of this unfortunate incident, Hesse's letters to the family bear no mention of Heinrich Jennen's name until six months later, and then for the last time. Thus, readers of the painstakingly compiled and transcribed letters contained in *Kindheit und Jugend* are deprived of what should have been a significant source of information about a quite important friendship of the young Hermann Hesse. As his later reminiscences stress, many of the central experiences of Hesse's Basel years were often gained in the company of Heinrich Jennen. In his "Basler Erinnerungen," the sixty-year-old writer devoted a lengthy passage to this brother-like friend from the Basel days:

> Ein anderer neugewonnener Freund, mit dem ich eine Zeitlang auch eine gemeinsame Wohnung an der Holbeinstraße hatte, war der junge rheinländische Architekt Jennen ... ein überschäumend lebensfroher junger Mensch, der mich Einzelgänger und Asketen in manche Genüsse und Behaglichkeiten des materiellen Lebens einführte. Wir haben in den elsässischen und badischen Wein- und Spargeldörfern manche Schlemmerei veranstaltet, im Storchen

Billard gespielt und in der Wolfsschlucht ... sowie im Helm am
Fischmarkt (es ist der *Stahlhelm* im *Steppenwolf*) häufig jene Studien
getrieben, deren Ergebnis die Camenzindschen Hymnen auf den
Wein waren.[29]

[Another new friend, with whom I shared an apartment on Hol-
bein Street for a while, was the young architect Jennen from the
Rhineland ... an exuberant and happy young person who intro-
duced this loner and ascetic to some of the pleasures and comforts
of the material life. In the wine and asparagus areas of Alsace and
Baden, we treated ourselves to some real culinary excesses. We also
played billiards in the Storchen ... and conducted studies in the
Helm down at the fish market (that's the Stahlhelm in *Steppenwolf*)
which led to the hymns of praise for wine that can be found in
Peter Camenzind.]

In the context of his prose masterpiece, *Der Steppenwolf*, Hesse's
allusion to the Basel experiences shared with Heinrich Jennen lends
rather indisputable legitimacy to the significance of that friendship.
In a short-story fragment written in 1900 or 1901, *Das Rathaus*, Her-
mann Hesse paid further tribute to Jennen. According to Marta
Dietschy, the two main characters in this sixty-two page manu-
script, Niklas and Veit, are modelled on Heinrich Jennen and Her-
mann Hesse, respectively.[30] It is somewhat puzzling that Hesse, to
judge by all available evidence, did not maintain any correspon-
dence with Jennen, especially since there is no indication that the
two had any sort of falling out. When he wrote of his Basel experi-
ences in later years, however, Hermann Hesse often mentioned Jen-
nen, while never alluding to either of the Baeschlin brothers.

Another close friend during Hesse's Basel years was fellow
bookseller Otto Drasdo, whom Hesse met during 1901 in Basel.
Hesse's unpublished correspondence to Drasdo, written between
1903 and 1910, reveals clearly that "Otti" (as Hesse addressed
him) was a member of the small clique that named itself *Die Ent-
gleisten*. Indeed, Drasdo seems to have been the author's source of
news from the group's members, for Hesse regularly thanked him
for passing along greetings from the *Wolfsschlucht*, the group's reg-
ular pub in Basel. Drasdo became business manager of Geering's
bookstore and antiquarian shop sometime after Hesse left Basel in

29. Hermann Hesse, "Ein paar Basler Erinnerungen," *Basler Nachrichten*, Basel,
4 July 1937, Sunday supplement. Reprinted in its entirety in *Kindheit und Jugend*,
2: 614ff.

30. Marta Dietschy, "Hermann Hesse und das Basler Rathaus," in *Basler Woche*,
11 February 1977, no. 7.

1903, and he often assisted Hesse in matters of business that had to be attended to in Basel, sparing Hesse burdensome trips from Gaienhofen. In the spring of 1908, for example, he entrusted Drasdo with power of attorney so that the latter could withdraw money from Hesse's account at a Basel savings bank.[31]

31. Unpublished letter of 12 April 1908 from Hermann Hesse to Otto Drasdo, Hesse Archives, Marbach.

ELISABETH

Aside from the Rudolf Wackernagel family, Hermann's most important social contact during his early days in Basel was another of his parents' circle of acquaintances from the days when they had lived in Basel two decades earlier, the family of Pastor Emmanuel La Roche-Stockmeyer, who had died in 1887. Although he did not visit the widow La Roche until 29 October 1899, Hesse met the two La Roche daughters, Elisabeth and Marie, at the home of Rudolf Wackernagel on 1 October.[1] Elisabeth, the youngest of the four La Roche offspring, was a year older than Hermann Hesse, and the two had met as children in the summer of 1893, when the Hesse family had vacationed with the Wackernagels and La Roches near Basel. Hesse was apparently soon fascinated by Elisabeth, an exceptionally talented musician whose piano virtuosity he regularly witnessed at the Wackernagels and greatly admired. She quickly supplanted Julie Hellmann as the author's fervently adored but unattainable love, although his letters to friends and family scarcely betray a hint of the depth of his feelings for her.

By mid-summer 1900, he seems to have realized the unlikelihood of Elisabeth's reciprocating his love for her. In a never-published, lengthy *novella*, *Der Dichter*, Hesse dealt with the relationship

1. The Hesse Archives in Marbach contain Dr. Rudolf Wackernagel's first invitation to Hermann Hesse to join the Wackernagels on a Sunday evening. Dr. Wackernagel dated the invitation only with "9. 1899," but sometime later Hesse himself noted on the envelope that his first invitation from Dr. Wackernagel and his first meeting with the two La Roche sisters was in September 1899. Since he had already paid a brief, introductory visit to Dr. Wackernagel after church on Sunday, September 24, Hesse surely refers here to his first evening invitation on 1 October 1899.

between a talented pianist named Elisabeth and the young poet Martin. In what is clearly an exaggerated depiction of his own relationship with Elisabeth La Roche, Hesse portrays the fictional Elisabeth's rather mocking rejection of Martin's attempt to interest her in his own literary creation, a flowery poem of admiration for a woman. After a period of withdrawal and self-pity, Martin again approaches Elisabeth, confessing his love for her in a poem. During a summer meeting at Lake Vierwaldstätter, he lures her into a nearby villa where they spend weeks of bliss together, revelling in each other's art. Elisabeth must leave for a concert tour, though, and when she fails to return, the young poet disappears into the snow-covered mountains, presumably never to be heard from again.[2]

Another unpublished manuscript from about the same time was given the title *Briefe an Elisabeth*. It is a cycle of six letters that were likely originally intended for inclusion in *Der Dichter*, since most of the letters touch upon themes and motifs central to that *novella*'s plot. While the references to Elisabeth in the two manuscripts unmistakably parallel Hesse's friendship with Elisabeth La Roche,[3] one can only speculate as to the biographical accuracy of the various actions of the young woman. There is little doubt, however, that the passion, frustration, and occasional anger expressed by the first-person author of *Briefe an Elisabeth* were Hesse's own deeply felt emotions. If Elisabeth La Roche indeed behaved toward Hermann Hesse as the Elisabeth of the *Briefe* does, at least implicitly, toward the writer of those letters, then the latter's quite pointed characterizations of her "gruesome nature" might be deserved. It is much more likely, though, that the consistently emotional tone of the *Briefe* reflects Hesse's inability to express his feelings directly to the real Elisabeth. In the heavily autobiographical *Lauscher* chapter, "Tagebuch 1900," the young author dealt more soberly – and more honestly – with his attraction to

---

2. *Der Dichter*, unpublished manuscript, 133 pp., Hesse Archives, Marbach. According to Joseph Mileck, Hesse submitted the story to the *Neue deutsche Rundschau* on 12 March 1902, where it was rejected. See Mileck, *Hermann Hesse: Biography and Bibliography*, 2: 1042.

3. The first line of the first page of the *Briefe* makes reference to Friday evening. Hesse regularly saw and heard Elisabeth La Roche at Wackernagels on Fridays. *Briefe an Elisabeth*, unpublished manuscript (two, nearly identical versions), 18 pp., Hesse Archives, Marbach. Quoted here from a typescript transcription in the Hermann Hesse Editor's Archives, Volker Michels, Offenbach, 2.

Elisabeth La Roche

Elisabeth La Roche and with the anxiety that would prevent his ever making his adoration known to her:

Liebe? Ich weiß nicht. Es ist nur ein Name. . . Oder soll ich dabei an Elisabeth denken? Ist das denn Liebe, daß ich manchmal Lust habe ihr mehr zu sagen, als man sonst Mädchen sagt? Daß es mich zuweilen traurig macht, wenn ich mir vorstelle, ich mache ihr Geständnisse und führe mit Schande von dannen?[4]

[Love? I don't know. It's only a word. . . Or should I think of Elisabeth when I hear it? Is it love, when I sometimes desire to tell her more than one ordinarily tells young women? Or that it occasionally makes me sad, when I imagine confessing my feelings to her only to leave in shame?]

There is no evidence to indicate that Hesse was able to master the fear of being rejected by Elisabeth La Roche that is unmistakably discernible in this passage; in his fictionalized accounts of his encounter with Elisabeth, of course, he could avoid the psychological obstacles that plagued him in reality.

In an interesting study of the interplay between Hesse's handwriting and the content of some of his early, unpublished writings, Günther Gottschalk takes a different view of Hesse's thinly fictional rendering of Elisabeth La Roche. Despite the indisputable similarities between the real and the fictional Elisabeth, Gottschalk argues, "one is not actually dealing here with the real Elisabeth, but rather with the conflict between a real person and the ideal of the perfect woman, as well as with the author's difficulty in establishing a satisfactory, indeed redemptive balance within this duality."[5] Several passages from the second and third letters of the *Briefe an Elisabeth* bear out the astuteness of Gottschalk's observation, for example:

4. Hermann Hesse, *Hermann Lauscher* (Frankfurt/M., 1976), 124.
5. Günther Gottschalk, *Dichter und ihre Handschriften – Betrachtungen zu Autographen des jungen Hermann Hesse im Marbacher Archiv* (Stuttgart, 1979), 81.

> Ich zweifle oft an der Wirklichkeit der sogenannten sichtbaren Welt, die hinter meinen Lidern und meiner Stirn in wilden, lohen Farben flammt. . .
>
> [I]n meiner inneren Welt sind Sie auch vorhanden. Kein Spiegelbild, denn Sie waren dort, ehe ich Sie im "Leben" fand.[6]
>
> [I often doubt the reality of the so-called visible world, which brightly burns within my own mind's eye in wild and blazing colors ...
>
> And you are also present in my internal world. Not as a reflection, for you were there before I found you in "real life."]

As Gottschalk concludes:

> Es geht hier ... um das beabsichtigte Zerrbild des Lebens und der Leidenschaft, das seinen Darsteller mit Verzweiflung erfüllt und mit dem Wunsch, hinter dieser "Wirklickheit" eine andere und höhere Wirklichkeit zu finden.[7]
>
> [One is dealing here ... with the intentional distortion of real life and real passion, which fill the author with despair and create the desire in him to find, behind this "reality," a different, higher reality.]

There is no doubt that *Der Dichter* and *Briefe an Elisabeth* reflect the notion of an aesthetically intense, "inner" reality that dominated Hermann Hesse's early creative endeavors and would continue throughout his life to inform his idea of the "internal" origin of creative and aesthetic impulse. Indeed, the young Hermann Hesse can be said to have shared some aesthetic concepts with expressionism and other abstract, nonrepresentational styles such as typified at the time by the Parisian *fauves*.[8] There is even, at times, a somewhat shamanistic aspect to Hesse's inward aesthetic journey, in which the poet as "medium" achieves, as it were, "contact" with his own inner spirit world. The search for a path to that inner

---

6. *Briefe an Elisabeth*, 2.

7. Gottschalk, 82.

8. That this was no passing aesthetic fancy of Hermann Hesse is confirmed by a passage in *Demian*, which appeared nearly two decades later and in which Sinclair receives the following wisdom from Pistorius: "Es gibt keine Wirklichkeit als die, die wir in uns haben. Darum leben die meisten Menschen so unwirklich, weil sie die Bilder außerhalb für das Wirkliche halten und ihre eigene Welt in sich gar nicht zu Worte kommen lassen." Hermann Hesse, *Demian, Werke*, 5: 112. ["There is no reality except the one contained within us. That is why so many people live such an unreal life. They take the images outside them for reality and never allow the world within to assert itself." Hermann Hesse, *Demian*, translated by Michael Roloff and Michael Lebeck (New York, 1965), 96.]

realm may well also have whetted Hesse's curiosity about the effects of hallucinogenic agents during the *Steppenwolf* period.[9]

Nonetheless, as Gottschalk himself implicitly acknowledges, one is confronted here with the "real" Hermann Hesse in his early twenties, an insecure, highly sensitive, and obviously shy young man who desperately desired interpersonal contact. His various protestations of the need to separate himself from his social surroundings can thus be interpreted as a kind of rationalization for his occasional very real inability to interact comfortably with others, especially with young women. Viewed from this perspective, Hesse's "inner" world may have been primarily a place of spiritual refuge that, to a considerable extent, owed its existence to the young poet's "flight" from the frequent unpleasantness of the external world. One can quite justifiably question, in other words, whether Hesse's "inner" world was really very much more than a place of escape from the difficulties of everyday life, born, to be sure, of a highly aestheticized and fantasy-driven creativity, but at the same time necessitated, in effect, by an almost instinctive compulsion for psychological survival.

In reality, Hermann Hesse's friendship with Elisabeth La Roche remained cordial and platonic, and his love for Elisabeth was most probably never expressed in any direct manner. In his occasional diary (*Bagels Geschäftskalender 1899*), Hesse noted on 5 February 1901:

> Bis über den Winter 99/1900 hinaus litt ich stark am Heimweh nach Lulu. . . Das Wilde und Quälende jener Liebe zerfloß zunächst in meiner neuerlichen Skepsis, dann auch durch die Bekanntschaft mit Elisabeth, die mich zu halber Liebe reizt, deren sehr wahre Schilderung Lauschers Tagebuch enthält.[10]

> [Through the winter of 1899–1900 and beyond, I longed greatly for Lulu. . . The passion and torment of the love I felt did begin to diminish, first because of my emerging skepticism and then due to meeting Elisabeth, who aroused mild feelings of love in me, which are honestly described in Lauscher's diary.]

As his forward to the second edition of *Lauscher* (1907) makes clear, Hesse had intended in this work to put the "dreams of his youth" behind him.[11] It is not clear to what extent Elisabeth La

9. As Joseph Mileck has taken great pains to determine, there is no conclusive evidence that Hermann Hesse ever used hallucinogens or any nonprescription drugs. There is no doubt, though, that Hesse was knowledgeable about the effects of opium, hashish, and mescaline. See Mileck, *Hermann Hesse: Life and Art*, 181f.

10. *Kindheit und Jugend*, 2: 524.

11. *Lauscher*, 156.

Roche figured in Hesse's "Jugendträume," for their relationship
was substantially different than the friendship with Julie Hell-
mann that had developed the previous summer, though Hesse's
quite different behavior toward each may well have been the
result of his acknowledgment of the very different social status of
the two young women: Julie, the orphaned child of little more
than peasant origins, and Elisabeth, the educated and talented
daughter of a prominent Basel family.

At any rate, *Lauscher* provides evidence that Hermann Hesse
was not only aware of the futility of his love for Elisabeth but had,
indeed, subjected his own behavior to a rather critical analysis:

> Bölsche könnte an mir einen eklatanten Fall von Distanzliebe
> konstatieren. Prüfe ich mich genau, so muß ich sagen, daß die
> Anziehungskraft, die Elisabeth auf mich übt, vom ersten Augen-
> blicke an auf einer einzigen frappanten Profillinie beruhte, na-
> mentlich auf der raffiniert eleganten Kontur des Halses und des
> Kinns im Profil. . . Ich besitze die Schönheit meiner Liebe in
> dieser Linie, wie man ein Meisterbild nach reichlicher Anschau-
> ung besitzt.[12]

> [Bölsche would diagnose in me a striking case of "love from afar." If
> I am quite honest with myself, I have to say that the attraction that
> Elisabeth exerts upon me has been based from the outset on a single,
> remarkable profile view of her; to be precise, it is based upon the
> exquisitely elegant contour of her throat and chin, as seen in pro-
> file.... I possess the beauty of my love by possessing this image, just
> as one possesses a masterpiece of art after viewing it thoroughly.]

The second volume of Wilhelm Bölsche's then quite popular, if
somewhat pseudoscientific work, *Das Liebesleben in der Natur* (1900),
contains a lengthy section on the topic of *Distanceliebe*, in which
Bölsche synopsizes the concept as follows:

> Zur Distanceliebe werfen wir alle Liebesdinge, die bloß durch den
> Geist, durch vergeistigte Werkzeuge, durch Schallwellen, Licht-
> wellen, Sprache, Schrift, ästhetisches Empfinden und so weiter
> das Liebes-Individuum bauen und zusammenhalten.[13]

> [We mean by the term "love from afar" all those notions of love that
> are solely intellectual constructs, the products of spiritualized ana-
> lytical tools, of sound waves, light waves, language, the printed

12. Ibid., 136.
13. Wilhelm Boelsche, *Das Liebesleben in der Natur*, 3 vols. (Jena, 1900), 154ff.
Hesse had apparently read the first two volumes of the work, which appeared in
1898 and 1900, respectively.

word, aesthetic sensitivity, and so on, and that have the purpose of perpetuating the love object.]

While Hesse's adoration of Elisabeth La Roche seems rather fittingly depicted here, his may have been, in Bölsche's taxonomy, an even more extreme case, that to which the latter referred as the "most chaste" form of *Distanceliebe*:

[A]lso [die] vergeistigste Unschuldsliebe per Distance, die den Mischakt [Zeugungsakt] eventuell gar nicht als möglich ahnt, mindestens ihn ignoriert als ihren Gegenpol.[14]

[That is to say, the most spiritualized and innocent form of "love from afar," which in some cases cannot even imagine the sexual act, or at least ignores it as the dialectically opposite pole to itself.]

Almost certainly, Hermann Hesse would have considered any sexual interaction with Elisabeth an impossibility; by transforming her into a kind of aesthetic construct of his own "inner" reality, he avoided – consciously or not – the potential pain of rejection. Indeed, his portrayal of Martin's treatment at the hands of Elisabeth in *Der Dichter* may fairly be viewed as a fictional projection of the reaction that he feared from the real Elisabeth.

As for Elisabeth La Roche, she appears to have been unaware of Hesse's amorous interest in her, at least until the first edition of his unpublished *Notturni* appeared in October 1900. Even in the set of *Notturni* dedicated to Elisabeth's mother, however, none of the poems is entitled "Elisabeth," although two of them would be included in a four-poem cycle bearing the name of Hesse's beloved. In her unpublished memoirs, Elisabeth La Roche recalled those years around the turn of the century, when she and Hermann Hesse were often guests of the Wackernagels, and offered an assessment of Hesse and of her personal situation at the time:

Es war zu jener Zeit, daß ich mit Hermann Hesse wieder zusammentraf, von dem in der Familie Wackernagel schon viel die Rede gewesen war. Der junge Dichter schien sich in diesem Milieu sehr wohl zu befinden, und die ganze Familie Wackernagel war ihm sehr zugetan. Aber ich hatte damals meinen Kopf und meine Gedanken immer noch ... in Gardone, und so war mein Interesse an Basler Bekanntschaften nicht sehr lebhaft.[15]

14. Ibid., 151ff.
15. "Hermann Hesse und Elisabeth," *Basler Nachrichten*, 10 October 1971, compiled from Elisabeth La Roche's unpublished memoirs by Marta Dietschy. Quoted here from *Kindheit und Jugend*, 2: 618f.

[It was then that I met Hermann Hesse once again, about whom there was much talk in the Wackernagel family. The young poet seemed to do well in this milieu, and the entire family was fond of him. At that time, however, my head and my thoughts were still in Gardone, thus my interest in making new acquaintances in Basel was not strong.]

Nothing in this passage indicates that her meeting with Hermann Hesse was anything more than a passing and cordial acquaintanceship, despite its importance for the poet himself. La Roche's mention of Gardone, by the way, is most likely a reference to Gardone Riviera, the international resort on the west bank of Lake Garda in northern Italy, where – befitting her social station – she had presumably spent a vacation before meeting Hesse in Basel in the fall of 1899.

According to Hesse's "quite true" depiction of his friendship with Elisabeth in *Lauscher*, his infatuation was rather intense well into the fall of 1900. By early 1901, however, as his diary entry indicates, that intensity had waned considerably, perhaps in reaction to Elisabeth's plans to leave for England later that year, where she was to spend three years employed as a social companion and music teacher. By the time she returned to Basel in 1904, Hermann Hesse had met Maria Bernoulli, to whom he became engaged in May 1903; he moved back to Calw in October of that year, never again to reside in Basel.

Taking a Critical Look at Basel: *Das Rathaus*

From shortly after his arrival in Basel in September 1899 until early fall one year later, Hermann Hesse's private life was anchored in the Wackernagel family. His letters of the period repeatedly make reference to his feeling completely at home there, and on more than one occasion he noted that Elisabeth Wackernagel was like a mother to him.[16] Outside of his contact with the Wackernagels, though, Hesse's attitude toward Basel society was decidedly skeptical. As he discovered early on, not everyone in Basel was as hospitable as the Wackernagels and their immediate families:

16. See, for example, the letter of 26 December 1899 to Johannes and Marie Hesse, *Kindheit und Jugend*, 2: 431.

Über diese Wackernagel'schen Familien hinaus reicht meine Bekanntschaft noch nicht – die echten Basler sind gegen Fremde, besonders junge Unbekannte, steif und mißtrauisch.[17]

[My circle of acquaintances doesn't yet extend beyond the Wackernagels – typical Baslers are formal and distrustful toward outsiders, especially toward young people they don't know.]

Increasingly, too, Hesse was reminded of the class discrepancy between him and many of those people with whom he came into contact through the Wackernagels. After a formal dinner party at the home of Prof. Jakob Wackernagel, Hesse wrote home:

Ein ganzes Haus voll Professoren in schwarzen Fräcken und Professorinnen in Staatskleidern bewegte sich in dem geräumigen und schönen Hause ... umher. Ich junger Pilz – ich war weitaus der Jüngste – saß etwas angeödet dazwischen.[18]

[The house was filled with professors in black jackets and their wives in elegant gowns, all circulating through the spacious and well-appointed rooms. As the youngest in the group, I sat in the middle of it all, somewhat bored.]

This and similar Basel experiences figure in Hesse's *Peter Camenzind* (begun in November 1901), in which the autobiographical protagonist is often at odds with a society into which, socially speaking, he does not fit. In a 1951 letter to French students working on *Peter Camenzind*, Hesse all but admits the heavily autobiographical essence of his first novel, and his remarks reveal quite strikingly the manner in which he had reacted to the Basel reality of the turn of the century:

Peter Camenzinds Unzufriedenheit und Sehnsucht richtet sich nicht auf die politischen Verhältnisse, sondern teils auf die eigene Person ... teils auf die Gesellschaft, an der er auf jugendliche Weise Kritik übt. Die Welt und Menschheit ... ist ihm zu satt, zu selbstzufrieden, zu glatt und normiert, er möchte freier, heftiger, schöner, edler leben als sie, er fühlt sich zu ihr von Anfang an im Gegensatz, ohne eigentlich zu merken, wie sehr sie ihn doch lockt und anzieht.[19]

[Peter Camenzind's dissatisfaction and yearning are not directed at the political circumstances of the time, but rather, in part, at himself

---

17. Letter of 3 December 1899 to Johannes and Marie Hesse, *Kindheit und Jugend*, 2: 419.

18. Letter of 1 February 1900 to Johannes und Marie Hesse, *Kindheit und Jugend*, 2: 443.

19. Hermann Hesse, "Über *Peter Camenzind*," *Werke*, 11: 25.

… in part at a society of which, in his youthful way, he is critical. He finds people in the world around him too contented, too self-satisfied, too polished and normal; he wishes to live more freely, more intensely, more aesthetically attuned, more nobly than they do. From the outset, he sees himself in opposition to them, without noticing, however, how much he really is attracted to their world.]

Perhaps as a result of his growing awareness that he did not and could never permanently "belong" to the society of the Wackernagels and the La Roches, perhaps also as a reaction to the futility of his longing for Elisabeth (who, of course, was leaving Basel anyway), Hermann Hesse began to withdraw from this circle of friends and acquaintances. His correspondence from the years 1901 and 1902 reflects rather clearly that even his contact with the Wackernagels was gradually curtailed. In fact, Hesse's last visit to the home of Rudolf Wackernagel occurred in November 1902, nearly a full year before the former's final departure from Basel in October 1903. In an explanatory and apologetic letter of 19 November 1903 – written in the relative security of his father's home in Calw – he assured Wackernagel that his absence during the preceding year (and, implicitly, his departure from Basel with no word of farewell) was mainly attributable to his own "strangeness":

Daß ich Ihr Haus so undankbar vermied, hat zum Hauptgrunde mein komisches Wesen, das mich immer hie und da gesellschaftsuntüchtig macht. So war ich wieder einmal feig und floh in die Wüste, denn ich ließ nicht nur meinen Verkehr bei Ihnen, sondern auch überall anderwärts ganz eingehen.[20]

[My having so ungratefully avoided your home was mainly due to my strange nature, which now and then renders me unfit for social contact. Therefore, in my cowardly way, I fled once again into the desert, causing not only my contact with your family to wither but that with all my other acquaintances, as well.]

In fact, Hesse had written a quite similar letter to Wackernagel more than a year earlier, on 19 October 1902, in which he apologized for not visiting the Wackernagels "during the past year." Apparently, the poet had begun to avoid social engagements in

20. Letter of 19 November 1903 to Dr. Rudolf Wackernagel, *Briefe*, 1: 113. Hesse listed here, among his other reasons for "disappearing," his serious involvement with a woman. It is surprising that he did not mention Maria Bernoulli by name, since Wackernagel would almost certainly have been aware of Hesse's friendship with Maria, whom he most likely had met in the Wackernagel home! One can, of course, only speculate as to the reasons for Hesse's hesitation to reveal his marriage plans, but he was definitely not entirely decided that he indeed wanted to marry.

Basel in late 1901 or early 1902. As an explanation for his absence, Hesse noted, probably quite honestly:

> Daß ich im letzten Jahr mich nie mehr blicken ließ, verzeihen Sie mir, da es nicht nur aus Laune, sondern meist wirklicher Krankheit wegen geschah. Dazu kam, daß meine alte nervöse Scheu vor dem unleidlichen Geschwätz größerer Abendgesellschaften usw. sich wieder mächtig regte und zu einer richtigen Angst vor allem Gesellschaftlichen wurde.[21]
>
> [Please pardon my having not been in contact during the past year. It was not just moodiness on my part, but mostly due to real health problems. Along with those, I was stricken anew by my old neurotic aversion to the unbearable prattle that always accompanies evening parties etc.; indeed, it turned into an outright fear of all social interaction.]

A much more candid epistle, written to Karl Ernst Knodt the beginning of December 1901, reveals a surprising cynicism on the part of the young poet:

> Die Geldnöte dauern einstweilen fort, doch komme ich mit Frechheit und Entsagung eben durch und taxiere die paar Häuser, in denen ich noch Verkehr pflege, nach dem Speisezettel. Trägt das Souper die verlorene Abendzeit und das Stiefelwichsen nicht materiell ein, so bleibe ich aus.[22]
>
> [My money problems continue, but thanks to my cockiness and some self-deprivation, I am making do, having learned to rank the meal offerings of the few homes in which I still have any social contact. If the meal doesn't pay off for the lost time and the preparations (shining my boots, for example), then I stay away.]

The very real financial "distress" mentioned by Hesse here can only have exacerbated his sense of being an outsider, since many of the families with whom he had most frequent contact were among the truly wealthy of Basel society. In the fragmentary *novella*, *Das Rathaus*, the autobiographical protagonist, the poet Veit, seems at times to reflect the author's own undeniable envy of those well-placed members of the Basel social structure, particularly the material security and status that were virtually guaranteed to the younger Basel generation. The figure of Gerhard, scion of an old and prominent family, functions as a kind of *Gegenspieler* to the Veit-Hesse character, and the author's various descriptions

---

21. Letter of 19 October 1902 to Dr. Rudolf Wackernagel, *Briefe*, 1: 91.
22. Unpublished letter of first week of December 1901, to Karl Ernst Knodt. Copy in Hermann Hesse Editor's Archive, Volker Michels, Offenbach.

of Gerhard reveal that Hesse intended him as a representative of the younger generation of the city's patrician class as, for example, in the following, subtly ironic introductory description of Gerhard:

> [D]iese klaren und guten Augen glänzten in jener Art von Fröhlichkeit, die fast so ständig wie eine Maske ist und nur für ein umfriedetes, sturmloses Dasein genügt.[23]
>
> [These good, clear eyes shone with the sort of cheeriness that is almost as fixed as a mask and really only suffices for someone who enjoys a peaceful and storm-free existence.]

Veit's status within the youthful group betrays with unfailing accuracy the author's mildly cyncial view of his own position in Basel society:

> [E]in schmaler, klug aussehender junger Mensch. Er hieß Veit, war ein stiller Gelehrter und Dichter und wurde, ohne eben viel zu gelten, von den Freunden oft als Quelle für Auskünfte gelehrter Art benützt.[24]
>
> [A slender, clever-looking young person. His name was Veit, he was a quiet, studious type and a poet, and without enjoying any particular status in the group, he was nonetheless often called upon by the friends as a source of learned information.]

In one of the fragment's central passages, Veit and Gerhard confront each other verbally as Veit challenges the latter's plan to organize the group of friends formally into a kind of social society. Gerhard's rejoinder provides an unmistakable reflection of Hermann Hesse's notion of his own status in the eyes of the privileged youth of patrician Basel society:

> Freundlich, doch mit etwas spöttischem Ton antwortete Gerhard. Er spielte den Lebenskenner und Praktiker gegen den Idealisten aus und hatte als beredter, witziger Sprecher den Beifall der meisten.[25]
>
> [In a friendly yet somewhat sarcastic tone, Gerhard answered. He assumed the role of the practical person, experienced in life. Thus pitting himself against the idealist, Veit, he gained the applause of most in the group.]

---

23. Hermann Hesse, *Das Rathaus, Aus Kinderzeiten – Gesammelte Erzählungen* (Frankfurt/M., 1977), 1: 53. It should be noted that, while Hesse does not mention Basel by name, his descriptions of various city landmarks make it clear that his story is set there. See Marta Dietschy, "Hermann Hesse und das Basler Rathaus," in *Basler Woche*, 11 February 1977, 3f.

24. Ibid., 60.

25. Ibid.

Another significant autobiographical feature of *Das Rathaus* is the introduction of Veit's close friend, the physician Ugel, who is based on Hesse's real-life friend Ludwig Finckh; that the author stopped short of identifying himself by name with the story's main character, Veit, thus becomes rather irrelevant. In fact, the sixty-two-page, unfinished manuscript, almost certainly written during 1902, contains a very accurate picture of Hesse's friendships with Finckh and Jennen (the architect Niklas in *Das Rathaus*) and may well bear witness to Hesse's need to articulate his strong attraction to these two entirely different young men and to differentiate between the two friendships. Veit and Ugel are presented as sharing an almost identical, critical perspective vis-à-vis Gerhard's proposal, a view that places them alone, outside the group:

> Die beiden einzigen, welche Gerhards Stimmung and Absichten herausfühlten und sich darüber Gedanken machten, waren der Arzt Ugel und sein neben ihm sitzender Freund ... Veit.[26]
>
> [The only two in the group who sensed what Gerhard was up to and were concerned about it were the physician, Ugel, and his friend, Veit, who was seated right next to him.]

In all, Ugel plays a rather peripheral role in the story, quite as Ludwig Finckh did at that time in Hesse's real circle of Basel friends and acquaintances. Living in Freiburg, Finckh was more than an occasional visitor in Basel, though his visits were limited, for the most part, to weekends and holidays. As the only "holdover" from the *petit cénacle*, Finckh's friendship was greatly cherished by Hermann Hesse, and there is no doubt that the two men grew increasingly closer during Hesse's four years in Basel.

It must be emphasized, however, that "Ugel" Finckh makes a rather token appearance in *Das Rathaus*, for the focus here is on the relationship between Hesse and Heinrich Jennen, the architect Niklas in the story:

> Die Freundschaft der beiden war von eigentümlicher Art. Aus der Blüte seines kraftvoll naiven, gesunden Lebens heraus bemitleidete Niklas den schmächtigen, schmalbrüstigen Kameraden, dessen geräuschlos fleißiges Bücher- und Gedankendasein ihm fremd, unbegreiflich und fast verächtlich erschien. Sobald ihm aber ein zuverlässiges Urteil fehlte oder eine tiefere Lebensfrage ihn beschäftigte, kam er zu Veit und erstaunte jedesmal über dessen Verständnis und tiefe Auffassung.[27]

26. Ibid.
27. Ibid., 66.

[The friendship between these two was unusual. In the prime of his robustly ingenuous and vigorous life, Niklas took pity on his slim, narrow-chested friend, who quietly and diligently toiled in a world of books and thought, a world that seemed foreign, incomprehensible, indeed almost contemptible to Niklas. Whenever he needed a reliable opinion, however, or was bothered by a deeper question about human existence, he came to Veit, whose understanding and profundity astonished him every time.]

Actually, as the lengthy passage continues, the relationship was quite complementary: what Veit (Hesse) lacked in physical strength and natural *joie de vivre* was provided "in abundance" by Niklas (Jennen), though the author emphasizes that Veit was "intellectually superior" to Niklas.[28]

Das Rathaus provides Hesse's most substantial fictional treatment of his Basel years. As mentioned above, close scrutiny of the text reveals unmistakably autobiographical insights into the young author's Basel friendships, as well as his status as an "outsider" who is rather indifferently tolerated by the younger generation of privileged Basel society, typified in the story by the character Gerhard. The latter's father may be viewed as a representative figure for the older generation, and his opinion about the presence of "artist" types among Gerhard's circle of friends undoubtedly reflects what a now more critical Hermann Hesse believed was the typical view of the father's generation. In a conversation with his son, Gerhard's father ("probably the most powerful man in the city") asks him to talk about his friends:

Du hast ja so viele, und ich gönne Dir's. Immerhin bin ich etwas erstaunt, so viele Fremde, so viele Künstler und Bücherschreiber darunter zu sehen. Ich schätze diese Leute. . . Aber sie sind unseßhaft, morgen verschwunden.[29]

[You have so many friends, and I am glad to see that. Still, I am somewhat surprised to see so many unusual types, so many artists and book writers among them. I do value these people. But they are unsettled, they'll be gone tomorrow.]

The father's reference to "unusual types" and his use of the mildly derogatory "book writers" describe precisely how Hermann Hesse

---

28. This "complementary" pair of friends anticipates a series of such pairs in Hermann Hesse's prose, for example Richard and Peter in *Peter Camenzind* and Hans Giebenrath and Hermann Heilner in *Unterm Rad*.
29. Ibid., 62.

believed he was viewed by many members of the older Basel generation.

Hesse's image of himself also emerges rather clearly in the *novella* in such phrases as "without enjoying much status in the group," "the unassuming person," and, especially, in his depiction of Veit's inner makeup:

> Daß hinter seinem maskenhaft trockenen Gesicht, seiner Unge-
> selligkeit und Redescheu verborgen eine starke, unersättliche
> Seele Qualen der Einsamkeit und Sehnsucht litt, wußten außer
> Ugel nur wenige.[30]
>
> [Aside from Ugel, only a very few knew that hidden behind his
> sober and mask-like face, behind his unsociable and taciturn exter-
> nal nature, a strong and insatiable soul suffered the torment of lone-
> liness and longing.]

The social environment depicted in *Das Rathaus* is hardly con-
ducive to a successful overcoming of such inner turmoil, and one
can justifiably ask if this nearly completed *novella* was not meant
as a vehicle for "working through" the frustations its author expe-
rienced in Basel. Indeed, one senses that Hesse may have too
pointedly striven here to project a differentiated portrait of Basel's
Bildungsbürgertum; while the individual parts of the work (the
group of youths, the Veit-Niklas friendship, Gerhard and his
father) are rather well rounded out, the main plot line remains
underdeveloped. Hesse may have realized that fact and decided
not to finish the story for publication. On the other hand, it may
have served the purpose of purging its author of his frustrations,
even in its incomplete form.

30. Ibid., 60.

NEW CONTACTS, NEW POETRY
The *Notturni*, the *Gedichte*

A s Hermann Hesse began during 1901 and 1902 to distance
himself from the Wackernagels, his Basel surrogate family, he
had already withdrawn to a great extent from his own family in
Calw. In fact, Hesse visited his family in Calw only five times dur-
ing his four years in Basel, although he could travel there in three
hours by train; between 1898 and 1903, he did not spend a single
Christmas in Calw! He also wrote home less frequently and, when
he did write, avoided topics that would have prompted criticism
or disapproval on his parents' part. He had discovered much ear-
lier, for example, that complaints about health problems were sure
to meet with sympathy and concern in Calw, although his reports
of insomnia and chronic headaches were hardly exaggerated. By
the time his mother died on 24 April 1902, Hesse had removed
himself to such a degree from the activities and interactions within
the family that he did not travel to Calw for the funeral. In addi-
tion, in the case of his mother, Hesse almost certainly harbored
some resentment, if only subconsciously. As Ralph Freedman
accurately puts it:

> He could not engage himself in his mother's death, just as for the
> past two years, since her rejection of his poetry, he could not fully
> engage himself in her life.[1]

That he nonetheless felt considerable remorse about failing to
travel to Calw for Marie Hesse's funeral, indeed about having left

1. Freedman, *Hermann Hesse: Pilgrim of Crisis,* 100.

so much unresolved between them, is reflected rather clearly in *Peter Camenzind*, when the autobiographical hero happens to enter his parents' bedroom during the night of his mother's death. Peter kneels beside her bed, where he passes with her the final two hours of her life. In Hesse's depiction of Mother Camenzind's eyes meeting Peter's one last time, the author undoubtedly projected his own wish for a kind of final absolution from his own mother.[2]

In his first contact with the family after learning of his mother's death – a postcard sent on 25 April – he informed them that he had decided, "after a difficult inner struggle," not to come to Calw.[3] He did not mention, however, the real reason for staying in Basel. As Freedman states:

> Joining his family at that time would have drawn Hesse into a vortex he feared most, that palpable awareness of loss from which he tried to protect himself all his life.[4]

Despite having voluntarily distanced himself from his family and from the Wackernagels, however, Hesse did not isolate himself completely from society. Indeed, given his friendships with Heinrich Jennen, Otto Drasdo, the Baeschlins, and the circle of artists and musicians around Maria Bernoulli and her younger sister, Mathilde, it would seem that he did not want for social companions and activity. As late as November 1902, he would make the acquaintance of yet another Basel artist, the young painter Rudolf Löw, who had sought him out after reading his just published *Gedichte*, though Hesse predicted quite accurately that the friendship would not last, since Löw, like Hesse himself, had definite "loner tendencies."[5]

Still, the need for a family tie was strong in Hermann Hesse, and the young man was rarely without an older male friend – teacher, colleague, employer – who filled his need for a father figure. As his bonds with the family in Calw weakened, and as the attraction of Basel society wore thin, Hesse obviously welcomed the chance to establish new friendships outside of Basel and Calw.

2. Hermann Hesse, *Peter Camenzind, Werke*, 1: 373.

3. Hermann Hesse did not return to Calw until September 1902, where he attempted to follow doctor's orders to rest and refrain from reading and writing in order to allow his eyes to heal. After nearly two months there, he returned to Basel in early November.

4. Freedman, *Hermann Hesse: Pilgrim of Crisis*, 100.

5. Unpublished letter of 21 December 1902 from Hermann Hesse to his family in Calw. Copy in Hermann Hesse Editor's Archive, Volker Michels, Offenbach.

Such an opportunity presented itself in the fall of 1900, when Hesse first came into contact with Karl Ernst Knodt.

The *Waldpfarrer* and His Friends

On 9 October 1900, Ludwig Finckh wrote to Hermann Hesse, offering to enlist the assistance of Karl Ernst Knodt in finding potential subscribers for Hesse's initial edition of the *Notturni*.[6] Hesse apparently did not avail himself of his best friend's offer, for the six extant copies of the collection – as well as orders for nearly a dozen more – would indicate that all of the twenty-five hand-written sets were probably purchased by Hesse's friends and acquaintances in Basel and the neighboring areas of Germany, quite in keeping with the young poet's desire to avoid the critical risks of broader public exposure. Nonetheless, late in the fall, he did contact Knodt (known as the *Waldpfarrer* or "pastor of the woods"), and by Christmas 1900, the two men had established a correspondence that would develop into one of Hesse's most extensive exchanges during his remaining years in Basel. Who was Karl Ernst Knodt?

> Wer Karl Knodt ist? Darum muß man uns junge Dichter fragen. . . Wir kennen ihn fast alle. Er hat uns, als wir noch hoffnungsvoll unbekannte Lyriker waren, herzliche Briefe geschrieben und uns eingeladen, und wir kamen auf unseren Wanderungen immer gern in sein Pfarrhäuschen in dem kleinen Odenwalddorf Ober-Klingen, weit abseits von Welt und Eisenbahn. . .
>
> Der "Waldpfarrer" schrieb nicht nur Kritiken über unsere Bücher – das taten andere auch. Aber er schonte, wenn einer von uns ange-wandert kam, nicht das Huhn auf dem Hofe, noch den Wein im Keller, noch die Gans im Stalle – und er war und ist doch nichts weniger als ein Krösus.
>
> Er saß mit uns Jungen abends beim Wein, lief mit uns in seine Wälder, richtete uns zur Nacht ein Bett und hat manch warmen Sommernachmittag mit uns in träumerisch lässigen Gesprächen und manch heitere Abendstunde in frohen Scherzen zugebracht.[7]

6. Unpublished letter of 9 October 1900 from Ludwig Finckh. Original in the Hesse Archives of the Swiss National Library, Bern.

7. Hermann Hesse, review of Knodt's *Fontes Melusinae* in *Neue Zürcher Zeitung*, 19 November 1904. Hesse's reference here to Knodt's village as "far from trains and city life," is no exaggeration. In an unpublished letter of 19 January 1901, Knodt described in detail how Hesse could travel by rail from Basel to Darmstadt, changing there to a local train to Lengfeld in the Odenwald region, from where he

[Who is Karl Ernst Knodt, you inquire? Well, ask any of us younger poets and writers . . . almost all of us know him, for when we were still struggling, unknown poets, he wrote us warm and hearty letters, inviting us to visit him, and we loved to come to his little parsonage in the village of Ober-Klingen in the Odenwald region, far from the world and far from the nearest train station.

The "pastor of the woods" didn't just write reviews of our work – others did that, too. But when one of us came wandering in, he spared neither the chicken from the barnyard, nor the wine from his cellar, nor the goose in the pen – he was (and still is) nothing less than a real Croesus.

He sat with us youngsters evenings over wine, hiked with us through his woods, fixed us up a bed at night, and spent many a warm summer afternoon in dreamily idle conversations and many a cheerful evening hour happily joking around with us.]

Karl Ernst Knodt was born on 6 June 1856 in Eppelsheim (Rhenish Hessia), the fourth son of Joseph Adam Knodt, a descendant of several generations of Lutheran theologians in the region. After grade school in his father's parish school, Karl Ernst attended *Gymnasia* in Darmstadt, Kreuznach, and Büdingen. Upon completion of his theological studies at the University of Strasbourg (1875 to 1878), he attended the pastor's college in Friedberg in 1879-80 and was ordained on 22 February 1880 as pastor and school deacon in Gernsheim on the Rhine.

In August 1880, he married Käthe Christmann from Nordheim (Heilbronn). After the birth of the first of their two children, Karl, on 14 June 1881, Knodt was called to serve as pastor to the village parish of Ober-Klingen in the Odenwald area at the foot of Otzberg mountain, some thirty kilometers to the southeast of Darmstadt. In this idyllic and little-known corner of Hessia, the family's second son, Theodor, was born on 21 October 1891. The Knodts remained in Ober-Klingen until 1904, when heart problems forced the *Waldpfarrer*'s retirement and a move to Bensheim, thirty kilometers south of Darmstadt.[8] There he died of a heart attack on 30

would have a forty-minute hike to the *Waldpfarrer*'s parsonage. Original in the Hesse Archives, Marbach. The *Waldpfarrer*'s door seems to have been permanently open to guests, some of whom stayed many weeks! See, for example, the unpublished letter of 3 October 1903 from Cesco Como to Hesse, in which the former mentions that Hans Bethge spent "three or four weeks" there. Copy of original in the Hesse Archives, Marbach.

8. A history of the fascinating Knodt family was published in 1967 by the family archivist at that time, Hermann Knodt (a nephew of Karl Ernst Knodt): *Familiengeschichte der hessischen Pfarrfamilie Knodt* (Limburg/Lahn, 1967).

September 1917, just weeks before he was to be awarded an honorary doctorate of theology by the University of Giessen. The words of dedication that accompanied the posthumous bestowal of the degree read:

> Dem Sohn des Hessenlandes, in dem seine Heimat wie das ganze Deutschland dankbar den Sänger der Sehnsucht des Menschenherzens nach dem Ewigen ehrt.[9]
>
> [To this son of Hessia, whose hometown and all of Germany gratefully pay honor to the singer who gave voice to the yearning of the human heart for the eternal.]

It was said of Karl Ernst Knodt that he had his knack for verse from his pastor father, although the latter's own poetic creations were apparently limited to light-hearted occasional poems that he often included in letters, a habit passed on to his son. According to Karl Adam Knodt, the older of the *Waldpfarrer*'s two sons, his father's first known poem was written while Knodt was a student in Strasbourg. In Ober-Klingen, with its unspoiled rustic landscape and its congregation of simple and hard-working farm families, Karl Ernst Knodt would flourish as pastor, teacher, and, increasingly, as a poet.

> Das Waldpfarrhaus ist recht eine Heimat für Vagabunden meiner Art. Ich verbrachte die ganzen Tage damit, mit des Pfarrers zehnjährigem Buben zu spielen, den Christbaum anzusehen und Musik zu hören. Gott segne das liebe Haus für seine schöne Gastlichkeit.[10]
>
> [The parsonage in the woods is an appropriate home for vagabonds of my ilk. I spent every day playing with the pastor's ten-year-old boy, looking at the Christmas tree, and listening to music. May God bless this dear house for its wonderful hospitality.]

Thus wrote an inspired Hermann Hesse to his new correspondent, the North German poet, Prince Emil von Schoenaich-Carolath, after a ten-day Christmas stay with the Knodt family in Ober-Klingen in 1901. Hesse owed Pastor Knodt his initial contact with the Prince, whom he mentioned in letters as one of his favorite living poets.[11] The *Waldpfarrer*, as Knodt was affectionately known

9. Quoted in *Familiengeschichte der hessischen Pfarrfamilie Knodt*, 33.
10. Unpublished letter of 30 December 1901 to Prince Emil von Schoenaich-Carolath. Original in possession of the Schoenaich-Carolath family, Haseldorf Castle, Schleswig-Holstein.
11. See, for example, Hesse's letter of 30 April 1898 to Helene Voigt (*Kindheit und Jugend*, 2: 253ff.) or his unpublished letter of 14 January 1901 to Karl Ernst Knodt, copy in the Hermann Hesse Editor's Archive, Volker Michels, Offenbach.

to all, would introduce Hermann Hesse to a great many writers, critics, and publishers of the period, including Carl Busse (who was to invite Hesse to publish *Gedichte* in 1901), Gustav Falke, Lulu von Strauß, Martin Boelitz, Hans Bethge, Jeanne Berta Semmig, and Agnes Miegel. The friendship that developed between Hesse and Schoenaich-Carolath, however, can be viewed as paradigmatic for Knodt's role as mediator, collector, and editor. As an unknown young poet still making his living primarily as a bookseller, Hermann Hesse had, by his own account, hardly any interaction with other writers in Basel:

> Der zunftmäßigen Literatur stehe ich ganz fern und habe auch hier in Basel keinen Literaturverkehr.[12]
>
> [I am quite detached from professional literary organizations, and I have no contact with literary figures here in Basel.]

It seems no exaggeration to state that Hesse longed for contact with an established poet such as Emil von Schoenaich-Carolath, yet Knodt's intervention here signified more than merely putting two writers in touch with each other: by linking those two men, Knodt at once bridged the generational gap (Schoenaich-Carolath was born in 1852) and brought a promising young poet from the southern end of the German-speaking world to the attention of an accomplished and respected North German poet. (Even Knodt's home in the Odenwald, some fifty kilometers southeast of Frankfurt am Main, afforded him a position near the geographical center of the German-speaking world.)

Hesse's Christmas 1901 sojourn was not his first visit to the *Waldpfarrer*, for he had eagerly accepted the latter's invitation to come the previous July, when he spent ten days in Ober-Klingen. He would return for Christmas in 1902, and members of the Knodt family – though never Pastor Knodt himself – would visit Hesse in Basel and Gaienhofen. The fact that Hermann Hesse spent Christmas with the Knodts two years in a row gives an indication of the close friendship that was developing. On a purely personal level, too, the Knodts (Käthe, the pastor's wife, and sons Theo and Karl) seem to have served Hesse as a kind of surrogate family, precisely at a time in the young poet's life when his own parents showed little understanding of his literary endeavors. Knodt himself would seem to have been an ideal substitute father for young Hermann,

---

12. Unpublished letter of 12 March 1902 to Prof. Jost Winteler. Copy in the Hermann Hesse Editor's Archive, Volker Michels, Offenbach.

Karl Ernst Knodt

for despite being nearly as old and most certainly as devout a Christian as the elder Hesse, Knodt, himself a poet, was obviously more tolerant of Hesse's literary notions.[13]

13. Hesse's parents were clearly pleased when their son set out from Calw in mid-July 1901, for his first visit in Ober-Klingen. They sent along a book for the

The correspondence between Hesse and Karl Ernst Knodt began in December 1900, when Hesse sent the pastor first a signed copy of the freshly published *Lauscher*, then Christmas greetings with a copy of his lengthy poem, *Meinen Freunden zur Weihnacht 1900.*[14] Knodt wrote a total of eighty-nine letters and cards to Hermann Hesse between 1900 and 1905. Unfortunately, fewer than twenty of Hesse's own missives to the *Waldpfarrer* during those years have survived, and it is nearly certain that many more were lost. Their letters sometimes dealt with literary topics – often multipage treatises – while others focused on purely personal matters, such as family, work, or the status of each other's health. When the mother of each man died in the spring of 1902 (Knodt's on 11 March and Marie Hesse on 24 April), the two consoled each other in lengthy letters. Hesse's own words of consolation to the *Waldpfarrer* seem less like the utterances of a twenty-four year old than those of a member of the forty-six-year-old pastor's own generation, reflecting distinctly how close the two friends had become in just over a year:

> Jeder Verlust, wie der Ihre, ist eine Wunde und ist unheilbar. Ein guter und wertvoller Mensch bleibt bei solchen Schlägen nicht heil. Aber Sie sind … ein Dichter. Und bei den Dichtern verwandeln sich nach altem wunderbarem Gesetz die Wunden, wenn sie ausgeblutet haben, in Quellen, aus denen 'Ströme lebendigen Wassers' springen.[15]
>
> [Every loss such as yours is an unhealable wound. A good and precious person can't help but feel pain in the face of such blows. But you are … a poet. And among poets, there is an old and miraculous law that proclaims that these wounds, when they stop bleeding, shall be transformed into springs of life-giving water.]

Similarly, Pastor Knodt had sought to ease the discomfort and frustration that Hesse's eye problems continually caused him, sending the poem "An Hermann Hesse" which contains the following lines:

Waldpfarrer, presumably from their own press. See the unpublished card of 16 July 1901 from Hermann Hesse and K. E. Knodt to Johannes and Marie Hesse. Copy in the Hermann Hesse Editor's Archive, Volker Michels, Offenbach.

14. Though Hesse's first letter has never been located, Knodt's thanks to the young poet in Basel for the copy of *Lauscher* and the Christmas poem are contained in Knodt's unpublished letter of 25 December 1900. Original in the Hesse Archives, Marbach.

15. Unpublished letter of 27 March 1902 to Karl Ernst Knodt. Copy in the Hermann Hesse Editor's Archive, Volker Michels, Offenbach.

> Kein Erbarmen kennt die Tiefe,
> Keinen Trost der Katarakt.[16]
> [The deepness knows no mercy,
> The cataract no comfort.]

In many letters, the two friends discussed authors and philosophers, often inspiring each other to read those they personally found interesting or at least provocative. At Knodt's urging, Hesse discovered Kierkegaard, while the younger man enticed the *Waldpfarrer* to delve into the works of the controversial, contemporary Italian philosopher and writer, Gabriele D'Annunzio, to which Knodt responded:

> Gabriele D'Annunzio wäre mir auch eine Gefahr – dennoch will ich ihn erleben.[17]
>
> [Reading Gabriele D'Annunzio would probably be dangerous for me – nonetheless, I want to experience him.]

His *Briefwechsel* with Knodt undoubtedly helped Hesse to emerge from the isolating aestheticism that marked his second year in Basel, and it is likely that Knodt's skepticism toward Nietzsche caused the young poet's passion for the philosopher to cool decidedly during the final two years of his Basel experience. The two men found common ground in their rejection of Tolstoy, of whom Hesse was particularly critical:

> Der Prophet von heute ist Tolstoi, für mich ein Odium. Er und alle Russen haben hinter sich die elementare Kraft kulturloser Völker.[18]
>
> [Today's prophet is Tolstoy, who is repugnant to me. He and all Russians are imbued with the elemental force that is characteristic of uncultured peoples.]

As these words reflect, their early letters frequently reveal that Hesse and Knodt were scanning the contemporary literary landscape in search of a prophet, a "seer," a "renewer," and lengthy epistolary passages were devoted to the evaluation of various "candidates" for those roles, for example, Nietzsche, D'Annunzio, Tolstoy, or Paul de Lagarde. Hermann Hesse also found his

16. Karl Ernst Knodt, *Neue Gedichte* (Mülhheim/Ruhr, 1902), 107. Originally sent by Knodt to Hesse on 29 January 1901, copy in the Hermann Hesse Editor's Archive, Volker Michels, Offenbach.

17. Unpublished letter of 19 January 1901 from K. E. Knodt to Hermann Hesse. Original in the Hesse Archives, Marbach.

18. Unpublished letter of 17 January 1901 to K. E. Knodt. Copy in the Hermann Hesse Editor's Archive, Volker Michels, Offenbach.

budding skepticism vis-à-vis what he termed the "formlessness of the modern" confirmed by the *Waldpfarrer*, whose own aesthetic principles were firmly anchored in nineteenth-century romanticism and realism.

Even before Hermann Hesse paid his first visit to the Knodt family in July 1901, the two began to forge plans to assemble an anthology of contemporary German verse. Although Hesse did not ultimately share the editing of the finished collection, his initial suggestion set the idea in motion:

> Dabei fällt mir ein, daß ich bei Ihnen anfragen wollte, was Sie von einer Liedersammlung moderner Sehnsucht halten würden. Sie wären der Mann zum Herausgeben oder Mitsammeln. Ich denke an Schoenaich, Falke, Finckh, Bethge, Busse-Palmer, Hesse, Knodt etc. Doch sollte, meine ich, das Buch keine Anthologie alter Sachen sein, sondern aus Ungedrucktem bestehen.[19]

> [It just occurs to me that I wanted to ask what you would think about a collection of poetry expressing the existential yearning of our modern age. You would be the man to edit or to help compile it. I'm thinking about poets such as Schoenaich, Falke, Finckh, Bethge, Busse-Palmer, Hesse, Knodt, etc. But the book should not be an anthology of old pieces, but should rather be made up of new, unpublished ones.]

Despite not yet having met Hesse in person, Knodt was immediately enthusiastic about the proposal, though he insisted he could not complete the project properly without Hesse's help:

> Und wie rasch würde der gemeinsame Gedanke reifen! Ich engagiere Sie jetzt schon zum in allen Stücken ebenbürtigen Mitredakteur des Sehnsuchtbuches, das ich *nur mit Ihnen zusammen gut* machen kann. Das sehe ich jetzt schon ein.[20]

> [How quickly this joint project would ripen! I hereby engage you as equal co-editor for all phases of the yearning book, which I can produce properly *only with your help*. I realize that already.]

The anthology appeared in print a year later. Twelve poems by Hesse were included (more than any other contributor), and the young poet found himself in rather prestigious company: R. M. Rilke, Ricarda Huch, Gustav Falke, Julius Hart, and Emil von Schoenaich-Carolath, among many others. Precisely why Hesse

---

19. Unpublished letter of 5 July 1901 to Karl Ernst Knodt. Copy in the Hermann Hesse Editor's Archive, Volker Michels, Offenbach.

20. Unpublished letter of 7 July 1901 from K. E. Knodt to Hesse. Original in the Hesse Archives, Marbach.

chose not to accept the task of coediting the work – his mother's death, his own health problems, the difficulty of working closely with Knodt on the editing because of the geographical distance between them – is not clear, but his letters indicate that he was repeatedly called upon by the *Waldpfarrer* for advice and assistance.

More than any other literary contact that developed as a result of his encounter with Karl Ernst Knodt, Hermann Hesse's *Brieffreundschaft* with Prince Emil von Schoenaich-Carolath stands as a monument to the young poet's swift arrival on the German literary scene. Hesse had known and treasured Schoenaich-Carolath's work at least since 1897, when he wrote to Helene Voigt:

> Sie kennen Schoenaich-Carolath? Er ist auch mir bekannt und lieb. Erinnern Sie sich seiner Verse –
> "O Schönheit, Schönheit, Danaergeschenk!
> Weh jedem, dem dein leuchtend Stirngehenk
> Als blitzend Stigma ward ums Haupt geschlagen!"[21]
>
> [You know Schoenaich-Carolath? He is known and dear to me, too. Do you remember the verse –
> "O Beauty, Beauty, most treacherous gift!
> Woe to him around whose head your banner
> Was wrapped quite like a shining stigma!"]

A scant three years later, now reviewing on a regular basis for the *Allgemeine Schweizer Zeitung*, Hesse referred to the "profound, gracious poetry of Schoenaich-Carolath" in his review of a new collection of poetry by Voigt.[22] In the fall of that year (October 1901), Hesse sent Schoenaich-Carolath a copy of *Hermann Lauscher*, and the Prince responded with a short note and a handsome present:

> Ferner erhielt ich hieher nach Oberklingen ein norddeutsches Paketchen, das ein Weihnachtsgeschenk des Dichters Emil v. Schoenaich-Carolath enthielt. Es war eine Schachtel raffiniert feiner Cigaretten und dazu ein sehr kostbares, schönes Etui mit Monogramm.[23]

21. Letter of 27 December 1897 to Helene Voigt, *Hermann Hesse, Helene Voigt-Diederichs. Zwei Autorenportraits in Briefen 1897–1900* (Köln, 1971), 19–20. See also Hesse's letter of 30 April 1898, 44f. in that collection. The passage is quoted from Schoenaich-Carolath's lengthy poem *Angelina*, contained in the first volume of his collected works (*Gesammelte Werke*, Berlin/Leipzig, 1922). Given the budding poet's almost obsessive aestheticism at this point in his intellectual development, his adoration of such verse is hardly surprising.

22. Hermann Hesse, "Unterstrom (Helene Voigt)," *Allgemeine Schweizer Zeitung*, Basel [Sunday supplement], vol. 6, 14 April 1901, 56.

23. Unpublished letter of 27 December 1901 to the Hesse family in Calw. Copy in the Hermann Hesse Editor's Archive, Volker Michels, Offenbach.

Prince Emil von Schoenaich-Carolath

[I also received, here in Ober-Klingen, a little package from north-ern Germany containing a Christmas present from the poet Emil v. Schoenaich-Carolath. It was a box of exquisite cigarettes, along with a monogrammed case.]

Thus the two writers began what was to become a regular corre-spondence that would endure until Schoenaich-Carolath's death on 30 April 1908.[24]

Emil Rudolf Osman Prinz von Schoenaich-Carolath-Schilden was born in Breslau (Silesia) on 8 April 1852, the offspring of mediatized princely lineage which ruled an area of nearly one hundred square miles in Silesia. He completed *Gymnasium* in

24. It is interesting that Ludwig Finckh, too, had already established a modest correspondence with Schoenaich-Carolath in 1898. In the early 1890s, Finckh and his sister, Cornelie, had come up with the clever idea of composing and sending

Wiesbaden, studied literature and art history at the University of Zurich for two semesters in 1870-71, and served as a cavalry officer (*Dragonerleutnant*) from 1872-74. After military service, he traveled to Rome and Egypt and made extensive journeys to the Orient, experiences that contributed to lending his work a distinctly Kiplingesque coloration. Schoenaich-Carolath established himself in the 1880s as a poet, novelist, and short-story writer, and his poetry, at least, was occasionally deemed worthy of mention in the same breath as that of his contemporary, Hugo von Hofmannsthal. His writing career spanned nearly thirty years and culminated shortly before his death in a seven-volume edition of his collected works (1907). Following his marriage to Katharina von Knorring in 1887, Schoenaich-Carolath and his bride lived at the family's castles in Denmark (Palsgard) and Haseldorf (Uetersen) in Schleswig-Holstein.[25] From 1895 on, the family maintained its permanent residence in the Haseldorf castle, where their six children grew up. Prince Emil is buried in the family cemetery on the castle grounds, and his descendants inhabit the castle to this day.

Around the turn of the century, Schoenaich-Carolath was one of a circle of north German writers and poets of neo-Romantic and naturalistic persuasion who enjoyed regular social interaction along with their lively literary exchange. The group included such established writers as Detlev von Liliencron, Richard Dehmel, Gustav Falke, Hans Bethge, and Gustav Frenssen, as well as little-known literary neophytes like Kurt Piper, who was to experience a short-lived but intense friendship with Hermann Hesse in 1902-03. In particular, the correspondence of Liliencron and Bethge from the early years of this century bears witness to the generous *Gastfreundschaft* of the Schoenaich-Carolaths toward the artistic community; indeed it can generally be said that the Prince's estate

---

short original poems in their Swabian dialect to well-known authors, artists, and musicians. Their intention was to encourage the recipients to return the favor, at least with an autograph, and according to Finckh, the two were amazingly successful. Unfortunately, almost the entire collection was destroyed in the fire that completely consumed the Finckh house in Gaienhofen in February 1907. Among them were notes from Wilhelm Raabe, Edvard Grieg, Theodor Fontane, Detlev von Liliencron, Gustav Falke, and Prince Emil von Schoenaich-Carolath. Ludwig Finckh, "So fing es an," *Familiennachrichten* [der Familie Finckh], No. 21, June, 1948, Hesse Archives, Marbach.

25. Technically, the *Schloß* Haseldorf was built as a *Herrenhaus* (the equivalent of an English manor house) near the beginning of the nineteenth century. Prince Emil von Schoenaich-Carolath inherited it from the Oppen-Schildens, his mother's side of the family.

was a gathering point for writers, artists, and musicians of the area. Haseldorf Castle was known quite beyond North Germany, however, and among its many guests during the period was Rainer Maria Rilke, who enjoyed the Prince's hospitality on three occasions, in 1898, 1901, and again in 1902, when he spent a good part of the summer there.[26] Haseldorf was the first of the several castles in which Rilke would temporarily abide during his adult life, "the first aristocratic family residence offered to him as a temporary refuge where he could be left to himself."[27] Since the Prince and his wife left, soon after Rilke's arrival there in May 1902, for a stay at the spa in Bad Pyrmont, southwest of Hanover, the poet was left quite to himself. The eloquent and vibrant depictions of the castle park contained in Rilke's letters from Haseldorf reveal his awe at the beauty and botanical richness of his surroundings, and he was similarly impressed by the extensive archival holdings of the castle library.[28]

As Schoenaich-Carolath's letters to Hesse make abundantly clear, the Prince was eager to welcome the young poet from Basel as his guest in Haseldorf. During the second year of their seven-year correspondence, Schoenaich-Carolath invited Hesse for the first time, expressing in his letter the desire to meet Hesse "face-to-face,"[29] and he would repeat the invitation time and again between 1903 and 1906, his letters comprising increasingly poetic and alluring characterizations of the estate grounds and, particularly, its extensive park. Having heard (probably from Karl Ernst Knodt) that Hesse was an avid angler, the Prince tried to tempt him with a depiction of the fish in his private streams, assuring Hesse in one letter that fifteen- to seventeen-pound

26. Rilke and Schoenaich-Carolath had met in Munich during the former's year of study at the university there, 1896/97. Rilke's recollections of his stays at Haseldorf are included in *Die Aufzeichnungen des Malte Laurids Brigge*. Indeed, Schoenaich-Carolath's manor house provided the model for the mansion of Malte's grandfather, described in the novel's opening pages: "Das lange, alte Herrenhaus. . ." ["The long, old manor house. . ."] Rainer Maria Rilke, *Die Aufzeichnungen des Malte Laurids Brigge* (Munich, 1962), 11. See William Small's *Kommentar zu den Aufzeichnungen des Malte Laurids Brigge* (Chapel Hill, 1983), 9f.

27. Wolfgang Leppmann, *Rilke – A Life*, trans. by Russell Stockman (New York, 1984), 145.

28. See, particularly, Rilke's letters from Haseldorf to his wife (5 June 1902) and to Otto Modersohn (25 June 1902) in: Rainer Maria Rilke, *Briefe und Tagebücher aus der Frühzeit (1899 bis 1902)* (Leipzig, 1933), 184ff. and 194ff., respectively.

29. Unpublished letter of 22 June 1903 from Prince Emil von Schoenaich-Carolath to Hermann Hesse. Original in the Hesse Archives of the Swiss National Library, Bern.

carp awaited his fishing rod,[30] while offering in another missive
a preview of the idyllic atmosphere that was in store for Hesse
in Haseldorf:

> Tiefe Ruhe, gänzliche Zwanglosigkeit, abends ein guter Trunk unter
> den Linden. Staffage: weite Land- und Stromflächen. Dem Angler
> können die schlauen, schweren Karpfen im Burggraben An- und
> Aufregung schaffen.[31]
>
> [Deep calm, complete informality, a good drink in the evening
> beneath the linden trees. The landscape: vast expanses of fields and
> river. The cunning, massive carp in the castle's moat will inspire
> and excite the fisherman.]

Apparently, Schoenaich-Carolath even enlisted the aid of their mu-
tual friend, Hans Bethge, to lure Hesse and his new bride to the
North, for some of Bethge's letters sound strikingly similar to
those of the Prince's own epistles. Just one week after Schoenaich-
Carolath had dispatched an invitation to Hesse in Calw on 23
July 1904 – and two days before Hesse's wedding to Maria Ber-
noulli in Basel on 2 August – Bethge also wrote, imploring his
young friend not to pass up an invitation to Haseldorf. Beyond its
amiable portrayal of Schoenaich-Carolath and his family (miss-
ing completely in the egocentric Rilke's missives), Bethge's depic-
tion of Haseldorf also offers a glimpse of the congenial atmosphere
to which the Prince's guests could look forward:

> Ferner möchte ich Sie bitten, falls Sie und Ihre Frau Gemahlin ein-
> mal eine norddeutsche Sommerfrische genießen wollen, sich doch
> beim Prinzen Schoenaich-Carolath auf Haseldorf einzuladen; ihm
> sowohl wie seinem prächtigen, feinen Frauchen würde es ein herz-
> liches Vergnügen sein, Sie beide als Gäste in Haseldorf zu beher-
> bergen; es ist dort ein sehr schöner alter Park, und die Gastlichkeit
> ist darum eine so angenehme, weil für die Gäste ein besonderes
> Haus vorhanden ist und jeder den Tag über tun und lassen kann,
> was er will; wenn man will, kann man also sogar arbeiten; die
> Gegend ist die Holsteinische, mit der Niederung der Elbe, doch ist
> die Geest in kurzer Zeit zu erreichen; ich war dort, ehe ich hierher
> nach Sylt kam, und wir sprachen von Ihnen und Ihrem *Peter Camen-
> zind*, der auch der Prinzessin ans Herz gewachsen ist; außerdem
> wird die kleine Lisi, meine besondere Freundin, bretonische Lieder

30. Unpublished letter of 23 July 1904 from Prince Emil von Schoenaich-Carolath.
Original in the Hesse Archives of the Swiss National Library, Bern.
31. Unpublished letter of 22 February 1905 from Prince Emil von Schoenaich-
Carolath. Original in the Hesse Archives of the Swiss National Library, Bern.

auf der Guitarre vorspielen, und sie werden sich sehr wohl fühlen in Haseldorf.[32]

[In addition, if you and your wife want to enjoy a north German vacation sometime, I would urge you to accept an invitation to Prince Schoenaich-Carolath's castle at Haseldorf; it would be a sincere pleasure for him and his splendid, elegant little lady to host the two of you in Haseldorf. There is a most beautiful old park there, and the hospitality is made the more pleasant in that guests there have a house of their own, and each can do whatever he wants all day; if you want, you can even work. The area is the Holstein region of the Elbe lowlands, though you can reach the coastal flats in short time. I was there before coming over here to Sylt, and we spoke about you and your *Peter Camenzind,* who has also found a place in the princess's heart. Besides everything else, little Lisi, my special girlfriend, will perform songs of Breton on the guitar, and you will feel quite comfortable in Haseldorf.]

In spite of these attempts to entice him to travel to North Germany, however, Hermann Hesse never visited Haseldorf. In fact, a brief stopover in Bremen during a public reading tour in the fall of 1909, a year after Schoenaich-Carolath's death, was the nearest Hesse ever came to the castle. Indeed, this 1909 excursion, during which he paid his personal respects to the aging Wilhelm Raabe in Braunschweig, was almost certainly the only journey to northern Germany in Hesse's entire life. Undoubtedly, the timing of the Prince's invitation during the weeks when Hesse was preparing for his wedding in Basel was a principal factor in his not availing himself of the opportunity. It is also entirely possible that, subconsciously at least, Hesse was apprehensive about being drawn once again into a milieu like that of the Wackernagel circle in Basel from which he had fled. While the Knodt family and their immediate circle of friends and acquaintances in Ober-Klingen obviously represented a comfortable contrast to the social whirl of the educated

32. Unpublished letter of 31 July 1904 from Hans Bethge to Hermann Hesse, original in the Hesse Archives, Marbach. (Bethge's "special girlfriend," Lisi, was the Schoenaich-Carolaths' daughter Elisabeth, their third child, born on 1 May 1893.) In another letter to Hesse, written after a visit to Haseldorf the previous summer, Bethge noted that guests of the Prince were also treated to gondola rides on the canal system that traversed the castle grounds at Haseldorf: "Ich komme soeben von einem sonnigen Aufenthalt bei dem Prinzen Schoenaich-Carolath zurück, wo wir sehr froh waren … auf kleinen Gondelfahrten unter Kastanien und Fliedern." ["I just returned from a sunny stay at Prince Schoenaich-Carolath's estate, where we had a wonderful time … taking little gondola rides among chestnut trees and lilacs."] Unpublished letter of 3 June 1903, original in the Hesse Archives, Marbach.

146 | A Poet or Nothing at All

Basel elite, the prospect of having to confront not only Schoenaich-Carolath, but also the literary sophisticates of the Prince's circle did not likely hearten the young poet. Nonetheless, Hermann Hesse's contact with Prince Emil von Schoenaich-Carolath, as will be seen below, marked a significant passage in the younger man's life.

The Knodts took Hermann Hesse into their family almost as one of their own, and the young poet also quickly became part of the *Waldpfarrer*'s sizeable "extended" family, which consisted of local friends and acquaintances, but also of writers, journalists, and people from the publishing trade. It was in Ober-Klingen that Hesse made the acquaintance of author and essayist Hans Bethge, a true "man of the world," although he was just a year and a half older than Hesse. Born a farmer's son in Dessau (Sachsen-Anhalt), Bethge studied in Halle and Erlangen, completing a doctorate in Geneva by the age of twenty-five with a dissertation on Molière. He traveled extensively during his younger years, visiting the Near East as well as Africa and the Orient, and worked for a time as a private tutor in Barcelona[33] before settling permanently in Berlin. There he made his living as a free-lance writer, author, and translator, earning a quite respectable reputation for his German transcriptions of Oriental poetry. He belonged to the Schoenaich-Carolath circle, was a regular guest at Haseldorf Castle, and, as detailed above, did his best to lure Hesse there.

When the two young men first met in 1902, Bethge had already published his first volume of poetry, a collection of neo-Romantic verse entitled *Die Feste der Jugend* (1901), to which Hesse had glowingly referred in one of his first reviews for the *Allgemeine Schweizer Zeitung*:

> Ich wohnte Leseabenden bei, an denen die weiche Süßigkeit Hof-mannsthals, die sehnsüchtig zarte Malerei Bethges ... auf einen engen Kreis empfänglicher Hörer Wirkungen übte, deren Zauber sich nur dem der Musik vergleichen läßt.[34]
>
> [I have attended poetry evenings where the mellow sweetness of Hofmannsthal or the yearningly tender poetry paintings of Bethge ... affected a small audience of receptive listeners in a magical fashion that can only be compared with that of music.]

33. Having assumed a somewhat Spanish appearance during his time in Spain, Bethge was good-naturedly referred to as "the Spaniard" at the Knodts' home in Ober-Klingen.

34. Hermann Hesse, review of "Unterstrom (Helene Voight)," in the Sunday supplement of the *Allgemeine Schweizer Zeitung* 6, 14 April 1901, 56.

It was at Hesse's suggestion to Karl Ernst Knodt that Bethge was included from the outset in the 1902 anthology *Wir sind die Sehnsucht*, and there are indications that Bethge was considered by Knodt and Hesse as a kind of third partner in the endeavor. When the volume appeared in late 1902, for example, Knodt and Hesse (who was visiting the *Waldpfarrer* during the Christmas week) each added a brief message to a postcard that they sent to Bethge in Berlin. Making use of the illustration that adorned the card (a picture of two dwarfs and a squirrel standing in the forest before some kind of monument), Hesse penned a short tale:

> Aus einem alten Poetenmärchen:
> " – der Rote legte den Finger an die Nase, räusperte sich zweimal und sagte: Ich bin die Sehnsucht. – Da erboste sich aber der Grüne, räusperte sich dreimal und sagte: Nein, ich bin die Sehnsucht." Siehe, da kam das weise schlanke Eichhorn seine 4 Treppen herabgesteigen, klopfte den Streitenden auf die Schulter und lächelte: Wir sind die Sehnsucht.
>
> Herzlich grüßt Hermann Hesse[35]
>
> [From an old poet's fairy tale:
> " – Red touched his nose with his finger, cleared his throat twice, and said: I am the yearning. Whereupon Green became quite annoyed, cleared his throat three times, and said: No, I am the yearning." Behold, then came the wise and slender squirrel down his four flights of stairs, slapped the two combatants on the shoulder, and smiled: We are the yearning.
>
> Hearty greetings from Hermann Hesse.]

Despite its levity, Hesse's short, fable-like anecdote clearly had the purpose of expressing his appreciation to Bethge, whose aid in getting the volume into print had exceeded mere technical assistance and had included helping to secure a publisher for the project. For his part, Hans Bethge penned one of the first reviews of *Peter Camenzind* – it appeared in the *Münchner Zeitung* on 4 March 1904, barely two weeks after the complete novel's publication – and, according to Hesse himself, his colleague repeatedly intervened on the novel's behalf:

> [D]anke ich Ihnen noch herzlich für Ihre mehrfache liebe Bemühung um das Buch.[36]

---

35. Unpublished picture postcard dated December 1902 from Hermann Hesse and Karl Ernst Knodt to Dr. Hans Bethge. Copy in the Hermann Hesse Editor's Archive, Volker Michels, Offenbach.

36. Letter of 26 December 1904, *Briefe*, 1: 133.

[I thank you again sincerely for all of your efforts on behalf of the book.]

After meeting personally in Ober-Klingen, Hesse and Bethge frequently exchanged cards and letters in the years between 1901 and 1904. In the last extant letter that Hesse wrote to Bethge (on 26 December 1904), he invited him to visit Gaienhofen. There is no indication that Bethge ever came, and there appears to have been no correspondence between the two men thereafter. Ironically, Hans Bethge would spend his final years in Kirchheim unter Teck, the setting of Hesse's "Lulu" interlude in the summer of 1899, having left Berlin sometime during World War II. He died in the hospital at Göppingen, fifteen kilometers northeast of Kirchheim, on 1 February 1946, without ever seeing Hesse again. Nonetheless, he came into Hesse's life at a most opportune moment, providing the budding writer from Basel with creative encouragement and serving, albeit briefly, as a literary model for Hermann Hesse. Almost certainly, Hans Bethge was the first Berlin writer Hesse ever met, and this at a time when, by his own admission, he had no contact with active *literati* in Switzerland.

Another rather worldly literary figure whom Hesse met through the Knodts was the German-French poet Jeanne Berta Semmig, the first of whose many stays with the *Waldpfarrer* and his family in Ober-Klingen (and later in Bensheim) occurred at Easter 1901 and preceded Hesse's initial visit by only a few weeks. Semmig was born in Orléans on 16 May 1867, the daughter of Dr. Friedrich Hermann Semmig, a teacher and writer who had fled Germany for France after participating in the "bourgeois revolution" of 1849 in Dresden. The family returned to Leipzig in 1871, where Jeanne Berta attended school and teacher's college. Never married, she taught school for more than forty years in Dresden, dedicating her free time to writing and traveling. Her oeuvre includes poetry (she was included in *Wir sind die Sehnsucht*), short stories, and two novels. At the time of her death in the former German Democratic Republic, she was called "the oldest living woman writer in Germany." In March 1958, at the age of ninety-one, she traveled to Berlin to attend International Women's Day ceremonies, where she was awarded the GDR's Clara Zetkin Medal in recognition of her long career. She died just four months later, on 28 July 1958.

In her autobiography, *Aus acht Jahrzehnten*, Semmig recalled her first impressions of pastor Knodt and his family as well as her surprise at the extent of the circle of literary friends, acquaintances, and contacts entertained by this modest and unassuming country parson. In his study, she was amazed to find letters, pictures, and manuscripts from writers throughout the German-speaking world: Schoenaich-Carolath, Gustav Falke, Maria Janitzschek, Gustav Schüler, Hans Bethge, Börries von Münchhausen, and Agnes Miegel. One morning, as he brought in the day's mail, Knodt called out to his wife, "Käthe, here's another letter from Hermann Hesse!" Noting that Käthe Knodt's eyes "lit up" at this news, Semmig asks rhetorically:

> Wer war das, Hermann Hesse? Einer, der augenblicklich heimatlos war, ein Schwabe nach dem Heimatort, aber nicht nach der Abkunft. Baltisches, süddeutsches, Schweizer Blut rann in seinen Adern. Er hatte sich nicht durch den schwäbischen Weg der Klosterschule Maulbronn zum Tübinger Stift hindurchgefunden. Er ging in die Welt. Augenblicklich arbeitete er bei einem Buchhändler in Basel.[37]

> [Who was this Hermann Hesse? Someone who was homeless at the moment, a Swabian by birth but not by descent. Baltic, south German, and Swiss blood ran through his veins. He hadn't been able to get through the Swabian preparatory course at the monastery in Maulbronn so that he could go to the seminary in Tübingen. He went out into the world. At the moment he was working in a Basel bookstore.]

Reflecting, as it undoubtedly does, the image of Hermann Hesse that he personally had presented to the Knodts – who had yet to meet him in the flesh – this description corresponds perfectly with Hesse's view of himself at the time, for he thought of himself, both literally and existentially, as a kind of vagabond. Too, he was writing now from Italy, on his initial journey through that land, and he enclosed a freshly written poem that would first be included in his second set of *Notturni* (1902):

> Dem Brief lag ein Gedicht bei, das erste Gedicht Hermann Hesses, das ich las und das ich stets mit heimlicher Bewegung wieder las: *Die Zypressen von San Clemente*. Die geistige Begegnung mit Hermann Hesse war das große Geschenk, das ich in den Ostertagen in der Waldpfarre empfing.[38]

> [There was a poem enclosed with the letter, the first poem of Hermann Hesse's that I ever read and one that I have always re-read with secret delight: *The Cypresses of San Clemente*. The spiritual

---

37. Jeanne Berta Semmig, *Aus acht Jahrzehnten* (Berlin, 1975), 166f.
38. Ibid., 167.

introduction to Hermann Hesse was the great gift that I received in those Easter days at the parish in the woods.]

The bond that developed between Hesse and Jeanne Berta Semmig was founded on their mutual friendship with the Knodts, although they were not to meet in person until the summer of 1907, when Semmig visited the Hesses and the Finckhs in Gaienhofen. In her autobiography, she describes a ferry ride across the Rhein to Steckborn, where the friends spent the afternoon partaking of Swiss red wine and toasting their many friends in the Knodt circle. As she departed later that day, she recalls, she had the feeling that the "delicate ties" between her and Hermann Hesse would endure, even though they were to see each other only once again, in the summer of 1930. Semmig found her way then to the *Casa Camuzzi* in Montagnola, where Hesse lived from 1919 until 1931. Their lengthy conversation, "just the two of them," focused primarily on news of the Knodt family and friends they had met through the *Waldpfarrer*, who had died ten years earlier. Before accompanying Semmig to her taxi, Hesse introduced her to Ninon Dolbin, who would become his third wife in November 1931 and who had occupied furnished rooms in the *Casa* since April 1927. Summing up that visit at the end of her autobiography, Semmig noted:

> Wir durften uns nicht wiedersehen von Angesicht zu Angesicht, aber viele Grüße sind zwischen uns hin- und hergegangen bis zu meinem neunzigsten und zu seinem achtzigsten Geburtstage [1957].[39]
>
> [We would never again see each other face-to-face, but many a greeting has been passed back and forth between us, right up to my ninetieth and his eightieth birthday.]

In the years leading up to and during the First World War, the two had little contact with each other, probably because Hesse had moved permanently back to Switzerland in 1912, first to Bern (1912–19), then to Montagnola, where he would spend the remainder of his life. It is interesting that it was not until 1917 that Hermann Hesse and Jeanne Berta Semmig began corresponding regularly, although that correspondence was fairly extensive and continued right up until Semmig's death in 1958. The latter's correspondence to Hesse, 127 letters written between 1917 and 1958, is preserved in its entirety in the Hesse Archives of the Swiss National Library in Bern; during those four decades, Hesse wrote more than one hundred letters and cards to Jeanne

39. Ibid., 294f.

Cesco Como

Berta Semmig.[40] As Semmig reports in her autobiography, she regularly sent her own work for Hesse's perusal, and the correspondence of each often included discussion of the other's writing, albeit gently critical in nature. It was an exchange of ideas and personal *Weltanschauung* that Semmig relished. She admitted to having followed Hesse "on his journey to the inner state" ("der Weg ins Innere"), and he reacted kindly to her comments:

40. This trove of Hesse missives, part of Jean Berta Semmig's literary estate, is housed in the *Stadtarchiv* in Döbeln (Saxony), some thirty kilometers west of Dresden

Er hatte freundlich meine Gedanken über die Werke aufgenom-
men, in denen er sich in die Tiefen, aber auch in die Abgründe
menschlicher Entwicklung versenkte.[41]
[He always reacted pleasantly to my comments on those of his
works in which he delved into the depths but also into the abysses
of human development.]

Like Prince Emil von Schoenaich-Carolath and Hans Bethge,
Jeanne Berta Semmig represented a broader spectrum of the
German-speaking literary world than Hermann Hesse had encoun-
tered up to that point in his life, and all provided him with
much-needed creative encouragement and personal friendship.
To some extent, certainly, they can also be considered as repre-
sentative of a much larger number of literary acquaintances and
intermediaries who, directly or indirectly, assisted in establishing
Hesse's literary identity in Germany. Of course, nearly all of these
contacts were, in the final analysis, the result of Hesse's interaction
and friendship with Karl Ernst Knodt.

On the other hand, it must be remembered that Hermann Hesse
was quite resolute in his determination to prevail as a working
writer, his self-portrayals as "vagabond" and "homeless soul"
notwithstanding. (In fact, this frequently assumed persona served
to authenticate the artist image he sought to project at the time.)
While Hesse rarely exhibited genuinely ambitious behavior on
behalf of his literary efforts, he seems to have consciously and
quickly availed himself of potential contacts in Germany. He was
surely aware that the literary career he so desired would depend to
a very considerable degree on gaining recognition in the German-
speaking world beyond Switzerland and Swabia.[42] In this regard,
the inclusion of a dozen of his poems in Knodt's anthology, *Wir
sind die Sehnsucht*, can be seen as symbolizing Hesse's literary
"arrival" in Germany. Not only did he find himself here in the
company of many established writers of the day, but his verses
were also literally surrounded there by those of poets from the
northern half of the German-speaking world, nearly eighty percent
of whom came from cities north of Frankfurt. It is also of no small
significance that the two works that established his reputation in

---

and close to Radebeul, where she spent much of her life. As of this date, there is no
record that this collection has ever been systematically studied.

41. Semmig, *Aus acht Jahrzehnten*, 292.

42. Hesse intimated as much in an early letter to Cesco Como: "In Basel z. B. habe
ich weder als Literat noch als Antiquar eine Zukunft. . ." ["In Basel, for example, I
have no future, neither as a writer nor as an antiquarian. . ."] *Briefe*, 1: 88.

the genres of poetry and prose, respectively, were both published in Berlin: *Gedichte* (1902) and *Peter Camenzind* (1903–4). Despite numerous "disclaimers" vis-à-vis the success of *Peter Camenzind*,[43] he most certainly enjoyed it, and this success was made possible by having established himself in Germany between 1900 and 1902, i. e., precisely during the years in which he lived in Basel! It would be difficult to imagine these successes, had Hesse not ventured out of Basel.

Along with this rather sudden and sizeable expansion of his circle of literary acquaintances and contacts, Hermann Hesse found a "soul mate" of sorts among the local members of the Knodt community, a young teacher named Franz "Cesco" Como. Born in Lämmerspiel (Offenbach) on 4 September 1877, Como was just two months younger than Hesse. They met at the Knodts' home during Hesse's third visit there at Christmas 1902, although they had exchanged letters since the beginning of that year. After an intensive and occasionally turbulent correspondence that lasted until 1905, the two friends lost track of each other until the year before Como's death on 13 November 1958.[44]

In January 1958, Josefa Michaelis-Como wrote to Hesse on her father's behalf after seeing the bundle of letters and cards Hesse had written to Cesco early in the century. Noting her father's delight at reading through the old letters and talking about his friendship with Hermann Hesse more than half a century earlier, Michaelis-Como also briefly summarized what had befallen her father after the National Socialists came to power in Germany:

> Vater, der nun wie Sie 80 Jahre alt ist, 1933 in Darmstadt als erster aus dem Schuldienst entlassen und später verhaftet wurde. . . Er ist

---

43. See, for example, Hesse's letter of 26 December 1904 to Hans Bethge: "Die übertriebenen Erfolge des Peter haben mich – vom Geld abgesehen – nicht eben gefreut, ich werde förmlich Mode, und das wollte ich nie." *Briefe*, 1: 132f. ["I am not exactly happy about the exaggerated success of my *Peter Camenzind* – aside from the money – since I am becoming downright fashionable, and I have never desired that."]

44. In her account of her visit to Hermann Hesse in 1927, Jeanne Berta Semmig noted that she and Hesse talked about what had become of Cesco Como, mentioning that he had eventually married the "love of his youth" but had gradually become estranged from his Protestant friends because, as Semmig put it, of "religious narrow-mindedness." Semmig offered no further details, though it would seem that the estrangement may well have had to do with Como's marriage (he was Catholic), since up to that time he had mixed quite comfortably with the largely Protestant circle around the Knodt family. Semmig, *Aus acht Jahrzehnten*, 293.

fast vereinsamt, weil seine Freunde gestorben oder von den Nazis
beseitigt worden sind.[45]

[Father, who like you is now 80 years old, was the first teacher to be
removed from his position in 1933, and he was later arrested and
jailed. . . He is quite lonely now, since his friends have died or were
done away with by the Nazis.]

When Cesco Como was in the hospital in March 1958, he wrote to
Hesse on 10 March, and Hesse sent him his *Aquarelle aus dem Tessin*
(1955) shortly thereafter.[46]

Both of Como's parents were of Italian descent, and he seems
to have prided himself on his proficiency in Italian, often embell-
ishing his correspondence to Hesse with greetings and passages
in Italian, even in his very first note on 6 January 1902. He had
missed the opportunity to meet the young poet from Basel dur-
ing Hesse's first two visits to Ober-Klingen the year before. Lis-
tening to the Knodt family and friends talk about Hesse, however,
and reading his poetry, Como became so fascinated with Her-
mann Hesse that he began work on a study of the poet that
would eventually be published in September 1903. Como lim-
ited his discussion there to Hesse's earliest works (*Romantische
Lieder, Eine Stunde hinter Mitternacht, Hermann Lauscher*), but he
showed a remarkable grasp of Hesse's meticulous, highly aes-
theticized style and did not shy away from critical comment:

> Diese Prosa, diese Verse muten einem wie venezianische Gläser an,
> duftig fein und zart, herrlich glänzend in ihrer Farbenwirkung, von
> unendlichem Reiz für das Auge, *aber das Herz kommt zu kurz.* Wäre
> er doch weniger aristokratisch, arbeitete und zisilierte er doch nicht
> so fein.[47]

> [This prose and these verses remind one of Venetian glass, delight-
> fully fine and delicate, splendidly shimmering in the effects of its
> colors, of endless fascination for the eye, *but the heart gets short-
> changed.* Were he only less aristocratic, if only he did not work and
> emboss so elegantly.]

On 7 March 1902, Karl Ernst Knodt wrote Hesse to request a
set of the latter's *Notturni* for Cesco Como, noting that Como

45. Unpublished letter of 12 January 1958 from Josefa Michaelis-Como to Her-
mann Hesse. Original in the Hesse Archives, Marbach.
46. In turn, Como thanked him with a note dated 26 March 1957. Since the letter
to Hesse initiating this final exchange was not sent by the daughter until January
1958, Como must surely have meant 26 March 1958.
47. Cesco Como, "Hermann Hesse, eine psychische Studie," *Deutsche Heimat*
(Leipzig/Berlin, 1903), 1672.

was quite fond of Hesse and was composing a study of him. Though seemingly somewhat amused that an admirer was putting together one of the first examinations of him as poet *and* person,[48] Hesse was also obviously flattered. He immediately sent the *Notturni* to Como, noting in his accompanying letter (his first to Como) that he had heard of Como's study, thanking him for it, and asking for a reprint when it appeared;[49] he also made mention of a short trip to Venice that he was planning for the fall. Clearly touched by Hesse's warm response and prompt dispatch of the desired collection of verse – especially the dedication of those *Notturni* to their author's "friends and supporters" – Como praised the poems and encouraged Hesse to seek a publisher for them.

That exchange marked the beginning of a flurry of cards and letters during the spring of 1902 as the friendship developed quite quickly. In what was an unusually impulsive gesture on his part, Hesse invited Como to join him on his proposed journey to Italy in the fall, even though he had not yet met Como in person and was writing to him for only the third time:

> Mit Ihnen hätte ich Lust, einmal eine Schweizer oder italienische kleine Reise zu machen. Ich hoffe, nächsten Herbst für zwei Wochen nach Venedig zu können. Wollen Sie nicht mit?[50]
>
> [I would like to take a Swiss or a little Italian journey with you sometime. I hope to be able to go to Venice next fall for two weeks. Don't you want to come along?]

By mid-spring, their trip to Italy was tentatively set for the following fall, but the death of Hesse's mother on 24 April and a recurrence of the severe eye strain and accompanying headaches that had plagued him since his early years in Tübingen made Hesse's participation impossible. After hearing nothing from Basel for several weeks in late summer, Como learned of Hesse's eye problems from Knodt's older son, Karl, who was also in Basel during May and June of that year. Writing to Hesse on 22 August 1902, Como

48. On 12 March 1902, Hesse wrote to inform Knodt that he had indeed sent a set of *Notturni* to Como and, obviously intrigued, inquired of the *Waldpfarrer*: "Was ist das für ein Blatt, in welchem er über mich herfallen will?" ["What type of journal is it, in which he is going to rake me over the coals?"] Unpublished letter to Karl Ernst Knodt, copy in the Hermann Hesse Editor's Archive, Volker Michels, Offenbach.
49. Undated letter written to Cesco Como between March 8 and 10, 1902, wrongly dated in volume one of *Gesammelte Briefe* as "circa summer 1903." See *Briefe*, 1: 101.
50. Letter of 6 April 1902 to Cesco Como, *Briefe*, 1: 88.

---

expressed his sympathy for his friend's suffering, but noted that he was "looking forward most eagerly" to their joint trip to Italy, to which Hesse – preparing to leave for a lengthy recuperative stay in Calw – responded immediately:

> Lieber Freund! Italien? – Venedig? Nein, leider nicht! Ich bin seit zwei Monaten augenkrank und werde viele Wochen lang weder zu lesen noch zum Schreiben etc. fähig sein, viel weniger zum Reisen.[51]
>
> [Dear friend! Italy? – Venice? No, unfortunately not. I have been down with eye problems for the past two months and will not be able to read or write for many more weeks, much less go on a trip.]

Como proceeded on his own, departing on 23 September, but was encouraged by Hesse to stop in Basel on his return journey:

> Höchstwahrscheinlich werde ich dann in Basel sein und würde so viele Stunden oder Tage, als Sie bleiben können, mit Freuden für Sie frei haben.[52]
>
> [Most probably I will be in Basel then and would gladly take as many hours or days off as you stay.]

These plans, however, were also to be foiled, since Hesse's recuperative stay in Calw lasted until near the end of October. Nonetheless, Como made a brief stopover in Basel and paid a quick visit to Hesse's living quarters there. While the two friends talked of a later journey together to Italy, that trip never came to fruition.

Although the pace of the Hesse-Como correspondence slowed noticeably during the second half of 1902, the mood of the letters grew increasingly intimate, even tender, through the early months of that year, a quite surprising phenomenon, given their not yet having met in person. In response to Como's short letter of condolence when Marie Hesse passed away, for example, Hesse wrote:

> Sie müssen ein guter, gütiger Mensch sein, daß Sie so zarte freundschaftliche Worte für mich fanden. Sie haben mir wohlgetan, ich spürte dabei, daß Sie im Herzen mein Freund sind.[53]

51. Unpublished letter of 22 August 1902 from Cesco Como to Hesse. Original in the Hesse Archives, Marbach. Unpublished letter of 24 August 1902 from Hesse to Cesco Como. Copy of original in the Hesse Archives, Marbach. Como apparently visited Italy several times, however, at least once in the company of Jeanne Berta Semmig, whom he introduced to the country of his family's origins in 1908. See Semmig, *Aus acht Jahrzehnten*, 179.

52. Unpublished letter of 17 September 1902 from Hesse to Cesco Como, dictated by the author in Calw to Adele or Marulla Hesse. Copy of original in the Hesse Archives, Marbach.

53. Letter of 7 May 1902 from Hesse to Cesco Como, *Briefe*, 1: 89.

[You must be a good and kind person to find such tender and amicable words. I needed them, and I sensed in my heart that you are my friend.]

Once they finally met face-to-face in Ober-Klingen at Christmas of 1902, they quickly opted for the familiar *du* form of address, thus certifying the close friendship that had already developed by mail. Their correspondence from the years 1903 and 1904, especially, bears witness to an almost brotherly relationship, and there seem to have been few secrets between them. Cesco Como was among the first, for example, to learn of Hesse's serious relationship with Maria Bernoulli. He was also one of the few friends from this period in Hesse's life who visited him in Calw, where he met Johannes Hesse and both of Hesse's sisters, and he would also visit the newly wed Hesses in Gaienhofen in the summer of 1905.[54]

As was occasionally the case with other male relationships during this phase of Hesse's life, the friendship between these two sensitive and somewhat willful young men was not without turmoil. Naturally, they held differing opinions from time to time about questions of literary aesthetics or authors, and they also had a running, albeit good-natured feud about the relative merits of Florence and Venice – Hesse emphatically preferred the former, Como the latter Italian city. It was a discussion of morality, though, specifically the notion of premarital chastity, that led to a spirited exchange of letters during the summer and early fall of 1903 and unquestionably strained what had become one of Hesse's closest friendships.

It all began quite innocently, when, almost simultaneously, each became seriously enamored of a woman. On 2 June 1903, Cesco Como wrote Hesse a card from Frankfurt with the following short poem and note:

Tragödie.

> War einst ein Jüngling unerfahren
> Den packt' einmal die Lesewut.
> Da stopft er voll in langen Jahren
> Den hohlen Kasten unterm Hut.
> Es wimmelt ihm vor Idealen,
> Bis glücklich die Komödie kam,

---

54. "Ich denke an den Tag, noch in Calw zurück, mit Freude…. Grüße mir, bitte, Deine Lieben von mir." ["I remember that day in Calw with great delight… Please give my best to your dear family."] Unpublished letter of 5 February 1904 from Cesco Como to Hermann Hesse. Original in the Hesse Archives, Marbach. See also Como's unpublished letter of 13 July 1905, original also in the Hesse Archives, Marbach.

Und dieser Jüngling wohlerfahren
Sich ein vermögend Weibchen nahm.
Ich glaub ich bins oder werds. Dein C. C.[55]

[Tragedy.
There once was an innocent boy
Who was seized with the urge to read.
And for many a year he stuffed full
The empty compartment under his hat.
He was teeming with ideals,
Until the comedy began,
And this once so innocent boy
Took himself a wealthy little lady.
I think that's me – or will be me. Your C. C.]

In his answer, Hesse commented briefly that Como's little verse had made him "extremely curious" since he, too, found himself "strolling along Cupid's paths," and he then described in rather surprising detail his budding affair with Maria Bernoulli:

Seit Jahren war ich nicht mehr verliebt und hatte keine Liaison mehr, pfiff vielmehr auf die Weiber und war der reine Puritaner. Seit kurzem aber halte ich allabendlich einen entzückenden, kleinen, schwarzen, wilden Schatz im Arm ... meine ganze Freizeit gehört dem kleinen Mädchen, das mir nur bis an den Bart reicht und so gewaltsam küssen kann, daß ich fast ersticke.[56]

[It has been years since I was last in love or had an affair, moreover I have rather shunned women and have been a complete Puritan. But the past few weeks, every evening, I have been holding in my arms a divine, little, dark, wild darling ... my entire free time belongs to this little girl, who only comes up to my beard and can kiss so powerfully that I almost suffocate.]

Noting that marriage was "out of the question," Hesse concluded the letter with a clearly unfortunate reference to "freshening up" his "rusty lovemaking skills."

He was doubtlessly quite taken aback at Como's response, a rambling and heavily moralistic admonishment nearly a thousand words in length, in which the latter expressed amazement at the "conversion" of his "Puritan" friend and, indirectly but unmistakably, took Hesse to task for "sinning against love" by entering a "union without love." Como concluded with almost sermon-like

55. Unpublished picture postcard of 2 June 1903 from Cesco Como to Hermann Hesse. Original in the Hesse Archives, Marbach.
56. Letter of 4 June 1903 to Cesco Como, *Briefe*, 1: 104.

fervor, imploring Hesse to exercise abstinence, to "leave the girl in peace," and to spare his "own heart further guilt."[57] At first glance, one might quite justifiably wonder that the two young men, who had repeatedly immersed themselves in soul-baring discussions during the preceding year and a half of correspondence, were so unaware of each other's moral views. As Hesse's words rather pointedly reveal, however, he had lived without female companionship "for years," certainly during the relatively brief time since he had become acquainted with the Knodt circle. Indeed, up until he met Maria Bernoulli, Hermann Hesse's association with young women in Basel – as has been previously discussed – was accurately characterized by the Bölschean term *Distanceliebe*. By Como's own rather clear admission, he, too, had been free of amorous encumbrances for some time, and it seems unlikely that either of these really rather proper young men had logged very extensive experience of an erotic nature with the opposite sex. Thus, they had scarcely discussed their individual sentiments regarding *real* relationships with women or their personal views on marriage.

Ever sensitive to moral dogma, however, Hermann Hesse bristled at his friend's chastizing, refuting Como's arguments and concluding with the question:

> Aber was ist "Sünde an der Liebe"? Ich verstehe darunter vor allem die Vergewaltigung seiner selbst, die Flucht vor jedem kräftigen und intensiven Erleben.[58]
>
> [But what is a "sin against love"? To me it means, above all, violating yourself, fleeing any strong and intensive experience.]

He also attempted to focus more sharply the vague impression of Maria Bernoulli that his first letter had obviously awakened, revealing in his depiction of Maria here the distinctly progressive and egalitarian attitude toward women that would typify Hermann Hesse throughout his adult life:

> Mein Schatz ist kein dummes Gretchen, sondern mir an Bildung, Lebenserfahrung und Intelligenz mindestens ebenbürtig, älter als ich und in jeder Hinsicht eine selbständige, tüchtige Persönlichkeit.[59]
>
> [My sweetheart is no naive Gretchen type but quite my equal in education, life experience, and intelligence; she is older than I and in every respect an independent and competent human being.]

57. Unpublished letter of 17 June 1903 from Cesco Como to Hermann Hesse. Original in the Hesse Archives, Marbach.
58. Letter of 21 June 1903 to Cesco Como. *Briefe*, 1: 106.
59. Ibid.

For three months, their correspondence all but ceased, picking up again only when Hesse sent a card in early October to inform Como of his move back to Calw, which would be his final departure from Basel. Como responded immediately to his friend's note, but began his lengthy missive with an inauspiciously obstinate defense of his earlier condemnation of Hesse's behavior, reiterating his conviction that the latter was "plunging into the sea of love ... without considering how it all will end."[60] Before Hesse could reply to his letter, however, Como learned from the Knodts of Hesse's engagement to Maria Bernoulli and responded with an effusively apologetic, yet quite heartfelt message that revealed very literally the depth of Como's feeling for Hermann Hesse:

> Ich habe Dich, habe Deine Liebe, Deinen Willen verkannt, jetzt bitte ich Dich innig, verzeihe mir und sei mir mein alter, guter Freund. – Ich gönne Dir vom Herzen Dein Glück, wenn auch im Anfang mein Egoismus sich recht sträubte und Dich gern unbeweibt, nicht andre liebend gesehen hätte. Ich war eifersüchtig.[61]

> [I misjudged you, your love, and your will power, and I plead with you to forgive me, my old and good friend. With all my heart, I wish you happiness, even though when this all started my ego rebelled, having rather seen you without a woman and not close to other people. I was jealous.]

In his response, while perceptibly grateful for his friend's honest apology, Hesse couldn't resist pointing out – with typical, biting irony – the hypocrisy implicit in Cesco's disavowal of his original reproach:

> Lieber Cesco!
> Danke für Deinen Brief! Den Streit über Deine seltsame Liebesmoral wollen wir ruhen lassen. Daß dieselbe Liebe, die Dir gestern gemein und schlecht erschien, heute, weil Du das Wort "Verlobung" hörst, auf einmal edel und erhaben ist, macht mich lachen. Das ist ja vorn und hinten Phrase, leere Phrase![62]

> [Dear Cesco!
> Thanks for your letter! As for the argument about your strange notions of romantic morality, we'll just let it be. I have to laugh, though, when I see that the same romance that seemed tawdry and bad to you yesterday is suddenly noble and exalted, because you

---

60. Unpublished letter of 3 October 1903 from Cesco Como to Hesse. Original in the Hesse Archives, Marbach.
61. Unpublished letter of 24 October 1903 from Cesco Como to Hesse. Original in the Hesse Archives, Marbach.
62. Letter of 26 October 1903 from Hesse to Cesco Como. *Briefe*, 1: 109.

have heard the word "engagement." That's nothing but rhetoric, empty rhetoric!]

Hermann Hesse's friendship with Cesco Como was almost certainly weakened by this episode, revealing as it had a moral righteousness on Como's part that must have reminded Hesse all too vividly of similarly moralistic admonishments he had frequently endured from his parents. Just as their moral chiding had unquestionably alienated Hesse from his family in Calw, this incident resulted in Hesse's distancing himself to some extent from Cesco Como, at least psychologically. True, Como would visit Hesse in Calw (January 1904) and again the following year in Gaienhofen (July 1905), but their correspondence appears to have stopped completely by the fall of 1905.

As detailed above, more than half a century would pass before Como's daughter, Josefa Michaelis-Como, would facilitate a final exchange of greetings between the two friends in 1958. Fortunately, that late contact provided a kind of reconciliation shortly before Como's death on 13 November 1958.

THE LAST *CÉNACLER*,
LUDWIG FINCKH

H ermann Hesse's introduction to the *Waldpfarrer*, which in large measure led to his subsequent recognition as a literary figure in Germany, was made possible by his one remaining close friend from the Tübingen *petit cénacle*, Ludwig "Ugel" Finckh. Karl Ernst Knodt's first letter to Hesse, at Christmas 1900, refers to Hesse's friend Ludwig Finckh, "indeed *our* friend Finckh, the one who brought the two of us together."[1] Almost from the moment of their first meeting at Heckenhauer's in Tübingen during the summer of 1897, Finckh and Hesse were fast friends, although, by all accounts, one could scarcely imagine more dissimilar types: Finckh was the gregarious and jovial optimist who could liven up any social occasion, while Hesse, rather prone to introspection and melancholy, often enough preferred to avoid social interaction, especially in larger groups.[2] Both did seem to thrive in small groups of like-minded companions, such as the *petit cénacle* in Tübingen had represented, but they also enjoyed each other's company without the encumbrances of the group.

They both left Tübingen in the fall of 1899, when Finckh began his study of medicine in Freiburg and Hesse assumed his new position at Reich's in Basel. For the next three years, the two friends were to remain nearly as inseparable as they had been in Tübingen, despite living some seventy kilometers apart. Unfortunately, the

1. Unpublished letter of 25 December 1900 from Karl Ernst Knodt to Hesse. Original in the Hesse Archives, Marbach.

2. For a balanced and informative portrayal of the Hesse-Finckh friendship, see Michael Limberg, "Hermann Hesse und Ludwig Finckh," in *Hermann Hesse und seine literarischen Zeitgenossen*, eds. Friedrich Bran and Martin Pfeifer (Calw, 1982), 39–56.

Ludwig Finckh and Hermann Hesse

personal correspondence between the two of them during this period is incomplete, since all of the cards and letters as well as a good many handwritten poems that Hesse sent to Finckh before 1907 were reduced to ashes in the February 1907 fire that literally burned Finckh's house in Gaienhofen to the ground. Finckh's letters to Hesse from this period, however, mirror and complement Hesse's missives to him and make regular reference to mutual weekend visits, when they could be found strolling through museums or attending concerts in Basel, or hiking, occasionally in Switzerland but more often in the Breisgau area between Basel and Freiburg, sometimes for two or three days at a time.[3] The excursions into nature, especially, suited these two "neo-Romantic" souls quite well, burdened as they both were with a day-to-day, city existence that each yearned to escape. While Finckh, by his own account, participated in the *Wandervogel* movement as a student in Tübingen, there is no indication that Hesse did so, which is hardly surprising, in view of his lifelong aversion to organized social activities.[4] In addition, of course, their own literary endeavors of the time, particularly Hesse's poetry from the years 1899 to 1902, reflected a conceptualization of nature that revealed influences that were sometimes pantheistic, sometimes incipiently symbolistic.

In their personal interaction, at least as revealed in letters, the two developed an intimacy that, at first glance, seems almost homoerotic in tone.[5] In fact, though, Hesse's close friendship with Finckh – not unlike that with Cesco Como at the same time – reflects rather a kind of glorification of male "bonding," as it were. In his retrospective depiction of the "Lulu" episode, Finckh attempted to delineate that male-male closeness from its male-female correlative:

Frauenliebe ist schön über alle Maßen, Männerfreundschaft ist schöner, beglückender.[6]

[The love of a woman is wonderful beyond measure, but male friendship is more wonderful, joyful.]

3. Finckh's letters to Hesse reveal that Badenweiler (some thirty kilometers south of Freiburg) was a favorite starting point, from which the hikers could reach several of the major mountains in the area: the Belchen, the Blauen, and the Bürgeln Castle. See, in particular, the unpublished letter of 17 June 1902, from Finckh to Hesse, original in the Hesse Archives of the Swiss National Library, Bern.

4. What Hesse had to say about Peter Camenzind and the Youth Movement of the turn of the century doubtless applied to the author himself: "Aber ... er gehört dennoch nicht zu den Wandervögeln und Jugendgemeinschaften, im Gegenteil, nirgends würde er schlechter eingeordnet sein." Hermann Hesse, "Über *Peter Camenzind*," *Werke*. 11: 26. ["But ... nonetheless, he doesn't join hiking groups and other youth organizations, on the contrary, no place would he fit in more poorly."]

5. Haile von Kutzleben, the youngest of Finckh's five children, mentioned having had a similar reaction when she first read some of her father's letters to Hesse from that time, though she rightly declared that both men were exclusively heterosexual. (Personal conversation with the author, 23 June 1994, in Gaienhofen/Hemmenhofen.)

6. Ludwig Finckh, *Verzauberung* (Ulm, 1950), 67. Hesse, too, put quite similar words into his autobiographical Peter Camenzind: "Ich weiß auch heute in der Welt nicht Köstlicheres als eine ehrliche und tüchtige Freundschaft zwischen Männern. ... " Hermann Hesse, *Peter Camenzind*, *Werke*, 1: 407. ["Even today, I know of nothing in the world more precious than an honest and solid friendship between men ... "]

Such an intimate companionship, of course, was subject to many of the emotional vicissitudes that typify any close friendship, regardless of gender. Hermann Hesse's friendship with Cesco Como, for example, was clearly affected by the latter's admitted jealousy vis-à-vis Hesse's budding relationship with Maria Bernoulli. In the Finckh-Hesse friendship during those years, it was Hesse who occasionally displayed what could only be termed jealous behavior.

Finckh soon had a sizeable circle of new friends in Freiburg, not due merely to his outgoing and sociable nature, but also because his study of medicine brought him into contact with many fellow students who were subjected to the same grueling training. In his early autobiographical novel *Der Rosendoktor*, for example, Finckh describes a group of students who meet while dissecting cadavers:

> Die Kameradschaft von der Leiche her bewährte sich. Man war bei der Arbeit aufeinander angewiesen, man wollte auch Farbe bekennen auf der Straße und im alltäglichen Leben … man unternahm Ausflüge und Bergfahrten, man streifte durch die Wälder und Dörfer, Sommer und Winter.[7]

> [The good companionship carried over from dissection class to our outside social life. We relied on each other in the lab, and we wanted to stick together on the street, in everyday life, too. We went on excursions and trips to the mountains together, hiking through forest and village, summer and winter.]

(Obviously, Hesse's daily routine did not include such intense interaction with his relatively few co-workers, and his Swiss hiking jaunts were usually undertaken alone.) It was precisely such a group of Finckh's student friends whom Hermann Hesse would join from time to time when he visited "Ugel" in Freiburg.

One of those Freiburg medical students who became a good friend of Finckh was Kurt Piper, a young north German who completed his medical studies in Kiel in 1904 only to abandon the traditional practice of medicine after World War I. Born in Hamburg-Altona on 23 December 1875, Piper was the son of a Germanist, Prof. Dr. Paul Piper (1844–1924), who achieved a certain notoriety when he discovered what he believed to be an original Goethe manuscript, though his claim was widely rejected by literary scholars of the time. On his mother's side, Piper was the direct descendant of the philosopher and writer Friedrich Heinrich Jacobi (1743–1819), a friend of the young Goethe.

---

7. Ludwig Finckh, *Der Rosendoktor*, 112f.

Like Finckh, Kurt Piper established a modest literary reputation while completing his medical studies, and his first volume of poetry, *Fegefeuer* (Sonnenblumen-Verlag, Leipzig/Berlin), appeared in print in 1903. A peripheral member of the literary circle around Detlev von Liliencron and Prince Emil von Schoenaich-Carolath, Piper had extensive contacts within the north German literary scene. He maintained a substantial correspondence with Liliencron that began in 1901 and lasted until shortly before the latter's death in 1909, and Liliencron edited and published Piper's 1905 collection of verse, entitled *Waffen und Wunden* (Schuster & Loeffler, Berlin/Leipzig). During the decade prior to the First World War, Piper was also in regular contact with Richard Dehmel and Karl Henckell. According to a handwritten family history,[8] he knew Thomas Mann and Otto Ernst personally, among other literary figures, and a number of his letters to Ludwig Finckh from the period 1900–5 were lost in the fire that leveled Finckh's home in 1907.

Kurt Piper served as a medical officer and field surgeon for the entire duration of the First World War, then assumed a position as staff physician at a sanatorium in Bad König (Odenwald) south of Frankfurt/Main. Here he resumed writing, though focusing now on essays of a poltical and cultural nature that appeared in journals of the time such as *Masken* and *Weimarer Blätter*. The culmination of his writing during this period was his *Bibelgold* (Hanseatische Verlagsanstalt, Hamburg), which he labeled a "retelling" of several Bible stories from both Testaments, published in 1921.

In 1922, at the urging of a patient in his care, Piper attended a series of lectures presented by Rudolf Steiner, an event that would change the direction of his life. He followed Steiner to Stuttgart, where he trained under Steiner's supervision and established an anthroposophic medical practice that would engage him until his death there on 3 August 1952.[9] He never completely abandoned his writing, contributing in particular to periodicals of the Anthroposophic Society and serving stints as editor of *Die Drei*, *Anthroposophie*, and *Die Morgenröte*.

8. In the possession of Dr. Hans-Felix Piper, Lübeck, who graciously allowed the author to peruse all of the materials passed along to him from his uncle Kurt Piper. Reference is made here to the 721-page, handwritten family history, *Geschichte der Familie Piper*, originally compiled by Dr. Paul Piper, Kurt Piper's father.

9. There is apparently only one introduction to Piper's life and work still in print today: Kurt Piper, *Vom lebendigen Wissen*, ed. Edwin Froböse (Stuttgart, 1975).

In the spring of 1902, Kurt Piper and Ludwig Finckh had become close friends, having discovered their mutual love for poetry and that each wrote verse himself. Piper was quickly fascinated by the poetry of "Ugel's" bosom friend in Basel, even memorizing Hesse's entire *Romantische Lieder*, according to Finckh.[10] At Finckh's suggestion, Piper sent Hesse one of his own poems ("Flammentod"), and Hesse responded with a copy of *Lauscher* and a sampling of his most recent verse, presumably some of the poems he was smoothing out for inclusion in the first draft of his *Gedichte* that he would send to editor Carl Busse just three weeks later. During the following eight months, Hesse and Piper would exchange letters and samples of their work, and Piper's letters, presumably all of them, are housed in the Marbach Hesse Archives. Unfortunately, Hesse's letters to Piper have never been located, except for the final letter written by Hesse and returned unopened by Piper in January 1903. Otherwise, only a few greetings and comments that accompanied Hesse's various literary mailings to Piper have survived. Thus, it is impossible to ascertain precisely what caused an almost immediate rift between these two young men. Nonetheless, Piper's letters to Hesse, combined with those written by Finckh between May 1902 and early 1903, reveal a rather distinct picture of an acquaintanceship marred from the outset by petulance, envy, and what may well have been outright jealousy.

Piper's letter of 15 May 1902 thanking Hesse for sending *Lauscher* and the poem selection just mentioned was the first full letter in their correspondence, and it may have touched a raw nerve in Hermann Hesse. Although flattering Hesse by noting that he had read everything Hesse had written up to then, Piper also made a rather derogatory reference to poet and editor Carl Busse (who was about to publish Hesse's *Gedichte*) as a "half talent" who was already "stagnating" before ever reaching his peak.[11] Since he had

10. Unpublished letter of 28 May 1902 from Ludwig Finckh to Hesse. Original in the Hesse Archives of the Swiss National Library, Bern.

11. Though Hesse and Busse were just getting to know each other personally, the importance of Busse's support for Hesse at this point in his career was quite comparable to that of Liliencron for Kurt Piper. It is possible that Hesse's emphatic and belittling rejection of Liliencron for Knodt's anthology, *Wir sind die Sehnsucht*, a few months later could have had something to do with the Piper episode: "Auf Liliencron können wir ohne Bedenken verzichten – wenn wir einmal ein Lyrikbuch für Sportsleute und Offiziere machen, soll er obenan kommen." Letter of 7 November 1902 from Hesse to Karl Ernst Knodt, *Briefe*, 1: 92. ["We can do without Liliencron with no hesitation – if we put together a book of verse sometime for athletic types and military officers, then he should be our lead author."]

Kurt Piper

been following Hesse's career, through Ludwig Finckh, on a nearly day-to-day basis, it seems unlikely that Piper did not realize that Hesse would take umbrage at this comment about his editor and friend. Piper's derisive remark may have been nothing more than envy, however, since he was finding it very difficult to write at the time, unable, as Finckh put it, to "tear himself away from medicine," though, as Finckh continued, "he lacks a poetic soul – he has a Nietzsche mentality."[12] Hesse may well have been equally affected, however, by Piper's remarks about his and Finckh's friendship:

12. Unpublished letter of 22 May 1902 from Ludwig Finckh to Hesse. Original in the Hesse Archives of the Swiss National Library, Bern.

Unser Finckh läßt Sie herzlich grüßen. . . Finckh ist mein einziger Freund hier.[13]

[Our friend Frinckh sends his hearty greetings. . . Finckh is my only friend here.]

Hesse must have felt at least a pang of jealousy at these words, since he tended, of course, to consider "Ugel" *his* only friend. In his letters to Hesse, Kurt Piper repeatedly alluded to his own friend-ship with Finckh, often rather pointedly mentioning plans that he and Finckh were making or noting that he was at Finckh's as he was writing to Hesse. Unfortunately, the good-hearted Finckh, cer-tainly without intending his best friend any harm, occasionally included comments that probably fueled Hesse's jealousy.

At almost exactly the same time as the first exchange was tak-ing place between Piper and Hermann Hesse, Finckh was busily lining up subscribers for Hesse's second edition of the *Notturni*, and Kurt Piper was among the first to place an order that Hesse filled immediately on 22 May 1902. The original set, now housed in the Marbach Hesse Archives, contains only Hesse's standard title for the 1902 version (*Notturni – Gedichte für meine Freunde* [Poems for my Friends]) and the personalized dedication to Piper (Herrn Kurt Piper mit herzlichem Gruß! [To Mr. Kurt Piper with hearty greetings!]). However, in his letter of response, written on 23 May, Piper referred to the letter Hesse had sent along with the *Notturni*, quoting passages verbatim from Hesse's letter:

> Sehr geehrter Herr Hesse,
> ich weiß genau, wo in Ihrem freundlichen Begleitschreiben die Ironie ihr Wesen treibt. . . Ich kenne aus Hermann Lauscher etc. die Ironie als integrierenden Bestandteil Ihres Wesens, und so ist es Sache allergewöhnlichster Toleranz, sie mir auch hier gern gefallen zu lassen trotz ihrer etwas persönlichen Nuance. Ich erwartete nichts "literarisch Apartes" sondern etwas Reinmenschliches und sah mich Gott sei Dank in meinen Erwartungen nicht getäuscht. . . Also von einem "erhebenden Gefühl des Almosengebens an einen armen Dichter" war bei mir keine Rede.[14]

> [Dear Mr. Hesse,
> I know precisely where your irony is at work in the friendly note you sent along. . . From Hermann Lauscher etc. I know that irony is an integral component of your being, thus it is a matter of most

13. Unpublished letter of 15 May 1902 from Kurt Piper to Hesse. Original in the Hesse Archives, Marbach.

14. Unpublished letter of 23 May 1902 from Kurt Piper to Hesse. Original in the Hesse Archives, Marbach.

common tolerance that I happily acquiesce to it here despite its somewhat personal tone. I did not anticipate anything "literarily out of the ordinary," but rather something pure and humane, and, thank God, my expectations were not dashed. . . For that very reason, I truly had no "feeling of providing charity for a poor poet."]

(Hesse was also probably not particularly pleased to be reminded once again, at the conclusion of the letter, of Piper's friendship with "Ugel": "Finckh and I hope to come to Basel in the next few weeks."[15] The same day, he also received a letter from "Ugel" that noted: "I am often amazed at how much Piper is like you, intellectually and existentially . . .")[16] Whatever may have motivated the sarcastic tone of Hesse's letter, it seems obvious that his gibes were indeed meant to be personal, a fact made all the more surprising by their having still not met; in no other letter accompanying his *Notturni* did Hesse avail himself of such an ironic and seemingly personal nuance. Aside from the letter, one of the poems in the set is also remarkable for its negative mood, and one is quite tempted to ascribe its inclusion to Hesse's clearly growing antipathy toward Kurt Piper and to speculate that Hesse might have written this poem with Piper in mind. At any rate, it is not to be found in any other extant *Notturni* collection, and it was included only in the first edition of Hesse's *Gedichte* (1902), under the title "Einem Unzufriedenen."[17]

> *Einem Verächter*
> Sieh, ich verstehe ja dein Fluchen.
> Aber die Welt bleibt wie sie war
> Dein Haß verändert an ihr kein Haar.
> Die Menschen sind eine verdorbene Brut,
> Aber du selber – bist du denn gut?
> Ich würde es mal mit der Liebe versuchen.[18]

> [To a Scornful One
> Look, I understand indeed your cursing.
> But the world will stay the way it was
> Your contempt won't change a thing about it.

15. Ibid.

16. Unpublished letter of 22 May 1902 from Ludwig Finckh to Hesse. Original in the Hesse Archives of the Swiss National Library, Bern.

17. According to Joseph Mileck, the poem appeared one other time, in the *Telegraph am Abend* (Berlin) on 4 August 1949, under title of "Bist du denn gut?" See Mileck, *Hermann Hesse: Biography and Bibliography*, 1: 659f.

18. Original version of "Einem Unzufriedenen," included in the Piper *Notturni*, original in the Hesse Archives, Marbach.

Human beings are all depraved,
But you yourself – are you then good?
I think I'd try a little love.]

Two letters from Finckh to Hesse the following week would seem to confirm that this poem might have suited well Piper's mood at the time:

Du, der arme Piper, sei gut zu ihm, er ist so verlassen und verbittert und ist *doch* was. (28 May 1902)

Piper sitzt hier auf meinem Sofa, der arme Kerl. Immer den Tod im Blick. (4 June 1902)[19]

[My friend, do be nice to poor Piper, he is forlorn and bitter, though he really *is* a good person.]

[Piper is sitting here on my sofa, the poor fellow. Always looking nearly suicidal.]

On 9 June, Hesse sent more poems to Finckh, perhaps an additional selection of pieces that were destined for publication in his *Gedichte*, which he had sent to Busse on 5 June. Finckh responded with a short letter of thanks and praise for the new poems (10 June), and at the bottom of the page, Kurt Piper added his own terse comment about a poem that Hesse had dedicated to him, objecting to Hesse's form of address:

12 Uhr nachts.
Wenn Sie mir, werther Herr Hesse, noch einmal so ein "undichtbares" Gedicht zustellen, so lassen Sie in der "Widmung" das verflixte "Herr" aus dem Spiele. Unter dieser Perspektive sind wir "Menschen" und keine Marionetten des *fin de siècle*. Nächstens bekommen Sie eine "poetische" Ladung von mir.
Ihr Kurt Piper
Wir lesen eben das Buch Ruth, meinen Liebling, zusammen.[20]

[12 o'clock midnight.
My esteemed Mr. Hesse, if you should send me another of your "unwritable" poems, please leave out that confounded "Mister" in your "dedication." In our present situation, we are "human beings" and not puppets of the fin de siècle mentality.
You will shortly be receiving a "poetic" package from me.
Your Kurt Piper

19. Unpublished letters of 28 May and 4 June 1902 from Ludwig Finckh to Hesse. Originals in the Hesse Archives of the Swiss National Library, Bern.
20. Unpublished letter of 10 June 1902 from Ludwig Finckh and Kurt Piper to Hesse. Original in the Hesse Archives of the Swiss National Library, Bern.

We are just reading the Book of Ruth together, my favorite.]

For Hermann Hesse, alone in Basel, still grieving the death of his mother just six weeks earlier, and plagued anew by increasingly severe eye strain and headaches, Piper's postscript to Finckh's letter must have been difficult to endure. The image of Piper and Finckh reading the Book of Ruth into the wee hours of the night, while likely a quite accurate reflection of the closeness of the Finckh-Piper friendship, may well have caused Hermann Hesse to infer that his status as Finckh's most intimate friend was threatened. On the other hand, even the most objective reading of Piper's concluding comment would have to acknowledge its openly flaunting tone. Thus, the rift between Hesse and Piper continued to widen, undoubtedly facilitated to a significant extent by what amounted to a kind of "competition" between the two for Finkch's friendship. Again, in his own innocuous way, Finckh would contribute to his best friend's apprehension, reporting on 11 June that Piper had rather abruptly found his poetic vein, writing "more beautiful poetry than ever."[21]

At Finckh's urging, Hesse arranged to come for a weekend of hiking in late June 1902, but to his likely dismay, he learned in a letter from "Ugel" just days before the trip that his friend would not be meeting him alone. After suggesting an itinerary for their outing, Finckh noted:

> Am liebsten wär' ich allein mit Dir dort, aber mein Schwanz Piper, Waldschrat und Rautendelein wird mitwollen. Na, wir können uns entziehen.[22]
>
> [I'd most prefer to be there alone with you, but my tail (Piper, Wood-goblin, and *Rautendelein*) will want to come along. Oh, well, we can slip away on our own.]

Finckh's reference to his "tail" (i.e., entourage of friends), while alluding to his own central status in the group, also reflects, in his and Hesse's use of nicknames for the others, the depth of their friendship. The names *Waldschrat* and *Rautendelein* were taken from Gerhart Hauptmann's "fairy-tale play," *Die versunkene Glocke* (1896), a work that was one of Hesse's and Finckh's favorites during their Tübingen years. (*Waldschrat* was in reality Karl Huck, a fellow medical student in Freiburg, as was *Rautendelein*, though

21. Unpublished letter of 11 June 1902 from Ludwig Finckh to Hesse. Original in the Hesse Archives of the Swiss National Library, Bern.
22. Unpublished letter of 17 June 1902 from Ludwig Finckh to Hesse. Original in the Hesse Archives of the Swiss National Library, Bern.

the latter was not identified by name in Finckh's letters.)[23] Finckh's words ("Oh, well, we can slip away on our own") could hardly reveal more clearly his own awareness of and sensitivity to the alienation that Hesse was feeling at the time. Too, "Ugel" could probably well imagine that Hesse and Piper, meeting in person for the first time, would have their difficulties. Unfortunately, no subsequent letter makes reference to that weekend, though it must be remembered that all of Hesse's and Piper's correspondence to Ludwig Finckh perished in the Gaienhofen fire in 1907. There seems to be good reason, however, to assume that the hike did take place and that Piper and Hesse did meet face-to-face.

Shortly thereafter, around mid-July 1902, Hesse heeded medical counsel and ceased most writing and reading in order to spare his eyes. In late August, he went home to Calw, entrusting himself to the care of his sisters and father, and remained there until the end of October. Understandably, his correspondence was drastically reduced during these months, and he often dictated letters to one of his sisters when he absolutely had to correspond. Thus, it is neither surprising nor particularly significant that no letter to or from Kurt Piper during the second half of 1902 is to be found in the Piper correspondence file in Marbach. A brief, final flurry of correspondence between the two in January 1903, however, makes it clear that they had either maintained written communication or had talked in person in the late fall of 1902. While only Piper's letters from their 1902 correspondence have been saved, Hesse's last letter to Piper has survived, thanks to Piper's having returned it unopened to Hermann Hesse, who dutifully entered it in his files, as he would do with so many thousands of other letters in his lifetime. Now completing his studies in Kiel, Piper wrote to Hesse on 21 January 1903, obviously responding to a recent exchange of letters or a discussion in person:

Sehr geehrter Herr Hesse,
    Sie bekehren mich nicht, und ich bekehre Sie nicht. Wir haben beide Recht und Unrecht. Nur soviel ist mir heute klar, daß wir uns nie hätten berühren dürfen.[24]

23. The significance of Hauptmann's play was brought to the author's attention by Haile Finckh von Kutzleben, Ludwig Finckh's last living offspring. She noted that Dr. Karl Huck set up practice in Singen, just twenty kilometers to the northwest of Gaienhofen, and maintained regular contact with the Finckh family in Gaienhofen. When Finckh became severely ill in October of 1950, he was treated in the hospital in Singen by Huck.
24. Unpublished letter of 21 January 1903 from Kurt Piper to Hesse. Original in the Hesse Archives, Marbach.

[Dear Mr. Hesse,

You are not going to convert me, nor I you. We are both right and both wrong, but it is clear to me today that we should never have had anything to do with each other.]

He then referred to a recent poem he had sent to Hesse, presumably the undated poem contained in the correspondence file in Marbach entitled "An Hermann Hesse," noting that it "was not meant to be ironic," though Hesse must have found it offensive. Citing a similar poem written about Ludwig Finckh, Piper assured Hesse that he is not the only one who suffered as a result of Piper's "manner":

Ich wünsche es keinem, in meinen "Dunstkreis" zu treten. Ich darf keine Freunde haben. . . Eine Freundschaft schließt sich so leicht, aber das Zerreißen geht nie ohne Blut ab. . . Ich danke Ihnen von Herzen für die tiefe Freude, die mir Ihr Buch [*Gedichte*] bereitet hat. . . Ich wünsche Ihnen alle Menschen zu Freunden, nur keinen

Kurt Piper[25]

[I would not wish upon anyone to enter my "atmosphere." I should not be allowed to have friends. . . Friendships are so easy to form, but breaking up a friendship always brings blood. . . I thank you from the bottom of my heart for the profound joy that your book has brought me. . . I wish that you may have all people as your friends, all except

Kurt Piper]

Hesse's response, written on 24 January 1903, lends credence to the assumption that a rather intense exchange – either written or verbal – had occurred much more recently than mid-summer 1902, when the two had last exchanged post. Still, Hesse's letter makes clear his desire to maintain the correspondence, even as Piper's missive had expressed no such willingness, but not without excluding rather forcefully any possibility of a full-fledged friendship:

25. Ibid. The poems referred to here could indeed be read as "ironic," even somewhat satirical in nature. However, without the full background context of the complete correspondence among Hesse, Finckh, and Piper, one must resort to more than a little speculation in attempting to interpret them. On the other hand, Piper does seem to capture some salient features of the two other men. He refers to Finckh as the "little king" and "peace maker" of his group, while the Hesse poem bears allusions to his "never satisfied yearning," the "higher reality" of Hesse's "inner worlds," as well as an inauspicious reference – given Hesse's eye torment – to his "mortal eye." Ironically, Finckh added a brief greeting at the end of the poem, "from Kurt Piper's lair." ("An Hermann Hesse," unpublished poem by Kurt Piper, undated [late 1902], original in the Hesse Archives, Marbach.)

Lieber Herr Piper ...
   Ihr Brief hat mich traurig gemacht. Wenn Sie mir nicht mehr schreiben wollen, kann ich's ja nicht erzwingen. Doch bitte ich Sie, unsre Beziehungen doch einstweilen zu lassen wie sie sind. . . Und dann sprechen Sie von "Freunden," die Sie haben oder nicht haben. An mir finden Sie keinen Freundschaftsenthusiasten. In gewissem Sinn habe ich alle Menschen gern. Aber ich habe nur einen Freund – das ist Finckh. Er ist der Einzige, für den ich Opfer bringen oder sterben würde. . . Sehen Sie, deshalb ziehe ich Bäume, Landschaften, Tiere etc. den Menschen vor – man kann sie liebhaben, ohne daß es Szenen gibt.[26]

[Dear Mr. Piper ...
   Your letter made me sad. If you don't want to write me anymore, I cannot force you to do so. Still, I do ask you to leave things between us as they are for the time being. . . And then you speak of "friends," whom you have or do not have. You won't find in me an enthusiastic supporter of friendships. In a certain sense, I like all human beings, but I have only one friend – that's Finckh. He is the only one whom I would make personal sacrifices or die for. . . You see, that's why I prefer trees, open countryside, animals, etc. to human beings – you can be fond of them without their causing any scenes.]

As already mentioned, Piper never read this letter, returning it unopened on 26 January with a short letter of apology:

Bitte, werter Herr Hesse, beruhigen Sie sich doch und betrachten Sie das leidige Gedicht als ungeschrieben. Ich beschwöre Sie, mir meine Ungezogenheit nicht zu verübeln, wenn ich Ihnen Ihr heutiges Schreiben uneröffnet wiederschicke, aber ich mag nicht mehr, wirklich nicht. . . Denken Sie nicht gar zu schlecht von mir. Ich leide am meisten unter mir selbst.

Ihr ergebener KP[27]

[Please, esteemed Mr. Hesse, do calm yourself and consider the offensive poem unwritten. I beg of you not to consider it too rude of me if I return today's letter to you unopened, but I don't want this to continue, really I don't. . . Please do not think ill of me. I suffer most from myself.

Your devoted KP]

In the absence of the full correspondence between the two men, the discussion of their relationship has been, of necessity, mildly

26. Unpublished letter of 24 Jan 1903 from Hesse to Kurt Piper. Original in the Hesse Archives, Marbach.
27. Unpublished letter of 26 January 1903 from Kurt Piper to Hesse. Original in the Hesse Archives, Marbach.

speculative here, though there seems to be sufficient evidence to indicate that these two sensitive and highly talented young men, who were by no means immune to emotional insecurity and immaturity, were apprehensive about each other from the beginning, both as regarded their friendship with their mutual "best" friend and their individual literary efforts. In a letter to Liliencron on 6 January 1903, Piper praised Hesse's *Gedichte*, alluding rather directly to his envy of Hesse's skill, albeit not without a touch of irony:

[...] Aber das Buch ist unglaublich schön, seine Verse durchsichtig wie Krystall und glänzend wie flüssiges Gold. Ich konnte mal so recht sehen, was er hat und was mir fehlt, um vor dem kunstkonsumierenden Publikum Gnade zu finden. Keine Zeile, die dem Durchschnittsleser direkt unverständlich sein könnte.[28]

[(...) But the book is unbelievably beautiful, its poems as clear as crystal and shimmering like liquid gold. I could see here quite well what he has and what I lack in my own work in order to find favor among the art-consuming public. There is not a single line that could really fail to be understood by the average reader.]

How mutually rewarding a friendship might have developed between these two men, had they only met under different circumstances!

As for Piper's friendship with "Ugel" Finckh, it would appear that they quickly lost contact after Piper left Freiburg.[29] Nonetheless, Finckh created a character in his autobiographical novel, *Der Rosendoktor*, who rather distinctly resembles the Kurt Piper whom Finckh and Hesse knew, right down to his physical description, although, unlike Piper, his talent is musical:

Einer von ihnen war mir besonders lieb geworden, Hans Knaster, ein Musiker und Komponist, mit einer hohen Stirn und wilden traurigen Augen. Hinter diesem Kopf sah's schön und trübe aus. Er spielte mir viele Nächte vor, Phantasien von großer Schönheit, aber wirr und zerrissen. . . Seine Schwermut und seine Trauer waren erschütternd. Er hatte wenig Freunde und suchte sie auch nicht.[30]

[I became particularly fond of one of them, Hans Knaster, a musician and composer with a high forehead and wild, sad eyes. In his head things looked both beautiful and murky. Many nights he

---

28. Unpublished letter of 6 January 1903 from Kurt Piper to Detlev von Liliencron. Original in the Liliencron Archives of the State Library of Schleswig-Holstein, Kiel.
29. Haile Finckh von Kutzleben cannot recall ever hearing her father mention Piper's name, nor is she aware of any correspondence between the two. Personal conversation with the author, 23 June 1994.
30. Ludwig Finckh, *Der Rosendoktor*, 119.

played for me, fantasies of great beauty, but confused and ragged....
His melancholy and his grief were pathetic. He had few friends
and really didn't look for any.]

Like Piper, Knaster one day leaves "for the north, where he would
complete his studies."[31]

Hermann Hesse's friendship with Ludwig Finckh would grow
ever stronger over the next decade, and the poet could scarcely have
found a more loyal and selfless comrade at this time in his life than
Finkch. He owed his contact with the Knodt circle and, by exten-
sion, with the literary world of Germany to Finckh, and, as will be
discussed in more detail below, "Ugel" was instrumental in finding
subscribers and in distributing both versions of Hesse's *Notturni*. In
1902, though, Finckh proved his friendship in another, equally sig-
nificant way. Eye problems and accompanying headaches had trou-
bled Hesse for years. During his last summer in Tübingen, he had
been under doctor's orders to refrain from reading and writing for
several weeks, and his ultimate exemption from military service in
July 1900 was based on a diagnosis of severe nearsightedness. The
official diagnosis of the recurring eye problems was made in July
1902, "muscular cramping of both eyes, left eye weakened."[32] As
Finckh wrote to a concerned Karl Ernst Knodt near the end of
August 1902, the prescribed treatment was failing to produce
improvement, due in large part to Hesse's own refusal to follow the
recuperative regimen and to his excessive wine consumption:

Die Augen wollen nicht heilen; daran ist aber weniger der Wein
schuldig als der *Mangel der rechten Pflege*. . . Er müßte längere Zeit
in wohltuender Klinikbehandlung sein, ohne sich um etwas küm-
mern zu müssen, und er müßte jemand zum Lesen und Schreiben
haben; dann würd's rascher gehen und dann brauchte er sich nicht
mehr durch Wein zu betäuben.[33]

[His eyes just won't heal, but it is not so much the wine that is caus-
ing that as it is the *lack of proper care*. . . He ought to be receiving
really beneficial treatment in a clinic, where he would not have to
worry about anything, and he also ought to have somebody to read
and write for him. Then things would get better faster, and he
would not have to deaden himself with wine against the pain.]

31. Ibid., 127.

32. Letter of 8 July 1902 from Hesse to Carl Busse, *Briefe*, 1: 90. Hesse apparently
refers here to the diagnosis of a physician he sought out in Basel.

33. Unpublished letter of 26 August 1902 from Ludwig Finckh to Karl Ernst
Knodt. Copy in the Hermann Hesse Editor's Archive, Volker Michels, Offenbach.

Shortly thereafter, Ludwig Finckh was evidently successful in convincing Hesse to see a well-known German eye specialist, Dr. Axenfeld, under whose supervision Finckh would complete his doctoral dissertation a year later:

> Da war ich nun froh, ihn zu einem großen Augenarzt bringen zu können. . . . Axenfeld konnte den Bedrückten beruhigen: es lag am Tränenkanal, hatte nichts zu bedeuten, wenn man sich Schonung auferlegte. Aber Hesse und Schonung!"[34]
>
> [Then I was happy to be able to get him to a first-class eye doctor ... Axenfeld was able to calm him: it was a problem with the tear ducts, not at all serious, if one simply took it easy. But you know Hesse and "taking it easy"!]

The Knodts were overjoyed when they received a letter from Hesse (dictated to his sister on 11 September 1902), in which the young poet indicated that he was, finally, following the prescribed treatment and recuperating in Calw. The *Waldpfarrer* himself waxed biblical in the expression of his happiness, adding a note to the bottom of Hesse's letter and sending it on to Cesco Como:

> Freuen Sie sich, lieber Cesco Como, mit uns! Denn dieser mein Sohn war tot und ist wieder lebendig geworden! Und Er wird leben in Ewigkeit! O Gott, was für ein goldner Morgen![35]
>
> [Rejoice with us, dear Cesco Como! For this my son was dead and has come to life again! And He will live in eternity! Oh, Lord, what a golden dawn!]

During the difficult months from late April, when Hesse's mother died, until the end of 1902, it would again be Ludwig Finckh who, time and again, came to his friend's aid. The year had begun on a quite positive note with the prospect, through publisher Eugen Diederichs, of a position in the Leipzig Museum of Books and Publishing at a salary nearly double his monthly income of one hundred francs at Wattenwyl's.[36] In March, Hesse decided not to

34. Ludwig Finckh, *Himmel und Erde*, 11f.

35. Unpublished letter of 10 September 1902 from Hermann Hesse to Karl Ernst Knodt, including Knodt's own note to Cesco Como at the end. Copy in the Hermann Hesse Editor's Archive, Volker Michels, Offenbach.

36. The position in Leipzig, according to Hesse, would carry an annual salary of 1,800 marks, the equivalent at the time of more than 2,200 Swiss francs. Unpublished letter of 2 March 1902 from Hermann to Johannes Hesse, copy in Hermann Hesse Editor's Archive, Volker Michels, Offenbach. (The exchange rate between the stronger German mark and the Swiss franc remained around 1.23 francs to the mark until the end of the decade.)

pursue the offer further, despite the attractive salary and working conditions, for he was now able to supplement his modest income in Basel through regular payments he received from journals and newspapers that published individual poems by him, as well as occasional literary reviews and travel articles he wrote. As the condition of his eyes worsened, however, he was compelled to limit reading and writing to the requirements of his job, which precluded authoring such small pieces for publication. When he was directed by his physician to curtail reading and writing entirely in order to promote the healing of his eyes, he took a two-month leave of absence from Wattenwyl's and went home to Calw. Thus, he found himself with little or no income throughout the summer and fall of 1902, a situation that he sporadically noted in remarks to friends.

In the spring, however, he had composed a new master set of *Notturni*, planning to sell handwritten copies of these on a subscription basis to raise funds for his hoped-for trip with Cesco Como to Italy. By early June, several orders had been garnered and a few filled, but the painstaking reproduction of each set by hand became more and more difficult as Hesse's eyes increasingly rebelled. By August, Finckh and Karl Ernst Knodt decided to act on their friend's behalf, agreeing that Finckh would copy sets of the *Notturni* and that both would seek subscribers.[37] They were successful in finding at least six or seven buyers, among them Schoenaich-Carolath, Como, Jeanne Berta Semmig, and the *Waldpfarrer* himself. According to a letter from Finckh to the *Waldpfarrer* ("the Prince has acted most princely!"),[38] as well as from Knodt to Hesse himself, it appears likely that the Prince contributed to the ailing poet beyond the price of the *Notturni*:

> Ihr Finckh ist ein wahrer Goldfink. Wissen Sie auch, woher Ihnen die anderen Goldstücke geflossen sind? Von Haseldorf her, von Carolath, der Sie sehr lieb hat.[39]
>
> [Your Finckh is truly a golden finch. Do you know where the other pieces of gold came to you from? From Haseldorf, from Carolath, who is very fond of you.]

37. Unpublished letter of 26 August 1902 from Ludwig Finckh to Karl Ernst Knodt. Copy in the Hermann Hesse Editor's Archive, Volker Michels, Offenbach.
38. Unpublished letter of 2 September 1902 from Ludwig Finckh to Karl Ernst Knodt, copy in the Hermann Hesse Editor's Archive, Volker Michels, Offenbach.
39. Unpublished letter of 23 September 1902, from Karl Ernst Knodt to Hesse. Original in the Hesse Archives, Marbach.

When Hesse sent Schoenaich-Carolath his just published *Gedichte* two months later (along with a depiction of his plans for the spring), the Prince's response made it clear that he would be prepared to come to his young compatriot's aid again, at least in the form of a loan:

> Wandern, Genießen, Studieren, Hoffen – wie glücklich sind Sie, und was will dagegen alles Andre bedeuten, selbst Armuth, so hart sie stundenweise drücken kann. Kommt Ihnen einmal eine solche Stunde besonders schwer vor, so schreiben Sie mir, bitte. Leider bin ich nicht reich, doch ein paar Goldstücke kann ich einem jungen "zigeunernden" Wegbruder immer noch leihen.[40]
> [Hiking, enjoying life, reading, hoping – how fortunate you are. What significance does all the rest of it have compared to that, even poverty, difficult though that can be at times. Should such a time come again, when things seem especially hard, please write to me. Unfortunatly, I am not rich, but I can always come up with a few pieces of gold to lend to a young, "gypsying" compatriot.]

Hermann Hesse had survived the most difficult year of his life since the turbulence of his early adolescence in Maulbronn and Calw. He could find solace in his improved health, in the publication of his *Gedichte* in November 1902 as well as his inclusion in Knodt's *Wir sind die Sehnsucht* in December of that year, and in the knowledge that he could rely on a circle of close friends for support and encouragement, even in his darkest hours. Two among those friends were especially loyal comrades, without whose staunch backing and unwavering faith in his creative potential Hermann Hesse could not have achieved his literary breakthrough so quickly: Karl Ernst Knodt and Ludwig Finckh.

The *Notturni* and the *Gedichte*

> Einem alten Wunsche nachgebend habe ich mich entschlossen, von zwei Dichtungen, welche mir in diesem Jahr zu vollenden vergönnt war, nur die eine der Öffentlichkeit zu übergeben, die andere aber nur einer ganz kleinen Zahl von namentlich eingeladenen Gönnern handschriftlich zu überreichen.

40. Unpublished letter of 4 December [1902] from Emil von Schoenaich-Carolath to Hesse. Original in the Hesse Archives of the Swiss National Library, Bern. The Prince was undoubtedly making a slightly tongue-in-cheek reference to the lead poem in the set of *Notturni* 1902 he had purchased. That poem is entitled "Zigeuner" [Gypsy].

Um diese intime Art der Mitteilung habe ich gewisse handschrift-
liche Literaturen, namentlich die persische, immer beneidet. Sie
gewährt mir den Vorteil: meine Dichtung unberührt von vermit-
telnder Mechanik, der Spekulation des Handels und dem Geschwätz
der Presse entzogen, nur von Wohlgesinnten gelesen zu wissen.[41]
[Yielding to a long-held desire, I have decided to offer to the pub-
lic only one of the two works I have been fortunate enough to
complete this year, but to pass along the other one in handwritten
form to a small number of patrons who are being invited, by
name, to subscribe.

I have always envied the handwritten literatures of certain cul-
tures, specifically the Persian, for this intimate form of communica-
tion. For me, it provides the advantage of knowing that my poetry
is untouched by any mechanical medium, that it is removed from
commercial speculation and journalistic nattering, and that it will
only be read by those sympathetic to me.]

From the time of his earliest literary activity, Hermann Hesse had
made it a practice to present short pieces of his writing to family
and friends. As a teenager in the 1890s, Hesse had begun to com-
pose small sets of poetry to give away; of these collections, written
between 1892 and 1897, eight are still in existence, six in the Hesse
Archives in Marbach and the other two in private hands.[42] Simi-
larly, the young bookseller had presented his mother and father
with fifty-five-page autograph collections on the occasion of their
birthdays in October 1897 and June 1898, respectively. After the
move to Basel in the fall of 1899, Hesse sporadically continued
this practice, now "packaging" his collections more elegantly. For
example, his *Verse aus einem Wanderjahr – Ein Weihnachtsgruß 1901*
were written, as Hesse noted on the title page of each set, on paper
produced at the end of the eighteenth century.[43]

41. Unpublished cover page for *Notturni* sets (October 1900), Hesse Archives,
Marbach. Three of these cover or title pages, unused, are located in the Marbach
archives. Unlike the *Vorlage* (Hesse's master set of the poems themselves), which
was obviously composed without particular care, these title pages were composed
in his best hand. Apparently these are extra copies, as he prepared more cover
pages than he needed. (See Appendix A – 1 in back of book.)
42. Mileck estimates that Hesse put together "at least a dozen" such manuscripts
before the *Romantische Lieder* appeared in 1898. Mileck, *Hermann Hesse: Biography
and Bibliography*, 1: 466.)
43. The Hesse Archives in Marbach contain several of these sets, given by the poet
at Christmas 1901 to Käthe Knodt, Otto Drasdo, and Karl Lichtenhahn. The title
page of each includes the note: "Papier und Einband vom Ende des 18. Jahrhun-
derts." ["Paper and binding material are from the end of the 18th century."]

Hesse's decision in Basel to initiate "self-production" of auto-graph collections was, to some extent, financially motivated; his regular monthly income as a bookseller there never exceeded 150 francs (at Reich's), and he yearned to travel, especially to Italy. Of course, he now received an occasional honorarium for the publi-cation of an essay or an individual poem, but his first volume of poetry, *Romantische Lieder* (published in November 1898), had brought in little extra income; indeed, only fifty-four copies of the slim volume were sold during the first twelve months after its publication.[44] Thus, the sale of twenty-five sets of *Notturni* in October 1900 made possible Hesse's first Italian journey (25 March to 19 May 1901). As he wrote to Helene Voigt-Diederichs at Christmas 1900:

> Anfang Februar verlasse ich das Geschäft, um mehrere Monate für meine Arbeit, für meine notleidende Gesundheit und für eine Reise nach Oberitalien frei zu haben. . . Durch eine kleine Dichtung, die ich letzten Herbst in 25 handschriftlichen Exemplaren ausgab, hob sich mein Sparpfennig auf das erwünschte Niveau.[45]
>
> [The beginning of February I am leaving the shop, so that I can have several months free for my work, my depleted health, and for a trip to northern Italy. Thanks to the sale of a small collection of poems that I published last fall in 25 handwritten copies, my sav-ings can handle it.]

Similarly, the *Notturni* 1902 were intended to help finance Hesse's second journey to Italy, although his eye problems necessitated a postponement of the trip until April 1903.

His journeys to Italy, of course, were by no means mere vaca-tion trips. Steeped as he was by this time in the literary and cul-tural traditions of the preceding two centuries and influenced especially by Jakob Burckhardt's *Cicerone*, Hesse considered the excursion a kind of personal pilgrimage to the source of the cul-ture with which he more and more strongly identified. The initial

44. According to the accounting statement sent to Hesse by the E. Pierson Verlag on 18 January 1900, first-year sales of fifty-four copies of *Romantische Lieder* brought the writer a mere 35.10 marks. (Original letter from E. Pierson Verlag, Hesse Archives, Marbach.)

45. Hermann Hesse, *Briefe*, 1: 81. Though he never explained the choice of his title *Notturni*, the significance of the word, both literally and metaphorically, in the con-text of his life at that time seems rather obvious. Because of his work as a book-seller, he could only compose at night, thus these "night songs" or "night scenes" were mostly written at night. For Hesse the Romantic, of course, the night held a particular fascination, to say nothing of its function as a psychological metaphor.

trip in 1900 also kindled a fascination for Italy and its people that would last his whole life, and he would ultimately find his spiritual *Heimat* in Montagnola, where he spent the second half of his life, on the border, as it were, between the cultures of the Germanic and Mediterranean worlds.[46] Too, although he achieved passable proficiency in French and could read English adequately, Italian was the only foreign language he ever mastered.

Hesse's first Italian journey can thus be said to signify a kind of conclusion to his *Privatstudium*, providing a transition from the theoretical to the practical, while allowing him to accumulate creative inspiration and aesthetic impressions that would augment the *Stoff* for a body of poetry that was to establish his literary reputation. Put another way, Hesse used the money he earned from the first set of *Notturni* to travel to Italy, where he collected experiences and images that would substantially constitute the second *Notturni* (1902)! While he did not entirely neglect the prose genre during the phase, he limited himself, by his own account, to taking only mental notes for his first major novel, *Peter Camenzind*, until late 1901, when he began committing that work to paper.[47]

Ever sensitive to critical opinion and – after the failure of his *Romantische Lieder* – keenly aware of the fickleness of the marketplace, he opted to compose and distribute his *Notturni* privately. His original scheme was to vary each poem of a set of eight slightly, so that every set of eight was unique, if only by one or two words in each poem. As he informed his parents on 8 November 1900, he had completed the intended twenty-five sets in three weeks, working "night and day" to copy a unique set for each of twenty-five "subscribers" who had responded to the "invitation" he had personally mailed to each of them in early October.

In order to solicit orders for the *Notturni* 1900, Hesse composed the above-mentioned *Prospekt* or "invitation" separately from the activity of composing and varying the poems themselves. While he did not attempt to deny being the author – as he was so often prone to do – Hesse did claim to have entrusted the copying to another person, referred to on the invitation sheet variously as a "dear, poor scribe" or a "poet friend" who was

46. Despite his fascination, however, Hesse was certainly not incapable of casting a critical glance at the country. See, for example, his unpublished letter of 8 May 1903 to Cesco Como, written just after Hesse's return from Italy, in which he refers to Genoa as a *"Drecknest"* ["filthy hole"]. Copy of original in the Hesse Archives, Marbach.

47. Letter of 19 October 1902 from Hesse to Rudolf Wackernagel, *Briefe*, 1: 91.

himself "capable of better verses than these"; of course, the hand-writing in all the extant *Notturni* 1900 sets is unmistakably Her-mann Hesse's. It seems likely that Hesse was plying his irony here, since, after all, he knew most of his subscribers personally. Such a "tongue-in-cheek" nuance could also serve to lighten the mood and lessen the likelihood of disapproval on the reader's part. A further characteristic unique to the *Prospekt* for the *Notturni* 1900 is the inclusion of a quote from Hermes Trismegistos (the Greek name for the Egyptian deity Thot, the god of writing and learnedness):

> Die Erde mußt du scheiden vom Feuer, das Subtile vom Groben, lieblicher Weise mit großem Verstande.[48]
>
> [You must separate earth from fire, the subtle from the coarse, in a pleasant manner and with great discerning.]

The quote can obviously be read as another expression of the young poet's literary insecurity, as a plea for his readers to be gentle in their criticism. A note that accompanied the delivered *Notturni* sets also reveals that insecurity:

> Hier ist nun das erwartete Kuriosum. Ich wünsche den harmlosen Versen harmlose Leser.[49]
>
> [Well, here is the oddity you were expecting. I wish for these harmless lines of verse, readers who also mean no harm.]

In the balance of the brief message, Hesse explained to his patrons the procedure he had used, while showing that he had managed to maintain a sense of humor about his work:

> Die Exemplare sind sämtlich sowohl durch die Widmungszeilen wie durch absichtliche, zum Teil bedeutende Variationen im Text als *Unica* gekennzeichnet. Sollte Ihnen nun ein Vers besonders gefallen, so bitte seien Sie überzeugt, daß ich ihn speziell für Sie eingefügt habe. Bei weniger glücklichen Passagen aber mögen Sie sich sagen, daß ich mir das vermutlich in den übrigen Exemplaren besser überlegt haben werde.[50]

48. Unpublished *Notturni* manuscript, originally sold by Hesse to Professor Paul Mezger in Basel, October 1900. Original now in the Hesse Archives, Marbach.

49. Ibid. Hesse also often included a copy of his recently published *Romantische Lieder* with the note: "Nach alter schwäbischer Sitte muß man bei jedem Kauf etwas 'dreinkriegen'. Als solche Dreingabe möge das beiliegende Büchlein gelten." ["An old Swabian custom prescribes that every purchase should be accompanied by 'a little something extra.' May the enclosed little book fulfill that custom."]

50. Ibid.

[Each set of these poems is unique, both in the personalized dedication and in the frequent intentional, sometimes significant textual variations. Should you find a verse particularly to your liking, please know that I added it especially for you. In the case of less skilled passages, though, you may tell yourself that I probably did a better job in the other sets.]

Similarly, in his desire to assure that his verses found readers who were "well disposed" toward him, Hermann Hesse seems to have been immoderately wary of contacting potential subscribers outside of a rather restricted circle of friends and acquaintances. "Ugel" Finckh, from whom he solicited a list of addresses of "interested parties" at the outset of the enterprise, was immediately enthusiastic ("Ich bin Feuer und Flamme für Dein Projekt"),[51] offering to provide current addresses for the other members of the *petit cénacle* (Faber, Hammelehle, and Rupp). He placed an order for himself and suggested Schoenaich-Carolath and Hamburg poet Gustav Falke, as well as his sister Cornelie Goltermann-Finckh and a colleague in medical school, Martha Kannengießer. Hesse himself approached several of his Basel contacts (Professor Burckhardt-Schazmann, Esther La Roche-Stockmeyer, Professor Paul Mezger, Professor Jakob Wackernagel, and Dr. Rudolf Wackernagel-Burckhardt), as well as friends in Tübingen with whom he was still in contact (Professor Theodor Haering and Eberhard Goes). According to letters from the time, it seems certain that Hammelehle did not order the poems, and Eberhard Goes informed Hesse on 12 October that he could not afford to subscribe.[52] Of the remaining potential "subscribers," five sets have been located along with Hesse's *Vorlage* (master copy or working draft).[53] In March 1902, just weeks before beginning to compose his second "batch" of *Notturni*, Hesse would copy a set of the *Notturni* 1900 for his new friend at the time, Cesco Como; this is evidently the only set of the initial *Notturni* that he compiled beyond the original twenty-five copies.

51. Unpublished letter of 9 October 1900 from Ludwig Finckh to Hesse. Original in the Hesse Archives of the Swiss National Library, Bern. The expression "Feuer und Flamme" translates roughly as "aflame and on fire," i. e., very enthusiastic about something. Ironically, Finckh's own copy of the *Notturni* 1900 would be destroyed by fire when his Gaienhofen home burned in 1907.

52. In his notebook, *Bagels Geschäftskalender*, Hesse noted on 5 February 1901 that he had not heard from Karl Hammelehle since he had arrived in Basel. *Kindheit und Jugend*, 2: 524. Goes's remark is found in an unpublished letter of 12 October 1900, to Hesse. Original in the Hesse Archives, Marbach.

53. See Appendices C-1 through C-3 in the back of the book.

Despite Hesse's original intention of limiting his selection to the eight poems listed in his prospectus and slightly modifying each of them twenty-five times, only the *Vorlage* and one of the five extant *Notturni* 1900 collections conform to the author's initial design. Of the other four surviving collections, two contain three of the eight announced verses, and two contain only one of them. (No title is common to all five sets, and while the title "Inspiration" occurs in four of the five sets, two of those four sets use a second, completely different poem with that same title!) It must be remembered that only five of the original twenty-five sets have been located, hardly a representative sampling, but it is nonetheless striking that four of the five sets differ quite substantially from the poet's original scheme. These four copies comprise a total of forty-five poems – one set has five, two have thirteen, and one has fourteen – and in these four sets, there are only eight occurrences of poems announced in the prospectus. What prompted the young poet to deviate so notably from his initial plan is, of course, impossible to ascertain. Still, it seems plausible that when he actually set about the task of assembling separate collections of poems for readers whom he knew personally, he found it necessary to select verses that suited the individual patron who had ordered the set. This procedure, at least based on the five extant collections, resulted in the compilation of distinctly individualized sets of the *Notturni* 1900; that was, after all, what the poet had promised in his prospectus.

Hermann Hesse often referred to his earlier poems as experimental; his correspondence with Helene Voigt-Diederichs and Ernst Kapff, in particular, regularly contained discussions of rhyme and meter. The extant *Notturni* 1900 are also characterized, to an observable extent, by formal experimentation, especially as regards his attempts to employ a variety of stanza forms. Although he rarely employed sonnet form, two sets of the *Notturni* 1900 show attempts to achieve variations on the original Italian as well as on the Shakespearean sonnet. In the La Roche-Stockmeyer set, his poem "Rast haltend" conforms to the structure of the Italian sonnet with two quatrains, followed by two tercets, but uses iambic tetrameter rather than the prescribed pentameter.[54] Hesse also takes liberties with the rhyme scheme in the second quatrain, opting for new rhyme pairs (*abba cddc*) instead of maintaining

---

54. This poem, with slight variations, is included under the title "Über Hirsau" in *Die Gedichte* (1977), 1: 80.

those of the the original Italian sonnet (*abba abba*), and his tercet scheme is also altered (*eff egg*) in place of the original Italian that customarily adheres to *cdc dcd* or *cde cde*. In the Goltermann-Finckh set of the *Notturni* 1900, Hesse comes quite close to imitating the Shakespearean sonnet in "An meinen Zeigefinger,"[55] following the rhyme scheme exactly (*abab cdcd efef gg*) but substituting iambic tetrameter for pentameter.

Other examples of Hesse's experimentation with form in the *Notturni* 1900 would include the twelve-line poem "Elisabeth," in three stanzas of four lines each, but utilizing the playful dimeter rather than the often used tetrameter:

> Die Nacht fällt ein,
> Das Fest verloht,
> Die Fackeln im Garten
> Verleuchten rot. [. . .][56]
> [The night is falling,
> The party is ending,
> The garden's lanterns
> Are now dying out.]

Another noteworthy twelve-line "experiment," contained in the Wackernagel-Burckhardt *Notturni* 1900 collection, is the poem "Angelika," which comprises four tercets in tetrameter, a variation on the Italian *terza rima*. While the original Italian *terza rima* employs iambic pentameter (actually, an eleven-syllable line) and Hesse uses only his favored tetrameter, he does adhere to the original feature of a common rhyme between two stanzas:

> Spätsommer. Meine Birke regt
> Sich kaum. Mit blauen Flügeln schlägt
> Ein dunkles Wasserjungfernpaar.
> Im Weiher schaukelt weiß und rot
> Am Seile müßig sich mein Boot,
> Ist alles, wie es immer war. [. . .][57]
>
> [End of summer. My birch tree moves
> Just slightly. With blue wings beating
> A dark dragonfly couple flies past.
> On the pond my boot rocks gently

55. This poem is included in Appendix B at the back of the book.

56. This poem is included with no changes under the title of "Vorwurf" in *Die Gedichte* (1977), 1: 124.

57. This poem is included in Hesse's *Gedichte* (1902) under the title "Das Kreuzlein." Stanzas quoted here are from the Wackernagel-Burckhardt *Notturni* 1900 collection, original in the Hesse Archives, Marbach.

> White and red, tied to its rope,
> And all is just the way it always was.]

A final illustration of Hesse's attempt to adapt specific stanza forms to his own poetry is also found in the Wackernagel-Burckhardt collection, the poem "Eleanor,"[58] which is a nearly perfect example of the Italian *dezima*, a ten-line poem in two five-line stanzas. Only in the rhyme scheme here does the author take liberties, utilizing one nonrhyming line in each stanza (*abacb dedfe*).

As already alluded to, more poems in the *Notturni* 1900 sets are twelve-line stanzas set in tetrameter than any of the experiments. That Hesse chose, in addition, to try out several Italian stanza types is hardly surprising in view of his extensive study of Italian literature, both classical and modern. Having introduced his *Notturni* 1900 collections with a reference to his admiration for the Persian handwritten literature, it would be interesting to investigate in more detail the lengthy and somewhat amorphous pieces that make up the remainder of the *Notturni* 1900. A comparison with the most familiar, traditional form of Persian poetry, the *ghazel*, shows that Hesse did not have the *ghazel* in mind, typified as it is by two-line stanzas and exemplified in German writing by Goethe's *West-östlicher Divan*.

The most characteristic feature of the extant collections of this small cross-section of Hesse's *Notturni* 1900 is the disparity in the length of individual poems, which vary between 8 and 131 lines. It is precisely those extraordinarily lengthy poems that were never published (see Appendix B). It would seem that Hesse was seeking a kind of "free" ballad form, which would be entirely plausible in light of Schoenaich-Carolath's influence on the younger poet, yet the finished poems cannot be designated as ballads. Most striking among the five surviving *Notturni* 1900 collections is the Mezger-Leube set, consisting of the standard "Inspiration" and four extremely long poems, called *Gesänge* (songs or cantos): *Der erste Gesang: Von der Sonne; Der zweite Gesang: Von der Nacht; Der dritte Gesang: Von den Wassern, Wolken und Winden; Der vierte Gesang: Vom Heimweh.* [*The First Song: Of the Sun; The Second Song: Of the Night; The Third Song: Of the Waters, Clouds, and Winds; The Fourth Song: Of Homesickness.*][59]

---

58. This poem is included, with slight variations, under the title of "Porträt" in *Die Gedichte* (1977), 1: 67.

59. These long poems, never published, are contained in their entirety in Appendix B at the back of the book.

The first of the five Mezger-Leube *Notturni* poems, "Inspira-
tion" represents a substantially truncated version of the poem of
the same name contained in the poet's working draft (*Vorlage*),
consisting of only twenty-two lines, fewer than half the forty-six
lines which the draft version comprises, yet almost word for word
the same poem that was contained in the posthumous collection
Die Gedichte (1977). This version of "Inspiration" and the third and
fourth *Gesang* reflect a decided formal preference for the iambic
tetrameter that Hesse utilized extensively in his early poetry, but
the first and second *Gesang* betray an almost rigid adherence to
trochaic rather than iambic lines. And though the first twelve lines
of *Der erste Gesang* follow a strict pentameter, many of the remain-
ing forty-nine lines are in tetrameter, albeit almost exclusively
trochaic. The middle portion of *Der zweite Gesang* is set off from
the rest of the piece; except for the final two lines of pentameter, it
also follows a quite strict trochaic tetrameter. At 131 lines by far
the longest of the five pieces, *Der dritte Gesang* shows a mixture of
meter which typifies the entire piece, ranging from the two open-
ing lines of three feet each to the pentameter of the final two lines.
In the fourth *Gesang*, iambic tetrameter is clearly the dominant
meter, only occasionally alternated with iambic pentameter. Rhyme
schemes in the five pieces are, for the most part, quite traditional;
although not set in four-line strophs, the rhyming patterns are
largely fitted to four-line segments, with most showing schemes of
a b a b, a a b b, or *a b b a.*

   Anyone familiar with the imagery and the typical stylistic traits
of Hermann Hesse's early writing, be it poetry or prose, will prob-
ably find few surprises in these *Notturni*, for they employ many of
the derivatively romantic images and mirror the kind of subjec-
tively pantheistic relationship to nature that have come to be asso-
ciated with the young Hesse. At the same time, however, these
Gesänge contain passages that, stylistically, are clearly more sophis-
ticated than is characteristic of most other extant *Notturni* poems.
As Joseph Mileck has noted about Hesse's early poetry generally,[60]
the imagery is less pictorially descriptive than evocative, provid-
ing, on one level at least, a store of objective correlatives for the
author's considerably subjective focus. If there is, beyond Her-
mann Hesse's personal projections, a consistent, overall theme in
the Mezger-Leube *Notturni*, it seems to be the ephemerality of

---

60. Joseph Mileck, "The Poetry of Hermann Hesse," *Monatshefte* 46 (1954): 192ff.

human existence and earthly institutions, a theme that occupied Hesse repeatedly in his life and work.

The *Notturni* 1902, which Hesse began assembling in early May of that year, contain poems that Hesse had written during his first Italian journey – nearly two dozen bear specifically Italian title references – as well as verses written since the summer of 1901. As with the *Notturni* 1900, he offered these for subscription, relying again on Finckh to assist him in finding patrons. Unlike the lengthy prospectus that preceded or, apparently, sometimes accompanied the *Notturni* 1900, however, the eight extant sets of the 1902 version indicate, at most, only title, city, date, and a brief dedication to the recipient.[61] Work on these sets actually coincided with the compilation of his *Gedichte*, which he sent to Carl Busse on 5 June. Within a period of less than a month, therefore, Hesse was distributing as *Notturni* freshly written verses that were to appear in print in the *Gedichte* volume just five months later!

The list of subscribers to the 1902 sets of *Notturni* reflects, both in number and nationality, the author's new orientation toward Germany. While nearly all the *Notturni* 1900 were ordered by friends and personal acquaintances in Basel or Tübingen, the new version was requested overwhelmingly by Germans. Of the twelve orders that were filled, only three were from Switzerland (Dr. Theodor Engelmann and Otto Drasdo from Basel and a Hermann Löhnert from Bern). The list of German orders included Cesco Como, Agnes Finckh (Ludwig's mother), Cornelie Goltermann-Finckh (the latter's sister), Karl Ernst Knodt, Kurt Piper, Prince Emil von Schoenaich-Carolath, Jeanne Berta Semmig, and Helene Silber (a friend of Finckh).[62] In addition, Finckh and Piper solicited orders from Karl "Waldschrat" Huck, Walther Krug (a law intern and friend of Piper in Pforzheim), and Hermann Sinogowitz (a pharmacist whom Finckh knew in Olten, Switzerland.)[63]

---

61. See Appendices D-1 through D-3 in the back of the book.

62. Finckh's requests for *Notturni* to be sent to his friends provide evidence of the quite personal touch that Hesse lent to each set. In placing Helene Silber's order for the poems, Finckh added: "Du weißt, liebe, versöhnende oder kräftigende?" ["You know, sweet, consoling or invigorating ones."] In another request, for his sister, he wrote: "[A]uch so versöhnende und die Heimwehlieder." ["Also consoling ones and the homesick poems."] Unpublished letters of 4 June and 11 June 1902, respectively, from Ludwig Finckh to Hermann Hesse. Originals in the Hesse Archives of the Swiss National Library, Bern.

63. Unpublished letter of 4 June 1902 from Ludwig Finckh to Hesse. Original in the Hesse Archives of the Swiss National Library, Bern.

In his *Notturni* 1902, Hesse seems no longer to be experimenting, and the mere fact that relatively few poems of the second edition of *Notturni* would remain unpublished indicates that he was now composing with the aspiration of accumulating new verse for his *Gedichte* (1902). While the five extant collections of his *Notturni* 1900 contain thirteen different pieces that would never get into print, the eight surviving sets from 1902 include a total of only six short poems that were never to be published. By the same token, only twenty individual poems from the *Notturni* 1900 found entrance into the *Gedichte* (1902), while that anthology contains sixty different poems from the *Notturni* 1902 collections. (All but ten of the seventy-one individual poems in the extant *Notturni* 1902 are included in volume one of *Die Gedichte* [1977], in the section marked 1899–1903.)

Absent in the 1902 sets are the cumbersome and often unrefined, ballad-length pieces that typify the extant collections from 1900. With but three exceptions,[64] the *Notturni* 1902 are devoid of poems over eighteen lines in length, while the dominant stanza form is the three or four quatrain structure. In these new *Notturni*, as in the *Gedichte* (published in November of the same year), the poet makes much more frequent use of pentameter, seeming more secure now with that meter, though he clearly still favors tetrameter. (It is somewhat surprising that he chose not to employ any traditionally Italian stanza form – the sonnet, for example – in the many verses that recount or reflect upon his first Italian journey in 1901.) The Otto Drasdo set contains a poem translated by the young author from French, "Mon rêve familier (Aus dem Französischen des Paul Verlaine)," and the Kurt Piper collection bears a French title "L'autre a soif de l'avenir et s'élance vers l'inconnu! A. de Musset," although the poem itself is evidently Hesse's own.

The *Notturni* 1902, like many of the other poems of the *Gedichte*, also reveal a somewhat curtailed reliance on the nature imagery that had been the young poet's trademark in the poetry of the preceding several years, yet the importance of mountains, forests, sky, and clouds is still prominent, even in the verses written about Italy. Hesse's relationship to nature had intensified during the late 1890s, progressing from that of an enthusiastic observer to the status of a nearly disciple-like proponent of his natural surroundings

---

64. The Drasdo collection has a twenty-two line piece, *Das fernste Schiff (Bei Livorno)*, and the Löhnert set contains two twenty-four line poems, *Der Abenteurer* and *Odysseus – Ein Gondelgespräch*. All three poems are included, with slight variations, in *Die Gedichte* (1977), pages 134, 173, and 144f., respectively.

in the *Notturni* 1900 period, epitomized by the four *Gesänge* in the Mezger-Leube 1900 collection, paeans to nature that are almost exceedingly effusive. In another unpublished and exceedingly long poem, *Das blaue Wunder* (Goltermann *Notturni* 1900), Hesse created a ballad-like account of drowning in Lake Urner (based on his own near-drowning there in September 1900),[65] an idea that smacks distinctly of a romantic-pantheistic reunion with the universal spirit.

In his admirably thorough and interpretatively sensitive treatment of Hermann Hesse's lyric poetry, Peter Spycher distinguishes, in the poems of the *Notturni/Gedichte* period, between nature imagery as *Dingsymbol* and as metaphor (or, by extension, simile). As an example of the former, he cites the six-line poem, "Die leise Wolke" (*Gedichte* 1902), in which the observer seeks, implicitly, to convince another person to "feel the white coolness" of a cloud as it "passes through your blue dreams."[66] The personification of nature, so typical of Hesse's earlier poetry, is almost completely subdued here, hinted at only in the attributive adjective *leise* [quiet]. Spycher points to one of the Elisabeth poems, "Wie eine weiße Wolke" (*Gedichte* 1902, also in several *Notturni* 1902 collections), as representative of the nature image as metaphor. Indeed, given Hesse's almost spiritual veneration of nature, as well as his aestheic absorption with its myriad manifestations, his implied metaphor of Elisabeth as a "white cloud in the highest sky, so white and lovely, yet so far away" presents a compelling image that corresponds neatly with his own position vis-à-vis Elisabeth La Roche.

More often, though, nature is personified in Hesse's poetry of this period (rather in keeping with the author's distinctly pantheistic view of nature), and that device is evident in a large number of poems in the *Notturni* 1902. In fact, almost without exception, one can say that if nature occurs at all in the poetry of this period, it will be personified. The pieces in the Drasdo collection illustrate this well, for scarcely a "nature" verse among the sixteen poems in this set is without an example of personification: Clouds go upon their "dark journey, with neither moon nor stars as chaperon" ("Notturno"); "the sea sings," while "the humid west wind howls and laughs" ("Bei Spezia"); the night clouds "take mysterious

---

65. Hesse reported the incident to his parents in a letter dated simply September 1900. *Kindheit und Jugend*, 2: 490–91.

66. Spycher, *Eine Wanderung durch Hermann Hesses Lyrik*, 133. The poem can be found in *Die Gedichte*, 1: 90.

flight, like a spirit, homeless, seeking home" ("Fremde Stadt"); the wind "cradles the colorful lanterns" ("Fest").[67] Still, Hesse did not undertake in that poetry to articulate the more spiritual notion of nature that predominates in his novel of the time, *Peter Camenzind*, only implying that idea here through his use of the literary device of personification.

By almost any measure, *Camenzind* is an autobiographical novel, a *Bildungsroman* set in the Switzerland of the turn of the twentieth century and based upon actual experiences of Hermann Hesse that function as focal points around which variously fictionalized episodes take shape. The novel's characters, too, have their real models among Hesse's friends and acquaintances of the time: Peter's bosom comrade Richard, for example, is the fictional counterpart of Ludwig Finckh; Erminia Aglietti invites serious comparison with Maria Bernoulli, Hesse's first wife; and Hesse's Elisabeth is Peter's Elisabeth, who also lives in Basel and whom Peter meets at one of the gatherings in a home clearly fashioned after the Wackernagel circle. In many of its details, too, *Peter Camenzind* is unmistakably autobiographical: Peter, like Hesse, learns to play billiards with great skill and to enjoy the Italian Veltlin red wine; Richard copies pieces of Peter's work and sells them, much as Finckh had done with the *Notturni* 1902; and Peter even takes a long journey on foot through the Black Forest and the Bergstraße and into the Odenwald area (though evidently no character is based on Karl Ernst Knodt).

In its portrayal of Peter's obsession with nature, the novel is likewise highly autobiographical, and it is here more than anywhere else in his early work that Hermann Hesse revealed his extreme affinity for nature. In his well-known retrospective analysis of *Peter Camenzind*, written in 1951, the author elucidated Peter's (and his own) relationship to nature:

> Da er Lyriker ist, wendet er sich in seinem unerfüllten und unerfüllbaren Verlangen der Natur zu, er liebt sie mit der Leidenschaft und Andacht des Künstlers, er findet zeitweise bei ihr, in der Hingabe an Landschaft, Atmosphäre and Jahreszeiten eine Zuflucht, einen Ort der Verehrung, Andacht und Erhebung.[68]
>
> [Because he is a poet, he turns to nature with his unfulfilled and unfulfillable longing. He loves nature with an artist's passion and reverence, and sometimes, in his devotion to the open countryside,

67. Otto Drasdo *Notturni* 1902 collection, original in the Hesse Archives, Marbach.
68. Hermann Hesse, "Über *Peter Camenzind*," *Werke*, 11: 25–26.

the setting, and the four seasons, he finds a place of veneration, of piety, of elation.]

Peter's contact with nature, as Hesse continues, the actual method by which he confronts nature and attempts to recreate it, is "to mirror nature and the world in his own mind and experience them in his own new images."[69] In a passage from the novel, Peter provides, in his "own" words, what could well be considered the crux of Hesse's own passion for nature:

> Berge, See, Sturm und Sonne waren meine Freunde, erzählten mir und erzogen mich und waren mir lange Zeit lieber und bekannter als irgend Menschen und Menschenschicksale. Meine Lieblinge aber … waren die Wolken.[70]
>
> [Mountains, lakes, storms, and sun were my friends. They told me stories, they taught me, and for a long time I liked them and knew them better than any human being or any human problems. My favorites though … were the clouds.]

The tenacity with which Hermann Hesse had undertaken his "private studies" and the singleness of purpose that characterized his development as a poet while he fulfilled his utilitarian obligations to his trade had brought him to the threshhold of the career for which he had been preparing since childhood. With the completion of his second "batch" of *Notturni* in 1902, he had accumulated more than 150 poems that were new since the appearance of his first slim volume of verse, *Romantische Lieder* (1899). As delineated above, the extant poems in the two *Notturni* manuscript editions comprised almost half of the 166 poems that constituted Hesse's first major collection, *Gedichte*, edited by Carl Busse and published on 3 November 1902 by the G. Grote'sche Verlagsbuchhandlung in Berlin as the third volume of their "New Poets" series. However, there has only been sketchy information about the actual process through which Hermann Hesse established contact with Carl Busse.

On 26 September 1901, Hesse sent Busse a small collection of unpublished verse, noting that he would like to submit the small book ("Büchlein") for publication but had "neither an agent, nor a publisher, nor any money," and by the end of that year, Busse was evidently making plans to publish a comprehensive collection of

69. Ibid., 26.
70. *Peter Camenzind, Werke*, 1: 353.

Hesse's verse.[71] After becoming very ill in January 1902, Hesse spent three weeks in Grindelwald in the Bern Alps during February, composing there his lengthy, five-part "winter poem" *Hochgebirgswinter*, two sections of which are contained in the Goltermann-Finckh and Schoenaich-Carolath *Notturni* 1902. By the end of February 1902, the author was discussing format, font, and paper for the forthcoming volume.[72] The initial contact between Hesse and Busse may well have been a consequence of Busse's having read the poet's *Romantische Lieder*, as has been assumed, but it could also have been the result of efforts initiated by Karl Ernst Knodt.

On 9 July 1901, just before Hesse would pay his first visit to the Knodts in Ober-Klingen, the *Waldpfarrer* closed a letter to Hesse with the question: "How did you determine that Carl Busse is an 'arrogant' person – (which he is!)?"[73] Clearly, Hesse had mentioned Busse's name in a previous letter to the *Waldpfarrer*, probably in his letter of 5 July 1901, the second page of which has been lost. Since a main topic of discussion in the correspondence of the two men had been their plan for the anthology of contemporary poetry (*Wir sind die Sehnsucht*), Busse's name probably came up as a potential contributor, for nine of his poems are included in the *Sehnsucht* volume. Thus, although he may not yet have had any personal contact with Carl Busse, Hermann Hesse certainly knew more about him than one would gain merely from reading Busse's poetry.

At any rate, Hesse had mentioned his first *Notturni* edition to Knodt, as well as his plans to compose a second edition, which met with the *Waldpfarrer's* enthusiastic support; in his first communication with Hesse after the latter's visit, Knodt promised to look for a publisher.[74] On 30 July 1901, Knodt rushed a card to Hesse with the question:

Sind's die *Notturni*, die an Cotta abgegangen sind? Oder *Neue Gedichte*? Das müßt' ich natürlich doch wissen.[75]

71. Letters of 26 September and 30 December 1901 from Hermann Hesse to Carl Busse, *Briefe*, 1: 83 and 85.
72. Letter of 27 February 1902 from Hermann Hesse to Carl Busse, *Briefe*, 1: 85–87.
73. Unpublished letter of 9 July 1901, from Karl Ernst Knodt to Hesse. Original in the Hesse Archives, Marbach.
74. Unpublished letter of 25 July 1901 from Karl Ernst Knodt to Hesse. Original in the Hesse Archives, Marbach.
75. Unpublished letter of 30 July 1901 from Karl Ernst Knodt to Hesse. Original in the Hesse Archives, Marbach.

[Is it the *Notturni* that you sent off to Cotta or the *Neue Gedichte* – I really ought to know that!]

Presumably, the *Waldpfarrer* was attempting to assist Hesse with the placement of a new edition of *Notturni*, but his card makes it clear that Hesse was also trying to publish another collection, entitled *Neue Gedichte*. Though there are no other surviving letters from Hesse to Knodt until December 1901, Knodt addressed more than a dozen cards and letters to Hesse between 1 August and 1 December 1901, some of which are clearly in response to Hesse's own letters. In any case, the manuscript with the title *Neue Gedichte* was sent to Hans Bethge in Berlin, who attempted to find a publisher for it during the months of August and September 1901. On 12 September, Hesse received word from Knodt that there had still been no message from Bethge as to the fate of Hesse's "book."[76] (Since no Hesse publication by that title exists, Bethge was obviously unsuccessful.) Two weeks later, of course, Hesse would send a manuscript to Busse, which led to the compilation and publication of the *Gedichte*. Whether this "Büchlein" was the manuscript called *Neue Gedichte* that Hesse and Knodt had sent to Bethge remains unclear. There can be no question, however, that the *Gedichte* represent the accumulated *Notturni* 1900 and 1902 as their main component.

Just two weeks after his *Gedichte* appeared in print in November 1902, Hesse wrote the following letter:

> Wertgeschätzte Redaktion!
>   Soeben erschien (als dritter der "neuen Lyriker") bei Grote ein Band Verse von mir. Vermutlich ist auch Ihnen ein Exemplar zur Besprechung zugekommen. Ich bitte Sie, das Buch einer freundlichen Prüfung zu würdigen.[77]

> [Dear Editors:
>   A volume of my poetry has just come out at Grote Publishers, the third volume in the series "New Poets." Most likely you have received a copy for review. I would ask you kindly to submit the book to a friendly reading.]

Almost one year to the day later, as the fate of *Peter Camenzind*, in the author's opinion, remained quite uncertain, Hesse had seen his poetic talent and diligence affirmed in the overwhelmingly

76. Unpublished letter of 12 September 1901 from Karl Ernst Knodt to Hesse. Original in the Hesse Archives, Marbach.

77. Unpublished letter of 18 November 1902 from Hermann Hesse to an unidentified periodical. Copy in Hermann Hesse Editor's Archive, Volker Michels, Offenbach.

positive critical reception that had been accorded his *Gedichte*. Writing to his Basel friend Theo Baeschlin on 17 November 1903, he noted:

> Lieber Gott, wieviel Gedichte bekam ich jahrelang ... mit bösen Glossen von den Redaktionen zurück, und wie oft war der ganze Kram mir verleidet! Und heute, wo ich als Lyriker anerkannt zu werden beginne, erlebe ich mit meinen Prosasachen wieder dieselbe Tragikomödie.[78]

> [Dear God, how many poems I got back over the years that had nasty comments by editors, and how often I was just sick about the whole business! And today, now that I am beginning to be recognized as a poet, I am going through the same tragicomedy with my prose.]

Hermann Hesse would be no stranger to "tragicomedy" in his life, yet within less than a year, his *Peter* would establish him as a prose author in the German-speaking world. Within his lifetime, of course, he would come to be far better known for his prose works than for his verse. Still, it was his poetry that gained him his first successes, and these verses of his youth, born in nights of insomnia, in walks through rain-drenched woods, or on lazy summer afternoons as he lay watching ever-mysterious clouds, remained among his favorite and among his best.

78. Letter of 17 November 1903 from Hermann Hesse to Theo Baeschlin, *Briefe*, 1: 112.

APPENDIX A-1

Note: The *Notturni* poems are published here with the friendly permission of the copyright holder, Suhrkamp Verlag, Frankfurt/M., 1996.

Notturni 1900 Prospectus/Cover Letter
(Mezger-Leube Collection)

Einem alten Wunsche nachgebend habe ich mich entschlossen, mein jüngst vollendetes Manuskript nicht der Öffentlichkeit zu übergeben, sondern nur einer kleinen Zahl von Gönnern und Freunden, soweit diese es wünschen, handschriftlich zu überreichen.

Diese intime Art der Mitteilung ist mir längst an fremden handschriftlichen Literaturen, namentlich der persischen, anziehend und fein erschienen. Auch genieße ich so den Vorteil: meine Dichtung, der Spekulation des Handels und dem Geschwätz der Presse entzogen, nur von Freunden und Wohlgesinnten gelesen zu wissen.

Der vollständige Titel meiner Versdichtung findet sich am Schlusse der gegenwärtigen Mitteilung. Ich gedenke höchstens fünfundzwanzig Exemplare schreiben zu lassen, für deren Texttreue und Sauberkeit ich bürge. Ein mir sehr lieber, armer Skribent hat die Abschrift übernommen. Obwohl er selbst Poet und besserer Verse als der abzuschreibenden fähig ist, unterzieht er sich der nicht geringen Mühe mit selbstloser Treue. Den Erlös werden Dichter und Schreiber gleichmäßig teilen. Das Exemplar, mit persönlicher Widmung versehen, kostet zehn Franken. Bestellungen gehen an meine Adresse: *Basel*, Mostackerstr. 10. Bestellungen von nicht Eingeladenen behalte ich mir vor anzunehmen oder zurückzuweisen.

    Mit bestem Gruss   Hermann Hesse

Titel und Inhalt

1. Inspiration
2. Das blaue Wunder
3. Adagio
4. Zwei Lieder, der schönen Eleanor gewidmet
5. Ad astra
6. Ich und ich
7. Der rote Veltliner
8. An die Schönheit

APPENDIX A-2

Individual *Notturni* Poems Never Published (by title)

Notturni 1900
(Never published, with title of collection, number within individual collection, poem title, and first line.)

Note: Mileck = Joseph Mileck, *Hermann Hesse, Biography and Bibliography*, volume number, page number, poem listing number.

Vorlage (Hesse's working draft, from which he copied)

2. *Das blaue Wunder.* Mileck, 1: 685 (1046)
   "Im Urner See. Ich war ertrunken"
   **Never published, but included in *Kindheit und Jugend*, 2: 492–494
   (part of a letter written by Hesse in September to Eberhard Goes)
3. *Adagio.* Mileck, 1: 693 (1127)
   "Tief in einem finstern Hause"
   **Never published
5. *Ad astra.* Mileck, 1: 697 (1183a).
   "Wind, freier Wind!"
   **Never published
6. *Ich und ich.* Mileck, 1: 684 (1034)
   "Ich stand im Garten spät am Tag"
   **Never published

Goltermann *Notturni. Frau Cornelie Goltermann in alter Reutlinger Freundschaft überreicht. 12. Oktober 1900.*

3. *An meinen Zeigefinger.* Mileck, 1: 688 (1076a–1078).
   "Mein liebes Zeigefingerlein"
   **Never published
4. *Ich und ich.* Mileck, 1: 684 (1034)
   "Ich stand im Garten spät am Tag"
   **Never published

6. *Adagio*. Mileck, 1: 693 (1127)
   "Tief in einem finstern Hause"
   **Never published
7. *Das blaue Wunder*. Mileck, 1: 685 (1046)
   "Im Urner See. Ich war ertrunken"
   **Never published, but included in *Kindheit und Jugend*, 2: 492–494
   (part of a letter written by Hesse in September to Eberhard Goes).

La Roche-Stockmeyer *Notturni*. *Frau La Roche-Stockmeyer ergebenst überreicht.*
Basel, Oktober 1900

11. *Julia*. Mileck, 1: 692 (1117)
    "Seit ich Ihren Garten sah"
    **Never published
12. *Der Narr*. Mileck, 1: 679 (986)
    "Erlaube im Geheimen mir"
    **Never published

Mezger-Leube *Notturni*. *Herrn Professor Dr. Mezger ergebenst überreicht. Basel, 17.*
10. 1900

2. *Der erste Gesang: Von der Sonne*. Not in Mileck.
   "Menschen leben wenig karge Tage"
   **Never published
3. *Der zweite Gesang: Von der Nacht*. Not in Mileck.
   "Heute auch aus blauen Fernen"
   **Never published
4. *Der dritte Gesang: Von den Wassern, Wolken und Winden*. Not in Mileck.
   "Wo klang zum erstenmal"
   **Never published
5. *Der vierte Gesang: Vom Heimweh*. Not in Mileck.
   "Was ist der Seele tiefster Grund?"
   **Never published

Wackernagel-Burckhardt *Notturni oder vertraulich poetische Briefe an Herrn und Frau*
Dr. R. Wackernagel-Burckhardt in Basel. ex ungue autorem. Basel, Oktober 1900
(Latin phrase obviously a play on the phrase *ex ungue leonem* – "by the lion's
claw you shall know him" – "by the author's 'claw' you shall recognize him.")

1. *Der Tag ist um* (= first line, no title). Not in Mileck.
   **Never published
12. *An meinen Zeigefinger (statt 'Ad Astra')*. Mileck, 1: 688 (1076a–1078).
    "Mein liebes Zeigefingerlein"
    **Never published
13. *Marienlieder I–IV*. Mileck, 1: 744 (849–851).
    I "Auf deine Schwelle laß mich treten"

**Never published
II "Du Eine, Gnadenvolle nur"
**Never published

Notturni 1902
(Never published, with title of collection, number within individual collection, poem title, and first line.)

Engelmann *Notturni. Herrn Dr. Th. Engelmann in Basel am 29. Mai 1902 überreicht.*

1. *Herbst.* Not in Mileck.
   "Nachsinnend still und ernst bewegt"
   **Never published
2. *Ach, du weißt – .* Not in Mileck.
   "Meine Jugend war ein keckes Spiel"
   **Never published
4. *L'autre a soif de l'avenir et s'élance vers l'inconnu! A. d. Musset.* Mileck, 1: 676 (962A)
   "Du mit dem tiefen Glanz im Blick"
   **Never published

Goltermann-Finckh *Notturni.* Title page: *(Zweite Ausgabe.) Frau Cornelie Goltermann-Finckh in Frankfurt mit vielen Grüßen!* (Closing page: *Basel, Juni 1902*)

8. *Tröste dich.* Mileck, 1: 688 (1079)
   "Meine Seele, tröste dich!"
   **Never published
16. *Mutter.* Mileck, 1: 679 (993)
   "Es kam ein Tag, der war so schwer"
   **Never published

Piper *Notturni. Herrn Kurt Piper mit herzlichem Gruß!* (Mileck, 1: 469, 4a)

4. *L'autre a soif de l'avenir et s'élance vers l'inconnu! A. d. Musset.* Mileck, 1: 676 (962A)
   "Du mit dem tiefen Glanz im Blick"
   **Never published
11. *Certosa di Val d'Ema.* Mileck, 1: 674 (928a)
   "Der Mönch an seiner Pforte thut mir leid"
   **Never published

APPENDIX B

Texts of Individual *Notturni* Poems Never Published (by title)

Notturni 1900
(never published, with title of collection in which contained)

Vorlage (Hesse's working draft, from which he copied)

Das blaue Wunder
Im Urner See. Ich war ertrunken
Im Sturm. Nun wölbte wieder weich
Die Bucht sich aus. Ich aber lag versunken
Einsamer Siedler in der Tiefe Reich,
Glaszart mit schwebenden Konturen
Sah jezuweil ein Berg herab,
Wie Träume ob dem Schläfer fuhren
Die Schiffe über meinem Grab.
O wär ich nimmermehr erwacht
Aus deinen unerhörten, satten
Glanzträumen, wundervolle Nacht,
Aus deinen silberblauen Schatten!
Da lag in bangem Z[w]itterlicht
    ["w" crossed out by Hesse in original]
Tiefblau ein Land fremdschöner Thale
Kühn wie ein fabelhaft Gedicht
Reich wie ein Lustbau aus Opale:
Zerflossen Form und Linie ganz
In schillernd blauen Perlenglanz,
In Spiele zarten Koselichts,
In Duft, in Dunst, in süßes Nichts.
Nicht Form, nicht Wesen, Schönheit nur
Floß Wohllaut ohne Sinn noch Ziel,
Nachwandelnd eigner Reize Spur
Gesetzlos hin in edlem Spiel
Wie ward ich da der Bürde los,

Wie quoll mir da aus jeder Welle
Ein harmlos zierer Spielgeselle,
Ein Schmuck, ein Reiz, ein Schillern namenlos
Durch Blick und Sinn und ausgestreckte Hand!
Ein tiefes, ewiges Blau ich fand:
Daraus in Strahlen, Schauern, Hauchen
Sah ich unendlich wechselreich,
Nun violett, nun silberbleich
In seligem Bad die Schönheit tauchen.
Ein Schatten fiel,
Ein Wind brach ein –
Ein neues Spiel,
Ein neuer Schein!
Ein schnellverrauschter Uferbach
Zog [silbern] quirlend feine Fäden nach,
    ["silbern" crossed out by Hesse in original]
Ein Fisch glitt grau vom Grund herauf,
Da glänzt' er alabastern auf,
Dann rötlich, dann in gelbem Golde,
Wie Licht es und Sekunde wollte.
Mir selber aber wunderbar
Hing voll Krystall Gewand und Haar,
Bald sah ich fahlweiß meine Hand,
Bald glühend violett entbrannt.
Ich sah's wie einen Schatz der Dieb,
Ich ward mir selber herzlich lieb,
Mein Will' und Ungenüge starben
Und lösten sich samt Geist und Leib
Zu einem Spiel brillanter Farben,
Mir selbst ich selbst zum Zeitvertreib.
O wie das wunderköstlich war,
So aller Sorge blank und bar
In müder Herrlichkeit zu schwimmen,
In Licht und Farbe zu verglimmen,
In Wollust ungezählter Chancen
Zu neuen, zärtlichen Nuancen!
So ist dein Lied, das hold vertönt
Es stirbt, ist nimmer und verschönt
Auszitternd noch sich und die Welt.
O süß, von keinem Wunsch gequält,
Weltfern, selbst Welt, in feinen, zieren
Lustwellen so sich zu verlieren,
So aller Ungenüge Pein,
So seiner selber ledig sein!

Die Nacht rauscht auf. Ich sitze da
Am Tisch, ich weiß nicht wie's geschah,
Der trüben Ampel zugewandt,
Die nasse Feder in der Hand.
Der Bücher und Papiere Schlamm
Umängstet mich wie Grab und Damm.

Komm, Schlummer, leichter, sanfter Tod,
Traumfährmann, nimm mich in dein Boot,
Den Knoten löse, der die Welt
Und mich noch wank zusammenhält.
Du Linnen weiß auf meinem Bette
Sei mir gegrüßt! Allnächtlich rette
Ich mich zu dir aus Lampentrüber
Poetenluft ins Träumeland hinüber.
Ein Hauch! Das Ämplein zuckt und zischt.
Und lischt.

Adagio
Tief in einem finstern Hause
Bin ich fremd und doch bekannt,
Vor den Fenstern mit Gebrause
Stürzt der Regen auf das Land.
Dämmerung mit fahlen Blicken
Scheint durch blinde Fenster her,
Eine Wanduhr hör ich ticken
Müd als wenn's mein Herzschlag wär.
Traurig kehrt mit allen Sinnen
Aus der bangen Dunkelheit
Sich mein Leben stumm nach innen,
Hört Herzensschlag und Stunde rinnen
Ohne Freude, ohne Leid.

Töne? Horch! Ein Saitenstreichen
Irgendwo erhebt sich zart,
Einer Liebe Gegenwart,
Einer sanften Freundin zu vergleichen.
Leise wie auf Diebessohlen
Tritt es aus der Nacht hervor,
Streift mit halbem Laut mein Ohr,
Grüßt mich fragend und verstohlen.
Schwellend nun erhebt es sich
Wächst heran mit vollerem Strich,
Zittert, wiegt sich wie auf Schwingen,
Will mir tief zur Seele dringen.
Senken muß ich meine Lider –
Einen Geiger sieht mein Traum,
Der entrückt das Lied der Lieder
Zaubern will aus dunklem Raum,
Der mit Einem [sic] Meisterstriche
Aller Lieder Reiz zu fangen,
– Alles Lachen, alles Bangen
Alles Edle auch und Königliche –
Dunkler Schätzekammer ausgegangen.
Seltsam zaubert seine Weise
Mich in ihre ahnungsvollen
Kühnen, dennoch zarten Kreise.
Alle alten Wünsche schwollen

Traumverwandelt, fieberfarb
Wieder auf in meinem Innern;
Was mir Liebes jemals starb,
Lebt empor in zitterndem Erinnern.

Kehrst du noch einmal mir wieder,
Heimwehtraum vergangener Nächte,
Lieblingstraum vom Lied der Lieder?
Komm! in deine alten Rechte
Komm zurück! Den schlanken Bogen
Gieb mir wieder in die Hand,
Den ich sehnlich oft gezogen.
Der mein Leid so wohl verstand.

Selber spiel' ich nur im Dunkeln,
Meine Geige an der Brust;
Meine Phantasieen [sic] funkeln
Durch die Nacht mit weher Lust,
Zittern von den alten, roten
Leidenschaften ohne Ziel,
Die vorzeit so brennend lohten,
Streifen frech im raschen Spiel
Alle Lüste, alle Wehen. –
Zage Liebe, herbes Hasten
Alles, was ich schweigend lang
Einsam trug durch fremde Gassen,
Soll mir nun in scharfem Klang
Jäh und lodernd auferstehen.

Jäh und lodernd! – Plötzlich sinkt
Mir die Geige aus den Händen.
Jene ferne Andre wieder klingt
Meines Liedes Melodie zu enden.
Und sie sänftet sich zu leisen,
Mutterzärtlichen, geheimen,
Tröstlich süßen Wiegeweisen,
Läßt in milden, milden Reimen
Allen Sturm und alle Frage,
Alles Weh und alles wilde Ringen
In unendlich fernen Duft verklingen
Wie in eine schöne fremde Sage.
Wie das schmilzt! Wie das sich selig rundet!
Wie sich lächelnd jeder Ton
Kaum erklungen, kaum entflohn
Einem andern schwesterlich verbündet!
Aber draußen brandet Regen
Gehet Sturmwind um und lacht,
Stößt um's Haus mit wilden Schlägen,
Schwillt aufstöhnend in die Nacht.

Wüßt' ich, wüßt' ich, wo ich fände
Meines angehob'nen Liedes Ende!

Ad astra
Wind, freier Wind!
Da hab' ich dich,
Da hast du mich,
Ich bin ein Vogel, bin dein Kind.
Wie fröhlich glänzt
Mein Flügelpaar!
Es ist aus weichem Federhaar
Und à la Schwalbe schlank geschwänzt
O Luft, Luft, reines Element,
Mein Wesen ganz in dir entbrennt!
Du hattest recht, ich wußte es,
Du hattest recht, mein Sokrates,
Da du der Höhe Hymnen sangst
Und von der Erde fortbegehrtest.
An jenem Tag, da deiner Freunde Angst
Dir traurig war und lächerlich zugleich,
Da du von Äthers reinem Reich
Den trägen Kebes Wunderdinge lehrtest.
(Der schlanke Phädon hörte zu,
Mit seinem Laken spieltest du.)
Fürwahr, die Erdluft war zu schwer
Für mich! Auch gingen dort umher
Beleidigend mich scheuen Dichter
So viel unleidliche Gesichter;
Ich wäre nimmer dort gewesen.
Nun aber schlägt mein ganzes Wesen
Mit breiten Schwingen, reckt sich weit
Und füllt sich ganz mit Herrlichkeit,
Mit Luft, mit Licht, mit Sonnenthau,
Mit selig wundersüßem Blau.

Die Welt ist schön! Ich wusst' es kaum,
Ich lag so lange ohne Licht
Schweratmend wie in engem Traum.
Nun seh ich dich! Nun plötzlich bricht
Das Leuchten deiner breiten Brust
Mit Macht in meine Seele ein,
Daß sie erbebt in namenloser Lust
So nah, so nah dem Ewigen zu sein.
Nun halt ich dich, nun bist du mein,
Wie eine Braut im schönen Reigen
Mit Blick und Herzschlag mir zu eigen,
Nun werd' ich erst ein Sänger sein!
Grüß' dich, du Weite ohne End,
Du goldhell überwölbtes Schloß,
Du nächtig schönes Firmament!
Grüß dich, O Schönheit! Nie genoß
Ich also dich im innern Wesen,
Nie war mein Blick so weit und groß,
So aller Trübe ganz genesen!

Tief unter mir – ich fliege hoch –
Liegt Basel wie ein großes Loch
Trübselig aus dem Nebel winkend
Aus schwärzlichen Kaminen stinkend.
Alleen und Straßen tief gekeilt
Von armen Bürgern übereilt,
Mein eigenes Schicksal dürftig hegend.
O arme Straßen, arme Gegend,
Das staubt und ächzt bei jedem Schritt!
Ihr tut mir leid, ich selber mit.
Ein Handbreit weiter schaut heraus
Aus Tannen meines Vaters Haus –
Wie zirkelte so eng im Kreise
Bis heute meines Lebens Reise!
Gottlob, es ist damit vorbei,
Mein Flügel rauschet, ich bin frei!
Zwar hängt mit feinen Fäden noch
Da drunten im verlassenen Loch
Vielfach von Menschenhand geschröpft,
Mein Glück und Schicksal angeknöpft.
Was thut's? Was ist's? Ein leer Getriebe,
Ein Amt, ein Traum von Kunst und Liebe,
Ein Freund, ein Haus, ein Mädchen oder zwei –
Was gilt's? Ich mach mich heut noch frei.
Weh wird es tun an Leib und Geist,
Mag sein – non dolet – Auf! – es reißt,
Es bricht, es läßt mich sacht hinan,
Mir ist, man zog mir einen Zahn.
Vorbei! Ein schmerzhaft Reissen war's,
Ich atme auf an Leib und Geist.

Ein roter Stern vorüber kreist.
Dein Name, Bruder? – Hesse – Mars.

Ich und ich
Ich stand im Garten spät am Tag.
Ein Erschlagener vor mir lag
Halboffenen Mundes, wirren Haars;
Ich kannte ihn – ich selber war's.
"Jetzt Hermann ist das Singen aus,
"Der Totenknecht kommt dir ins Haus,
"In Leinewand wirst du vernäht,
"Kein Hahn im Land mehr nach dir kräht.
"Du warst mir lieb, es thut mir weh,
"Daß ich dich so am Boden seh'.
"Doch ist der Tod des Lebens Lohn
"Und du warst ein verlorner Sohn.

Ich schwieg und ging. Ich lag verlassen
Im kühlen Sand mit meiner blassen,
Eiskalten Stirn. Der Abend kam

Und mich in seinen Mantel nahm.
Dann kam die Nacht. In meiner Seele
Stieg meines Erdenlebens Lauf
Buntfarb gewebt aus Recht und Fehle
In wundersamer Klarheit auf:
Blauäugig meine Kindertage,
Die Knabenzeit voll Trieb und Frage,
Der Jugend dunkelrote Feuer,
Der Kranz verliebter Abenteuer,
Der erste scheue Schritt ins Heiligtum,
Das erste Lied, der erste süße Ruhm,
Dann alles bis zum Säbelschlag,
Von dem ich noch am Boden lag
In meinem roten jungen Blut.
Mir schien es alles herzlich gut,
Eindämmernd nach dem lauten Thun
Fand ich den Tod ein süßes Ruhn.

Ich kam zurück und sah mich an –
"Da liegst du, armer Wandersmann!
"Du Ungeduld bist früh gegangen.
"Die Lieder, die du angefangen,
"Die Träume, die du halb geträumt,
"Sind ungeboren nun verschäumt.
"Wie süße Reime deine Kraft
"Noch barg, wie kecke Leidenschaft
"Dein Herz noch trug, wie heiß und frei
"Dein Aug' noch war, es ist vorbei!

Vorbei! Und wieder ging ich fort.
Ich lag allein am stillen Ort.
Der dumme Kläger ärgert mich,
Der mir so feig ums Feuer schlich.
Sonst aber war mir wohl zu Mut:
Am Himmel lief getreu und gut
Der helle runde Mond dahin,
Ein Vogel rauschte im Jasmin.
Ein Windlein, zart und sänftiglich
Mit Blumenduft beladen schlich
Vorbei und ließ im trägen Wallen
Mir Wohlgeruch hernieder fallen.
Vom Kirchturm freundschaftlich vertraut
Schwang sich herab ein Glockenlaut;
Ich zählte nicht, ob eins, ob zwei,
Es war mir wurst und einerlei.

Ich kam zurück und sprach zu mir:
"Du Lieber! Ach wie fehlst du mir!
"Wie schad um dich, Freund, Mensch, Poet!
– Der Schwätzer! Plötzlich hatt' ich halb
Im Sand den toten Kopf gedreht,

Ich schrak und stierte wie ein Kalb.
Ich regte mich – ich lief davon –
Da fasste mich's mit hellem Hohn,
Ich rief, ich lebte, sprang in's Haus
Mir nach – ich keuchte bleich vor Graus
Die Treppen auf und rief: Gespenster –
Ich faßte mich – ich war so leicht! –
Am Bein und schob mich stracks durchs Fenster.
Ein flottes Rennen, wie mir däucht!

Nun stand ich in dem Mondenlicht
Am Fenster. Drunten lag der Wicht
Gebrochen, blutig, ohne Regen,
Genau wie ich zuvor gelegen.
Ich lachte, schlug das Fenster zu:
In deinen Schanden schlafe du,
Freund ich, indessen ich genas!
Der schnelle Tausch gefiel mir baß,
Auch ging's so fröhlich, Zug um Zug,
Daß ich Erschlagener mich selbst erschlug.

Goltermann

An meinen Zeigefinger (statt Ad astra)
Mein liebes Zeigefingerlein,
Wo wirst du über's Jahr
Um diese selbe Stunde sein?
Vielleicht verwirrt in Frauenhaar?
Vielleicht auf einer Geigensaite?
Vielleicht auf einer Alpe Grat
Gestreckt in eine grüne Weite?
Vielleicht der Schönheit leisem Pfad
Nachspürend über Marmorgliedern?
Vielleicht am Säbel straff und stark?
Vielleicht in einem niedern,
Vergessenen Sarg?
Ich weiß es nicht, du weißt es nicht. –
Ist das auch ein Gedicht?

Ich und ich
[with slight variations, a few omitted lines, identical to poem
of same title in the *Vorlage*]

Adagio
[with slight variations, a few omitted lines, identical to poem
of same title in the *Vorlage*]

Das blaue Wunder
[with slight variations, a few omitted lines, identical to poem
of same title in the *Vorlage*]

La Roche-Stockmeyer

Julia
Seit ich Ihren Garten sah,
Kenn ich Sie genau;
Nimmer, schöne Julia,
Nehm ich Sie zur Frau.
Gott der Herr beschütze Sie,
Schönste, früh und spat,
Und Ihr holdes Potpourri:
Rosen und Spinat!

Der Narr
Erlaube im Geheimen mir,
Eh' ich als Narr mich vor Dir neige,
Daß ich für Augenblicke dir
Mein ungeschminktes Antlitz zeige.

Sieh Herr! Ein scharf und blaß Gesicht,
Mit ernsten Zügen zugeschnitten,
Nah beieinander Nacht und Licht,
– Wie Eines, der schon viel gelitten.
Und sieh, dies ernste Auge kennt
Die feinsten Falten deines Kleides,
Und dieses ernste Auge brennt
In Flammen eines wilden Leides –

Du mahnst mich früh.-! Die Maske vor!
Geruhet Herrin, zu verzeihen,
Und wollet fürder Euer Ohr
In Hulden meinen Späßen leihen.

Mezger-Leube

Der erste Gesang: Von der Sonne.
Menschen leben wenig karge Tage,
Bauen Städte, und die Bauer werden
Und die Städte selber werden Sage,
Und die Sage selber stirbt auf Erden.
Tiere regen sich und fallen nieder,
Bäume wachsen auf und breiten Äste
Über sie und fallen selber wieder:
Berge fallen mit, verschäumt wie Feste.
Unveränderlich und ohne Ende
Mißt darob die Sonne ihre Bahn,
Ewig in desselben Kreises Wende,
Ewig schön wie sie die Alten sah'n.

Sonne! Sonne! Jeden Tag
Triffst du unsre schweren Lider,
Immer wieder,
Mit dem wohlbekannten süßen Schlag,

Füllest Auge uns und Brust
Mit der süßen, wohlbekannten,
Ohnegleichen, dir verwandten,
Brennend schönen Tagesluft,
Lockst zu hellen Freudethaten,
Leuchtest vor auf Höhenpfaden
Zu verklärten Fernen, schmückst mit Kränzen
Heiße Stirnen nach erregten Tänzen.

Aller Künste Mutter du, geboren
Aus der Schönheit Schooß, wie stark
Pochest du an allen fernsten Thoren,
Wo ein Glanz, ein Reiz, ein Ton sich barg!
Durch die Wechselwolken dringend
Schufst du erster Farben Pracht,
Siebenfach mit Lichtes Macht
Siebenfache Nacht bezwingend.
Lächelnd wie ein Künstler auch
Lockst du aus den Wassern viele
Flüchtig bunte Zauberspiele,
Aus den Bergen Silberhauch,
Malst auf Wände, Wege, Matten
Zarten Laubes zarte Schatten,
Spielst auf Blumen, Wellen, Steinen
Spiele mit unendlich feinen
Tausendfach gebrochenen Scheinen.
Streiter lieben dich und Ritter,
Helle Helden, rasche Läufer,
Frohe Tänzer, ernste Schnitter,
Kluge Händler, kluge Käufer.
Auch der Kinder wolkenlose
Stirnen wenden sich und große
Augen fromm zu deinem Glanze,
Der mit seinem klaren Kranze
Gold den Augenblick verschönt
Und der Zukunft unbekannte
Ahnungsvolle Wunderlaute
Mit der Hoffnung Freudelichter krönt.

Sonne! Ewige, Verklärte, Wahre,
Schütze uns und unsre schwachen Gänge,
Leite uns im dämmernden Gedränge,
Einzig Makellose und Unwandelbare!
Deines Lichtes würdig lehr' uns streiten,
Herz und Auge lehr' uns nach dir weiten,
Rauhe Kriege lehre uns und leichte Reigen,
Siegbekrönte Stirnen lehr' uns vor dir neigen!

Der zweite Gesang: Von der Nacht.
Heute auch aus blauen Fernen
Kommst du leise,

Kommst du wundersamer Weise
Mit den schönen, fremden Sternen
Träumerisch in deinem langen
Schwarzen Kleide hergegangen,
Lenkst im Mondlicht die beglänzten
Wolken über blaue Räume,
Schüttest aus dem mohnbekränzten
Silberhorn den Flug der Träume,
Redest wie ein fernes Singen
Dunkel von geheimen Dingen,
Daß die Thäler atmend lauschen,
Daß die fernsten Wasser rauschen.

Dunkle, fremde Freundin, wieder
Wandelst du von Haus zu Haus,
Sänftigst alle lauten Kinder,
Löschest Herd und Ampel aus.
Komm! In alle Kammern wende
Deinen Gang und lege Hände,
Leise Mutterhände voll Erbarmen
Auf die Stirne jedem Müden,
Jedem Armen,
Dem ein Leid und Kummer ward.
Deine milde Gegenwart,
Deinen Frieden
Und den wundersamen, kühlen
Tröster Schlummer laß ihn fühlen.

Aber uns im Heiligen Hain
Rede du Verehrte, Bleiche,
Von dem fremden Heimatreiche,
Deß du dunkle Ahnung bist.
Laß uns deine Hörer sein,
Wenn von deinem ernsten Munde
Andrer Welt erschloß'ne Kunde
Rätselhaft ergreifend fließt.
Laß vom ewigen Vergehen
Dein Geheimnis uns verstehen,
Von des Todes Finsternissen,
Von des Lebens dunklem Schooße,
Wo mit schwerem Schwung das große
Ewig rege Rad sich wendet,
Das in unabänderlichem Triebe
Unser und der Welt Geschick vollendet.

Rede auch von jener Liebe,
Jener ewigen entbrannten,
Deren Stimme mit verwandten,
Holden Lauten
Unsern oft im Traum geschauten
Heimatbildern zärtlich rief,

Daß der ganzen Ahnung Fülle,
Die verschüttet uns im Innern schlief,
Überquellend alle strenge Hülle
Selig über allen Taggeschicken
Uns bedrängt in süßen Augenblicken.
– Heimat! Heimat!
                              Du allein,
Milde Nacht, mit deiner Sterne
Überflortem Zauberschein
Lässest uns in dunklen, bangen
Hoffnungen hinüberfragen
Mit unsäglichem Verlangen.
Schütte uns dein Silberhorn,
Stille Trösterin, ergieße
Aller Ahnung, aller Hoffnung Kern,
Daß er mit dem Strom der Träume fließe
Heimatwärts an selige Gestade:
Aus der Sehnsucht Reich in's Reich der Gnade.

Der dritte Gesang: Von den Wassern, Wolken und Winden.
Wo klang zum erstenmal
Und wann der süße Ton
Erster Musik, dem Zwang entfloh'n,
In irgendeinem unbekannten Thal!
Wann war's, daß erstmals schnöder Norm
Und freier Lust Vereinigung
Enthoben dem Gesetz der Form
Sich selbst empfand und mit errregtem Schwung
Anschwellend in's Unendliche zerfloß?

Wir wissen's nicht.
Wir sinnen manche Nacht
Im Sternenlicht, aus Traum zu Traum erwacht,
Und spüren flutend wie ein groß Gedicht
In uns verborgner Urkraft schwankes Sein
Zart wie Musik, flüssig wie Schein
Und dennoch schwer und dunkler Fremdheit voll,
Die unbewußt und namenlos
Dem Korn der Ewigkeit entquoll.

Dann langsam ringt sich wie aus Ketten los
Der Sinne Leben, und durch Nebelflor
Trifft aus der Finsternis Gesang
Mit brüderlich bekanntem Laut das Ohr.
Ihr seid's, mit eurem wechselvollen Lied,
Du Bruder Wind, du Bruder Fluß,
Du Sturm, du Meer! In eure Kreise zieht
Uns heute auch zu Qual und zu Genuß!

Ihr Heimatlose, nirgendwo Geborene,
Sehnsüchtig in's Unendliche Verlorene,

In euren Takten laßt uns Träumer lesen
Mit dunklem Ahnungsdrang das eigene Wesen.
Uns unerklärte Traurigkeit gebunden,
Als wäre alles, was wir thun und sind,
Nur Zufalls Werk und Flockenspiel im Wind.
Dann wieder leben wir gewohnt und leicht:
Ein Wunsch lockt an, erregt uns, wird erreicht,
Ein andrer dann und wieder einer bricht
Flackernd empor mit kurzem Lockelicht.
Dann eines Tags, wir wissen nicht woher,
Trifft uns ein Hauch, so weh, so todesschwer,
Daß alles Tageslebens laute Hast
Zu Tand und Ekel wird und schal erblaßt.
Dann steigt aus trüber Stunde Schooß
Fremd, unaufhaltsam, bleich und groß
Die ewige Frage auf, das ewige Leid.
Was Schatz und Wert war, wird zu Kot,
Was That und Sieg war, zu Erbärmlichkeit,
Und hinter allem steht und harrt der Tod.

Das ist der Herbst. Das ist die Wende
Der himmelüberwölbten Pracht
Der Jugendfröhlichkeit. Zu Ende
Geht Spiel, Gelächter, Tanz und Lust
In einer kurzen, sternelosen Nacht.
Du denkst, wie bald du sterben mußt,
Wie bald der grünen Berge Pracht
Dir nimmer lacht.
Du spürst es wohl, von allem Glanz
Der warmen, gold'nen Tage bleibt
Als Denkmal nur ein welker Kranz,
Den jeder nächste Wind zerstäubt,
Und alles, was du Leuchtendes erträumt,
Und alles, was du liebtest ohne Maß,
Ist nur ein Hauch, der quillend überschäumt
Und glänzt, und schwindet. Träume werden blaß,
Die gestern noch in lohem Rot
Emporgeflammt. Im letzten Thor,
Durch das der letzte Tröster sich verlor,
Steht mit dem herben Lächeln Nacht der Tod.

Heilige Nächte! Aller Seelen
Geschicke wendet ihr und weist
Aus der Bedrängnis zu erwählen
Zwei fremde Wege jedem Geist.
Wohl dem, der sich den rechten kor,
Der aus des Leides Nacht empor
Zu höchsten Wissens süßer Ahnung drang!
Ihr Wanderer! – und Wanderer sind auch wir.
Ihr Ruhelose! – ach, wir sind's nicht minder.
Ihr Unbeständige, ihr mutterlose Kinder,

Ihr Fremdlinge! – Und Fremde sind auch wir!
Wie ihr euch quält und wendet
Und keinen Zug
Und keinen Kreis noch Heimwärtsflug
Jemals vollendet,
So hat in mancher langen Nacht,
So hat an manchem bangen Tag
Ein drangvoll weher Flügelschlag
Auch uns entführt und müd gemacht
Und in die alten Tiefen,
Wo alle Rätsel schliefen,
Am Ende hoffnungslos zurückgebracht.

Und wie aus Drang und Ungenügen
Der großen Sänger Seele sprach
Und prachtvoll in beglänzten Flügen
Hindurch zum seligsten Zauber brach,
So wandelt über Wolkenstege,
In Winden, Sternen, Strom und Flut,
In hauchbewegter Spiegelglut
Die Schönheit ihre Lieblingswege.
Was ist so reich an wunderbarer Schau
Wie eines Wolkenhimmels Farbenflucht,
Wie eines Mittagssee's vertieftes Blau,
Das Spiegelzittern einer stillen Bucht?
Wenn irgendwo, so ist's in Eurer Flut,
Daß alles unerlöste Leben ruht,
Daß aller Vorzeit Seele klagt,
Daß aller Seelensehnsucht Stimme fragt.

Wie eines Schiffes zages Boot
Sich zwischen Sturm und Woge drängt,
So ängstlich von Geburt und Tod
Ist unser Leben eingeengt:
Ein Augenblick, ein halbbewußt
Hinträumen mit bedrückter Brust,
Und schließt doch in der Stunde Schrein
Den Schatz der Ewigkeiten ein.

Wind, Welle, Wolke, ohne Form noch Stand,
Ihr seid im innern Wesen uns verwandt,
Uns Wanderern, uns Seglern ohne Halt.
Seid auch so einerlei und mannigfalt,
So voll Begier und dennoch ohne Ziel,
Ganz Drang und Wille, dennoch ewig Spiel.
Wir schauen Euch mit fremdem Staunen nach;
Ihr rauscht ein Wort, das keine Lippe sprach,
Ihr malt in rastlos wanken Rätseln hin
Des Lebens Bild und seinen tiefsten Sinn.

Mit Euch, Geschwister, immer wieder
Jagt unsre Seele zitternd nach

Dem Kern der Lust, dem Lied der Lieder,
Bis ihr die letzte Brücke brach,
Und müht sich wund in schweren Flügen:

Der Born, an dem sie lechzend hängt,
Der wechselnd sie erquickt, versengt,
Des Lebens Born heißt Ungenügen.

Der vierte Gesang: Vom Heimweh.
Was ist der Seele tiefster Grund?
Wo hebt ihr dunkles Leben an?
Frag' nicht! Frag' nicht! Die Tage nahn,
Da wirst du einsam, zag und wund
Vor deines Rätsels Lösung steh'n
Und wirst des Schatzes Boden seh'n,
Der dir so unerschöpflich schien.
Dann wirst erschrocken du gewahr
Des Erdenlebens tiefsten Sinn,
Und alles, was dir köstlich war
Wird blaß in Traum und Duft zerrinnen.

Wir leben hie mit heißen Sinnen:
Tage verglüh'n in wundervollem Glanz
Und legen in den Schooß der Nacht
Verdämmernd ihrer Lüfte Kranz,
Wie sich ein Fürst entkleidet seiner Pracht.
Wir spielen Spiele, reden Worte viel
Und wechseln mit den Tagen Wunsch und Ziel.
Nur manchmal hält in bangen Stunden
Seliges Heimweh! Wundersamer Klang
Der Ewigkeit, vernehmlich jedem Sinn,
Du öffnest aus der Nacht zu Neubeginn
Der zagen Seele deinen milden Pfad.
Du redest uns mit heimatlichem Laut
Von jener Stadt aus Edelstein gebaut,
Der wir verlorene Bürger alle sind.
O fülle alle kranken Seelen du
Mit deinem Liede, das so köstlich rinnt
Wie Quellengruß verheißend Trank und Ruh!

Unselig, der dich Zarte überhört!
Du fliehst von ihm, du lässest ungestört
Im grauen Strom des Tags ihn ziehen;
Ihn locken immer weg und zart
In andre Welten deine Melodien.
Genügsam, enge, karg und hart
Rinnt ihm ein klanglos Leben,
Indeß des Auserwählten Taggeschicken
Sich ewige Mächte freundschaftlich verweben,
Indeß aus jeder leidesschweren Nacht
Ihm heimatlich vertraute Sterne blicken,

Ihn deine Stimme still und müde macht.
Seliges Heimweh, du aus Todesleid
Geborene Sehnsucht nach dem fernen Land,
Aus dessen Glanz für eine kurze Zeit
Wir Wanderer zur Freude sind verbannt,
Du hülle tiefer uns von Traum zu Traum
In deine Schleier, laß wie Duft und Schaum
Den lauten Alltag über uns zerrinnen,
Indeß wir ahnungsvoll und traumgewiß
Dem ewigen Feiertag entgegensinnen,
Dem deine linde Stimme uns verhieß!

Den Tag, die Nacht, die Welt und unser Handeln
Zu Bild und Ahnung wolle du verwandeln
Des ewig Wahren, das kein Wort ermißt
Und deß du Priesterin und Opfer bist!

Wackernagel-Burckhardt

Der Tag ist um
[no title listed in original]
Der Tag ist um
Die Nacht ist stumm,
In meinem Kopf
Geht schwer und dumm
Ein Mühlrad um – –

An Hermann's Zeigefinger
[with slight variations identical to *An meinen Zeigefinger* in
Goltermann collection]

Marienlied I
Auf deine Schwelle laß mich treten!
Nicht um zu beten.
Nur um mit wehevollen Schauern
Nach den verschmähten
Himmeln zu sehen, und um zu trauern.

– Nun hab' ich wieder dich gesehen,
Nun laß mich gehen
Und dunkle Pfade weiterfliehen.
In meinen Wehen
Laß mir den Traum, du habest mir verziehen.

Marienlied II
Du Eine, Gnadenvolle nur
Verstehend tröstend, was mein Herz
An namenlosem Reueschmerz
In jener und in dieser Welt erfuhr.

Du sieh mich liegen tief im Staub –
Mein Schmuck ist welk, mein Lied vertönt,

Mein frecher Mut der Jahre Raub,
Mein Herz versengt und unversöhnt.

Die ich in Weh, die ich in Grimm
Gesungen, Lieder ohne Zahl,
Der Lust, der Liebesnot, der Qual,
Zum gerngebrachten Opfer nimm!

Und auch den Ton der tiefsten Brust,
Und auch des Auges helle Zier
Und auch des Lebens vage Lust,
Gebenedeite, nimm von mir!

Notturni 1902
(never published, with title of collection in which contained)

Engelmann

Herbst
Nachsinnend still und ernst bewegt
Denk' ich an dich, der heimlich naht –
Da hast du schon auf meinen Pfad
Ein welkes Blatt gelegt.

In wunderbaren Farben flammt
Der Wald und bringt dir Sold,
Die Nähen sind wie eitel Gold,
Die Fernen mild wie Sammt [sic].

Mit wunderbarem Golde färbst
Du mir die Seele auch
Und doch mit einem dunklem Hauch
Der Trauer, schöner Herbst!

Ach, du weißt –
Meine Jugend war ein keckes Spiel,
Eine Bahn zu unbekanntem Ziel,
War ein Fest mit purpurroten Fahnen
War ein Segeln über Ozeanen.
Ach du weißt, was ich am Ende fand!
Stürmemüd ein heimatfernes Land,
Wo ich Segler karge Tage friste.

Ferne liegt und mir allein bekannt
Der verlorene Port, mein Glück und Weh.
Fremde Schiffe fahren über See,
Und ich irre träumend an der Küste.

L'autre a soif de l'avenir e s'élance vers l'inconnu! A. d. Musset.
Du mit dem tiefen Glanz im Blick,
Du unerlöster Jugendtrieb,
Du träumest immer noch vom Glück
Und hast das unerreichbar Ferne lieb!

Du sehnst dich immer noch nach Haus,
Obwohl du keine Heimat hast,
Und streckst verhärmte Hände aus
Und findest erst in meinem Sarge Rast.

Goltermann-Finckh

Tröste Dich!
Meine Seele, tröste dich!
Was du Gutes je besessen,
Webt und wirket unvergessen
Einen festen Schutz um dich.
Weine du, doch wisse immer:
Über dir sind mitternächtig
Freundliche Gewalten mächtig;
Du kannst gleiten – fallen nimmer!

Mutter.
Es kam ein Tag, der war so schwer,
Daß ich in seinem dunklen Schooß
Verzweifelnd beide Augen schloß –
Ich hatte keine Mutter mehr!

O wie das dunkel, dunkel war!
– Als läge, was es Lichtes gab,
Fern und vergessen hundert Jahr
In einem namenlosen Grab.
Dann aber warst du plötzlich da
Und legtest eine zarte Hand
Mir auf die Augen, und ich sah
Dich stehen noch und wohlbekannt.

Und seither kamst du jeden Tag
Und um mein Bette jede Nacht,
Und wenn ich ganz in Thränen lag,
Hast du mir Trost und Schlaf gebracht.

Piper

"– l'autre a soif de l'avenir e s'élance vers l'inconnu!" A. d. Musset.
[with slight variations identical to poem of same title in
Engelmann collection]

Certosa di Val d'Ema.
Der Mönch an seiner Pforte thut mir leid:
Er sah mir nach, wie ich am hohen Stab
Mich schwang den abendlichen Berg hinab,
Und seine Blicke redeten von Neid.

Und ich betrachtete sein keusches Kleid
Und lauschte seiner Glocke sanftem Lied.
– Er weiß nicht, daß von seiner Pforte schied
Der fremde Wanderer mit stillem Neid.

Appendix C-1

Notturni 1900 – All Titles, Alphabetical
(* = in *Gedichte* 1902)

Note: For titles included in more than one *Notturni* collection, each occurrence is listed.

Ad astra, Vorlage
Adagio, Goltermann
Adagio, Vorlage
* *Agnes*, Wackernagel-Burckhardt
Altmodisch, La Roche-Stockmeyer
* *An die Schönheit*, Burckhardt-Schazmann
An die Schönheit, Goltermann
An die Schönheit, Vorlage
An meinen Zeigefinger, Goltermann
An meinen Zeigefinger (statt 'Ad Astra'), Wackernagel-Burckhardt
Angelika, Wackernagel-Burckhardt
Auf deine Schwelle laß mich treten, Wackernagel-Burckhardt
Blondchen, Wackernagel-Burckhardt
Das blaue Wunder, Goltermann
Das blaue Wunder, Vorlage
* *Das war des Sommers schönster Tag*, Burckhardt-Schazmann
Deinem Blick darf meiner nicht begegnen, Wackernagel-Burckhardt
Der dritte Gesang: Von den Wassern, Wolken und Winden, Mezger-Leube
Der erste Gesang: Von der Sonne, Mezger-Leube
* *Der Geiger*, (Du braunes Holz ...), Burckhardt-Schazmann
Der Geiger, (Du braunes Holz ...), La Roche-Stockmeyer
Der Geiger, (Es geht kein Rauschen ...), Burckhardt-Schazmann
Der Geiger, (Es geht kein Rauschen ...), La Roche-Stockmeyer
Der Narr, La Roche-Stockmeyer
Der rote Veltliner, Goltermann
Der rote Veltliner, Vorlage
* *Der schönen Ungetreuen. Nach dem Fest*, La Roche-Stockmeyer
* *Der Sommerabend*, La Roche-Stockmeyer

Der Tag ist um, Wackernagel-Burckhardt
Der vierte Gesang: Vom Heimweh, Mezger-Leube
Der zweite Gesang: Von der Nacht, Mezger-Leube
Du Eine, Gnadenvolle nur, Wackernagel-Burckhardt
* *Einem schönen schlanken Mädchen*, Burckhardt-Schazmann
* *Einer schlanken Schönheit*, La Roche-Stockmeyer
* *Eleanor*, (Mit blassen Flatterwolken), Burckhardt-Schazmann
* *Eleanor*, (Ich hatte dir ein Lied gespielt), La Roche-Stockmeyer
* *Eleanor*, (In allem loderlohen Glanze), La Roche-Stockmeyer
Eleanor, (Hochmütig ...) Wackernagel-Burckhardt
Elisabeth, Wackernagel-Burckhardt
Elise, Wackernagel-Burckhardt
* *Erinnerung*, La Roche-Stockmeyer
* *Finale*, Wackernagel-Burckhardt
Ich und ich, Goltermann
Ich und ich, Vorlage
* *Inspiration*, (Nacht. Wolkensturm und Wipfeltanz), Burckhardt-Schazmann
Inspiration, Goltermann
Inspiration, Vorlage
Inspiration, (Nacht. Finsternis. In müder Hand), Mezger-Leube
Inspiration, Wackernagel-Burckhardt
Julia, La Roche-Stockmeyer
Lulu, Wackernagel-Burckhardt
* *Müde*, Burckhardt-Schazmann
O, du roter Wein, komm her!, Wackernagel-Burckhardt
O Nacht, du silberbleiche, Burckhardt-Schazmann
* *O reine, wundervolle Schau*, Burckhardt-Schazmann
* *Ohne Schmuck und Perlenglanz*, Wackernagel-Burckhardt
* *Rast haltend*, La Roche-Stockmeyer
Seelang stehen die welcken [sic] Stunden, Burckhardt-Schazmann
Sommerabend, Burckhardt-Schazmann
Trauer, Burckhardt-Schazmann
Trauer, La Roche-Stockmeyer
* *Was hold zu hören ist. Vom Hofnarren*, La Roche-Stockmeyer
* *Zwei Lieder, der schönen Eleanor gewidmet* (Das erste Lied, Das
   zweite Lied), Goltermann
Zwei Lieder, der schönen Eleanor gewidmet (Das erste Lied, Das
   zweite Lied), Vorlage

APPENDIX C-2

Notturni 1900 – First Lines, Alphabetical

"Auf deine Schwelle laß mich treten" *Marienlieder I*, Wackernagel-Burckhardt
"Auf marmorner Treppe" *Was hold zu hören ist. Vom Hofnarren.*
  (der schönen Eleanor), La Roche-Stockmeyer
"Aus dem Weiher blickt die Nacht" *Sommerabend*, Burckhardt-Schazmann
"Blätter gelb und rot sich drehen" *Das erste Lied* (*Zwei Lieder, der schönen Eleanor*
  gewidmet – Das erste Lied, Das zweite Lied), Goltermann
"Blätter gelb und rot sich drehen" *Das erste Lied* (*Zwei Lieder, der schönen Eleanor*
  gewidmet – Das erste Lied, Das zweite Lied), Vorlage
"Chopin's Nocturne Es-Dur! Der Bogen" *Erinnerung*, La Roche-Stockmeyer
"Das war des Sommers schönster Tag" *Das war des Sommers schönster Tag*, Burck-
  hardt-Schazmann
"Deinem Blick darf meiner nicht begegnen" *Marienlieder IV*,
  Wackernagel-Burckhardt
"Der Tag ist um" *Der Tag ist um*, Wackernagel-Burckhardt
"Der Tod ging nachts durch eine Stadt" *Finale*, Wackernagel-Burckhardt
"Die Nacht fällt ein" *Der schönen Ungetreuen. Nach dem Fest*, La Roche-Stockmeyer
"Die Nacht fällt ein" *Elisabeth*, Wackernagel-Burckhardt
"Dir liegt auf Stirne, Mund und Hand" *Einem schönen schlanken Mädchen*, Burck-
  hardt-Schazmann
"Dir liegt auf Stirne, Mund und Hand" *Einer schlanken Schönheit*, La Roche-
  Stockmeyer
"Dir liegt auf Stirne, Mund und Hand" *Agnes*, Wackernagel-Burckhardt
"Du braunes Holz, behutsam leg'" *Der Geiger*, Burckhardt-Schazmann
"Du braunes Holz, behutsam leg'" *Der Geiger* La Roche-Stockmeyer
"Du Eine, Gnadenvolle nur" *Marienleider II*, Wackernagel-Burckhardt
"Ein Kindermündlein lieb und lind" *Elise*, Wackernagel-Burckhardt
"Eine silberne Spieluhr spielte" *Altmodisch*, La Roche-Stockmeyer
"Erlaube im Geheimen mir" *Der Narr*, La Roche-Stockmeyer
"Es geht kein Rauschen übers Feld" *Der Geiger*, Burckhardt- Schazmann
"Es geht kein Rauschen über's Feld" *Der Geiger*, La Roche-Stockmeyer
"Gieb uns du die milde Hand" *An die Schönheit*, Burckhardt-Schazmann
"Gieb uns du die milde Hand" *An die Schönheit*, Goltermann

"Gieb uns du die milde Hand" *An die Schönheit*, Vorlage
"Heute auch aus blauen Fernen" *Der zweite Gesang: Von der Nacht*, Mezger-Leube
"Hochmütig, schön und rätselhaft" *Eleanor*, Wackernagel-Burckhardt
"Ich habe keinen Kranz ersiegt" *Müde*, Burckhardt-Schazmann
"Ich hatte dir ein Lied gespielt" *Eleanor*, La Roche-Stockmeyer
"Ich soll erzählen – " *Der Sommerabend*, La Roche-Stockmeyer
"Ich stand im Garten spät am Tag" *Ich und ich*, Goltermann
"Ich stand im Garten spät am Tag" *Ich und ich*, Vorlage
"Ich will mich tief verneigen ... " *Lulu*, Wackernagel-Burckhardt
"Im Urner See. Ich war ertrunken" *Das blaue Wunder*, Goltermann
"Im Urner See. Ich war ertrunken" *Das blaue Wunder*, Vorlage
"In allem loderlohen Glanze" *Eleanor*, La Roche-Stockmeyer
"Irgendwo in einem Walde war's" *Blondchen*, Wackernagel-Burckhardt
"Mein liebes Zeigefingerlein" *An meinen Zeigefinger*, Goltermann
"Mein liebes Zeigefingerlein" *An meinen Zeigefinger (statt 'Ad Astra')*, Wacker-
    nagel-Burckhardt
"Menschen leben wenig karge Tage" *Der erste Gesang: Von der Sonne*,
    Mezger-Leube
"Mit blassen Flatterwolken" *Eleanor*, Burckhardt-Schazmann
"Mit blassen Flatterwolken" *Das zweite Lied (Zwei Lieder, der schönen Eleanor
    gewidmet – Das erste Lied, Das zweite Lied)*, Goltermann
"Mit blassen Flatterwolken" *Das zweite Lied" (Zwei Lieder, der schönen Eleanor
    gewidmet – Das erste Lied, Das zweite Lied)*, Vorlage
"Nacht. Finsternis. In müder Hand" *Inspiration*, Mezger-Leube
"Nacht. Finsternis. In müder Hand" *Inspiration*, Wackernagel-Burckhardt
"Nacht. Wolkensturm und Wipfeltanz" *Inspiration*, Burckhardt-Schazmann
"Nacht, Wolkensturm und Wipfeltanz ... " *Inspiration*, Goltermann
"Nacht, Wolkensturm und Wipfeltanz ... " *Inspiration*, Vorlage
"O, du roter Wein, komm her" *O, du roter Wein, komm her!*, Wackernagel-
    Burckhardt
"O Nacht, du silberbleiche" *O Nacht, du silberbleiche"*, Burckhardt-Schazmann
"O reine wundervolle Schau" *O reine, wundervolle Schau"*, Burckhardt-Schazmann
"Ohne Schmuck und Perlenglanz" *Marienlieder III*, Wackernagel-Burckhardt
"Rast haltend unter Edeltannen" *Rast haltend*, La Roche-Stockmeyer
"Seelang stehen die welcken [sic] Stunden" (no title), Burckhardt-Schazmann
"Seit ich Ihren Garten sah" *Julia*, La Roche-Stockmeyer
"Spätsommers. Meine Birke regt" *Trauer*, Burckhardt-Schazmann
"Spätsommers. Meine Birke regt" *Trauer*, La Roche-Stockmeyer
"Spätsommers. Meine Birke regt" *Angelika*, Wackernagel-Burckhardt
"Tief in einem finstern Hause" *Adagio*, Goltermann
"Tief in einem finstern Hause" *Adagio*, Vorlage
"Trüb vor deinem leichten Schaum" *Der rote Veltliner*, Goltermann
"Trüb vor deinem leichten Schaum" *Der rote Veltliner*, Vorlage
"Wind, freier Wind!" *Ad astra*, Vorlage
"Was ist der Seele tiefster Grund" *Der vierte Gesang: Vom Heimweh*, Mezger-Leube
"Wo klang zum erstenmal" *Der dritte Gesang: Von den Wasser, Wolken und Winden*,
    Mezger-Leube

APPENDIX C-3

Notturni 1900 – Title Plus First Line of Each Poem

Notes: Mileck = Joseph Mileck, *Hermann Hesse, Biography and Bibliography,* volume number, page number, poem listing number; *DG* = *Die Gedichte,* 1977; 1902 = *Gedichte 1902;* 1921 = *Ausgewählte Gedichte.* Dates in brackets [ ] = *Gedichte 1902,* Hesse's own "dating" – as he entered it in pencil in his own copy of the work. Poems are in the same order as in originals.

Vorlage

1. *Inspiration* [1900] (*DG,* 102-03). Mileck, 1: 571 (388)
   "Nacht, Wolkensturm und Wipfeltanz ... "
   Textual variations in 1902, p. 110; = *DG*)
   **Not in 1921
2. *Das blaue Wunder.* Mileck, 1: 685 (1046)
   "Im Urner See. Ich war ertrunken"
   **Never published, but included in *Kindheit und Jugend* 2:492-494
   (part of a letter written by Hesse in September 1900 to Eberhard Goes).
3. *Adagio.* Mileck, 1: 693 (1127)
   "Tief in einem finstern Hause"
   **Never published
4. *Zwei Lieder, der schönen Eleanor gewidmet (Das erste Lied, Das zweite Lied)*
   [1900] (= *DG, Der böse Tag,* 116; *Fluch,* 98). Mileck, 1: 503 (56)
   "Blätter gelb und rot sich drehen"
   (= 1902, p. 95; = *DG*)
   "Mit blassen Flatterwolken"
   (Textual variations in 1902, p. 90; = *DG*)
   **Neither poem in 1921
5. *Ad astra.* Mileck, 1: 697 (1183a).
   "Wind, freier Wind!"
   **Never published
6. *Ich und ich.* Mileck, 1: 684 (1034)
   "Ich stand im Garten spät am Tag"
   **Never published

7. *Der rote Veltliner* (= *Tröster Wein, DG*, 159f.) Mileck, 1: 597 (506)
   "Trüb vor deinem leichten Schaum"
   (Textual variations in *DG*, p. 159f)
   **Not in 1902, 1921
8. *An die Schönheit* [1900] (*DG*, 95). Mileck, 1: 540 (226)
   "Gieb uns deine milde Hand"
   (Textual variations in 1902, p. 136; = *DG*)
   **Not in 1921

Burckhardt-Schazmann *Notturni. Herrn und Frau Professor Ch Burckhardt-Schaz-mann ergebenst überreicht. Basel 10. 10. 1900* (Only title page has been located, thus no textual comparisons.)

1. *Inspiration* [1900] (1902, 110; *DG*, 102-03). Mileck, 1: 571 (388)
   "Nacht. Wolkensturm und Wipfeltanz"
2. *Müde* [1899] (= *Wie kommt es*, 1902, 121; *DG*, 86). Mileck, 1: 545 (255)
   "Ich habe keinen Kranz ersiegt"
3. *Das war des Sommers schönster Tag* [1899] (= *August*, 1902, 28; *DG*, 78).
   Mileck, 1: 509 (84)
   "Das war des Sommers schönster Tag"
4. *Einem schönen schlanken Mädchen* [1900] (= *Elisabeth I*, 1902, 40; *DG*, 113).
   Not in Mileck under this title variation.
   "Dir liegt auf Stirne, Mund und Hand"
5. *Sommerabend* (= *Seeabend, DG*, p. 263. Not in 1902). Mileck, 1: 499 (41, 41a)
   "Aus dem Weiher blickt die Nacht"
6. *Trauer* (= *Das Kreuzlein*, not in 1902, *DG*). Mileck, 1: 662 (830)
   "Spätsommers. Meine Birke regt"
7. *Der Geiger* [1899] (= *Der Geiger IV*, 1902, 132-33; *DG*, 75-76). Mileck,
   1: 533 (195)
   "Es geht kein Rauschen übers Feld"
8. *Der Geiger* [1899] (= *Der Geiger III*, 1902, 131; *DG*, 75). Mileck, 1: 522 (147)
   "Du braunes Holz, behutsam leg'"
9. *An die Schönheit* [1900] (1902, 136; *DG*, 95). Mileck, 1: 540 (226)
   "Gieb uns deine milde Hand!"
10. *Seelang stehen die welcken [sic] Stunden* (Not in any other, available source).
11. *Eleanor* [1900] (= *Fluch*, 1902, 90; *DG*, 98). Mileck, 1: 569 (377)
    "Mit blassen Flatterwolken"
12. *O reine, wundervolle Schau* [1898] (= *Spätblau*, 1902, 16; *DG*, 82). Mileck, 1: 578 (419)
    "O reine wundervolle Schau"
13. *O Nacht, du silberbleiche* [1900] (Presumably, final eight lines of *Inspiration*, no. 1 above.) Mileck, 1: 578 (418a)
    "O Nacht, du silberbleiche"

Goltermann *Notturni. Frau Cornelie Goltermann in alter Reutlinger Freundschaft überreicht. 12. Oktober 1900.*

1. *An die Schönheit* [1900] (*DG*, 95). Mileck, 1: 540 (226)
   "Gieb uns du die milde Hand"
   Textual variations in 1902, p. 136; = *DG*)
   **Not in 1921

2. *Inspiration* [1900] (*DG*, 102-03). Mileck, 1: 571 (388)
   "Nacht, Wolkensturm und Wipfeltanz ... "
   Textual variations in 1902, p. 110; = *DG*)
   **Not in 1921
3. *An meinen Zeigefinger*. Mileck, 1: 688 (1076a-1078).
   "Mein liebes Zeigefingerlein"
   **Never published
4. *Ich und ich*. Mileck, 1: 684 (1034)
   "Ich stand im Garten spät am Tag"
   **Never published
5. *Der rote Veltliner* (= *Tröster Wein, DG*, 159f.). Mileck, 1: 597 (506)
   "Trüb vor deinem leichten Schaum"
   (Textual variations in *DG*, p. 159f)
   **Not in 1902, 1921
6. *Adagio*. Mileck, 1: 693 (1127)
   "Tief in einem finstern Hause"
   **Never published
7. *Das blaue Wunder*. Mileck, 1: 685 (1046)
   "Im Urner See. Ich war ertrunken"
   **Never published, but included in *Kindheit und Jugend*, 2: 492-494 (part
   of a letter written by Hesse in September to Eberhard Goes).
8. *Zwei Lieder, der schönen Eleanor gewidmet (Das erste Lied, Das zweite Lied)*
   [1900] (= *DG, Der böse Tag*, 116; *Fluch*, 98). Mileck, 1: 503 (56)
   Introductory stanza: *Nun brichst du dich nieder* – not in any published
   version of the poems.
   "Blätter gelb und rot sich drehen"
   (= 1902, p. 95; = *DG*)
   "Mit blassen Flatterwolken"
   = 1902, p. 90; = *DG*)
   **Neither poem in 1921

La Roche-Stockmeyer *Notturni. Frau La Roche-Stockmeyer ergebenst überreicht.
Basel, Oktober 1900*

1. *Der schönen Ungetreuen. Nach dem Fest* [1901] (= *Vorwurf, DG*, 124).
   Mileck, 1: 519 (128)
   "Die Nacht fällt ein"
   (Textual variations in 1902, p. 60 and 1921, p. 21; = *DG*)
2. *Der Geiger* [1899] (= *Der Geiger III, DG*, 75). Mileck, 1: 522 (147)
   "Du braunes Holz, behutsam leg'"
   Textual variations in 1902, p. 131; = *DG*)
   **Not in 1921
3. *Der Geiger* [1899] (= *Der Geiger IV, DG*, 75-76). Mileck, 1: 533 (195)
   "Es geht kein Rauschen übers Feld"
   (Textual variations in 1902, p. 132-33; = *DG*)
   **Not in 1921
4. *Altmodisch* (*DG*, 736). Mileck, 1: 636 (701)
   "Eine silberne Spieluhr spielte"
   **Not in 1902, 1921
5. *Erinnerung* [1899] (= *Nocturne, DG*, 71). Mileck, 1: 505 (64)
   "Chopin's Nocturne Es-Dur! Der Bogen"

(= 1902, p. 50; = *DG*)
**Not in 1921
6. *Einer schlanken Schönheit* [1900] (= *Elisabeth I, DG*, 113). Not in Mileck
under this title variation.
"Dir liegt auf Stirne, Mund und Hand"
(Textual variations in 1902, 40; = *DG*)
**Not in 1921
7. *Trauer* (= *Das Kreuzlein*). Mileck, 1: 662 (830)
"Spätsommers. Meine Birke regt"
**Not in 1902, 1921, *DG*
8. *Eleanor* [1900] (= *Purpurrose, DG*, 96). Mileck, 1: 546 (260)
"Ich hatte dir ein Lied gespielt."
(Textual variations in 1902, p. 55; = *DG*, p. 96)
**Not in 1921
9. *Eleanor* [1899] (= *Jahrestag, DG*, 73). Mileck, 1: 550 (286)
"In allem loderlohem Glanze"
(Textual variations in 1902, p. 58; = *DG*)
**Not in 1921
10. *Was hold zu hören ist. Vom Hofnarren. (der schönen Eleanor)* [1899]
(= *Narrenlied für die schöne Lulu, DG*, 72). Mileck, 1: 498 (36)
"Auf marmorner Treppe"
(Textual variations in 1902, p. 68; = *DG*)
**Not in 1921
11. *Julia*. Mileck, 1: 692 (1117)
"Seit ich Ihren Garten sah"
**Never published
12. *Der Narr*. Mileck, 1: 679 (986)
"Erlaube im Geheimen mir"
**Never published
13. *Rast haltend* [1898] (= *Über Hirsau, DG*, 80). Mileck, 1: 580 (433)
"Rast haltend unter Edeltannen"
(Textual variations in 1902, p. 7; = *DG*)
**Not in 1921
14. *Der Sommerabend* [1900] (= *Elisabeth II, DG*, 113). Mileck, 1: 548 (274)
"Ich soll erzählen – "
(Textual variations in 1902, p. 41 and 1921, p. 23; = *DG*)

Mezger-Leube *Notturni. Herrn Professor Dr. Mezger ergebenst überreicht. Basel
17. 10. 1900*

First interior page: *Die Erde mußt du scheiden vom Feuer, das Subtile vom
Groben, lieblicher Weise mit großem Verstande. (Aus der smaragdenen Tafel des
Hermes Trismegistus.)*

Das in der Einladung versprochene Titelprogramm konnte nicht eingehalten werden.

1. *Inspiration* (*DG*, 347). Mileck, 1: 571 (387)
"Nacht. Finsternis. In müder Hand"
**Not in 1902, 1921
2. *Der erste Gesang: Von der Sonne*. Not in Mileck.
"Menschen leben wenig karge Tage"
**Never published

3. *Der zweite Gesang: Von der Nacht.* Not in Mileck.
   "Heute auch aus blauen Fernen"
   **Never published
4. *Der dritte Gesang: Von den Wassern, Wolken und Winden.* Not in Mileck.
   "Wo klang zum erstenmal"
   **Never published
5. *Der vierte Gesang: Vom Heimweh.* Not in Mileck.
   "Was ist der Seele tiefster Grund?"
   **Never published

Wackernagel-Burckhardt *Notturni oder vertraulich poetische Briefe an Herrn und Frau Dr. R. Wackernagel-Burckhardt in Basel. ex ungue autorem. Basel, Oktober 1900* (Latin phrase obviously a play on the phrase *ex ungue leonem* -"by the lion's claw you shall know him" – "by the author's 'claw' you shall recognize him.")

1. *Der Tag ist um* (= first line, no title). Not in Mileck.
   **Never published
2. *Inspiration* (*DG*, 347). Mileck, 1: 571 (387)
   "Nacht. Finsternis. In müder Hand"
   **Not in 1902, 1921
3. *O, du roter Wein, komm her!* (= *Tröster Wein DG*, 159f.). Mileck, 1: 597 (506)
   "O, du roter Wein, komm her"
   (Textual variations in *DG*, p. 159f)
   **Not in 1902, 1921
4. *Elise.* Mileck, 1: 678 (975)
   "Ein Kindermündlein lieb und lind"
   **Not in 1902, 1921, *DG*
5. *Agnes* [1901] (= *DG*, "Elisabeth I", 113). Mileck, 1: 521 (140)
   "Dir liegt auf Stirne, Mund und Hand"
   (= 1902, 40; one word different, *DG*)
   **Not in 1921
6. *Elisabeth* [1901] (= *DG*, *Vorwurf*, 124). Mileck, 1: 519 (128)
   "Die Nacht fällt ein"
   **Not in 1921
7. *Eleanor* (= *DG*, *Porträt*, 67). Mileck, 1: 543 (244)
   "Hochmütig, schön und rätselhaft"
   (Textual variations in 1902, p. 57; = *DG*)
   **Not in 1921
8. *Angelika.* Mileck, 1: 662 (830), *Das Kreuzlein.*
   "Spätsommers. Meine Birke regt"
   **Not in 1902, 1921, *DG*
9. *Blondchen.* Mileck, 1: 648 (758), *Einmal.*
   "Irgendwo in einem Walde war's"
   **Not in 1902, 1921, *DG*
10. *Lulu* [Aug. 26, 1899 (Mileck)]. Mileck, 1: 646 (745), *An das Lulumädele II.*
    "Ich will mich tief verneigen ... "
    **Not in 1902, 1921, *DG*

11. *Finale* [1898] (= *Der Tod ging nachts, DG,* 89). Mileck, 1: 515 (113).
    "Der Tod ging nachts durch eine Stadt"
    (Textual variations in 1902, p. 117; = DG)
    **Not in 1921
12. *An meinen Zeigefinger (statt 'Ad Astra').* Mileck, 1: 688 (1076a-1078).
    "Mein liebes Zeigefingerlein"
    **Never published
13. *Marienlieder I-IV.* Mileck, 1: 744 (849-851).
    I "Auf deine Schwelle laß mich treten"
    **Never published
    II "Du Eine, Gnadenvolle nur"
    **Never published
    III "Ohne Schmuck und Perlenglanz" [1900]
    (= 1902, *Marienlieder II,* p. 103; = DG, p. 175)
    **Not in 1902
    IV "Deinem Blick darf meiner nicht begegnen" [1900]
    (Textual variations in 1902, *Marienlieder III,* p. 104; = DG, p. 176)
    **Not in 1902

Appendix D-1

Notturni 1902 – All Titles, Alphabetical
(* = in *Gedichte* 1902)

Note: For titles included in more than one *Notturni* collection, each occurrence is listed.

Ach, du weißt – , Engelmann
* *Ähren im Sturm*, Finckh
Ähren im Sturm, Löhnert
Ähren im Sturm, Schoenaich-Carolath
Albumblatt, Goltermann-Finckh
Albumblatt, Pfau
* *Ausklang*, Finckh
Ausklang, Goltermann-Finckh
Ausklang, Schoenaich-Carolath
* *Bei Spezia*, Drasdo
Beim Weiher, Piper
Certosa di Val d'Ema, Piper
* *Das fernste Schiff … (Bei Livorno)*, Drasdo
* *Das welke Blatt*, Pfau
* *Den Duft der Resede*, Engelmann
* *Der Abenteurer*, Löhnert
* *Der alte Geiger*, Pfau
* *Der Brief*, Engelmann
* *Der Duft der Narzisse*, Engelmann
Der Schmetterling, Finckh
Der Schmetterling, Schoenaich-Carolath
* *Der stille Hof*, Pfau
* *Die Cypressen von San Clemente*, Goltermann-Finckh
Die Cypressen von San Clemente, Piper
Drüben überm Berge, Piper
* *Dunkelste Stunden*, Löhnert
* *Einem Verächter*, Piper
* *Einer Schönheit*, Englemann
Einer Schönheit, Goltermann-Finckh

Einer Schönheit, Löhnert
Einer Schönheit, Piper
* *Einsame Nacht,* Engelmann
Einsame Nacht, Finckh
Einsame Nacht, Löhnert
Einsame Nacht, Schoenaich-Carolath
* *Elisabeth,* Drasdo
* *Elisabeth,* Drasdo
* *Er ging im Dunkel ...* , Drasdo
Er ging im Dunkel ... , Englemann
Er ging im Dunkel ... , Goltermann-Finckh
Er ging im Dunkel ..., Löhnert
Er ging im Dunkel ... , Pfau
Er ging im Dunkel ... , Piper
* *Es giebt so Schönes ...* , Goltermann-Finckh
* *Es wird dir sonderbar ...* , Engelmann
Es wird dir sonderbar ... , Löhnert
* *Fest,* Drasdo
* *Florenz,* Finckh
Florenz, Schoenaich-Carolath
* *Fremde Stadt,* Drasdo
Fremde Stadt, Goltermann-Finckh
* *Frühsommernacht,* Drasdo
Frühsommernacht, Engelmann
* *Gedächtnis,* Finckh
Gedächtnis, Löhnert
Gedächtnis, Schoenaich-Carolath
* *Gleichnisse,* Drasdo
* *Grindelwald,* Finckh
Grindelwald, Schoenaich-Carolath
* *Hafen von Livorno,* Pfau
* *Heimkehr,* Goltermann-Finckh
Heimkehr, Pfau
Herbst, Engelmann
* *Hochgebirgswinter,* Goltermann-Finckh
* *Ich möchte wohl ...* , Drasdo
Ich möchte wohl ... , Löhnert
* *Ich liebe Frauen ...* , Piper
* *Ist das schon Herbst?,* Pfau
* *Kennst du das auch?,* Drasdo
Kennst du das auch?, Finckh
Kennst du das auch?, Schoenaich-Carolath
Kennst du das auch?, Engelmann
* *Kreuzgang von Santo Stefano in Venedig,* Engelmann
L'autre a soif de l'avenir et s'élance vers l'inconnu! A. de Musset,
Engelmann
L'autre a soif de l'avenir et s'élance vers l'inconnu! A. de Musset., Piper
* *La belle qui veut ...,* Löhnert
* *Liebesgeschichte I/II,* Piper
* *Liebeslied,* Finckh
Liebeslied, Löhnert

Liebeslied, Schoenaich-Carolath
* *Ligurisches Meer*, Finckh
Ligurisches Meer, Löhnert
Ligurisches Meer, Schoenaich-Carolath
* *Meine Liebe*, Engelmann
Meine Liebe, Goltermann-Finckh
* *Mon rêve familier (Aus dem Französischen des Paul Verlaine)*, Drasdo
* *Müde*, Finckh
Müde, Schoenaich-Carolath
Müde nun ... , Piper
Mutter, Goltermann-Finckh
* *Nacht*, Pfau
* *Nachtgebet der Schiffer auf dem adriatischen Meer (zur Stella maris.)*, Finckh
Nachtgebet der Schiffer auf dem adriatischen Meer (zur Stella maris.), Schoenaich-
  Carolath
* *Nachtwanderung*, Finckh
Nachtwanderung, Schoenaich-Carolath
Notturno, Drasdo
* *Odysseus – Ein Gondelgespräch*, Löhnert
* *Pilger*, Engelmann
Pilger, Finckh
Pilger, Goltermann-Finckh
Pilger, Löhnert
Pilger, Schoenaich-Carolath
* *Reine Lust*, Finckh
Reine Lust, Schoenaich-Carolath
* *Rücknahme*, Engelmann
* *Sage*, Pfau
* *Schwarzwald*, Goltermann-Finckh
* *Spätblau*, Engelmann
Spätblau, Finckh
Spätblau, Schoenaich-Carolath
* *Tempel*, Drasdo
Tempel, Löhnert
Tröste dich, Goltermann-Finckh
* *Über die Felder*, Engelmann
Über die Felder, Goltermann-Finckh
Über die Felder, Piper
Vollendung, Goltermann-Finckh
* *Weiße Wolken*, Pfau
* *Wende*, Drasdo
Wende, Finckh
Wende, Schoenaich-Carolath
* *Wie eine Welle* ... , Drasdo
Wie eine Welle ... , Goltermann-Finckh
Wie eine Welle ..., Löhnert
Wie eine Welle ... , Pfau
Wie eine Welle ... , Piper
* *Wolkenflug und herber Wind*, Engelmann
* *Zigeuner*, Schoenaich-Carolath
Zigeuner, Finckh

Appendix D-2

Notturni 1902 – First Lines, Alphabetical

"Das fernste Schiff, das abendlich besonnt" *Das fernste Schiff ... (Bei Livorno)*, Drasdo

"Das sind die Stunden, die wir nicht begreifen!" *Dunkelste Stunden*, Löhnert

"Daß ich so oft mit dunklem Leid" *Ist das schon Herbst?*, Pfau

"Der König mit den Mannen saß beim Mahl" *Sage*, Pfau

"Der Mönch an seiner Pforte thut mir leid" *Certosa di Val d'Ema*, Piper

"Der Schneewind packt mich jäh von vorn" *Hochgebirgswinter*, Goltermann-Finckh

"Die ihr meine Brüder seid" *Einsame Nacht*, Engelmann

"Die ihr meine Brüder seid" *Einsame Nacht*, Finckh

"Die ihr meine Brüder seid" *Einsame Nacht*, Löhnert

"Die ihr meine Brüder seid" *Einsame Nacht*, Schoenaich-Carolath

"Die dunklen Büsche duften schwer" *Fest*, Drasdo

"Die Stunden eilen – Mitternacht!" *Nachtgebet der Schiffer auf dem adriatischen Meer (zur Stella maris.)*, Finckh

"Die Stunden eilen – Mitternacht!" *Nachtgebet der Schiffer auf dem adriatischen Meer (zur Stella maris.)*, Schoenaich-Carolath

"Dir liegt auf Stirn und schmaler Hand" *Einer Schönheit*, Löhnert

"Dir liegt auf Stirne, Mund und Hand" *Elisabeth*, Drasdo

"Dort am Horizonte kannst du sehen" *Odysseus – Ein Gondelgespräch*, Löhnert

"Drüben überm Berge" *Drüben überm Berge*, Piper

"Du mit dem tiefen Glanz im Blick" *L'autre a soif de l'avenir et s'élance vers l'inconnu! A. de Musset*, Engelmann

"Du mit dem tiefen Glanz im Blick" *L'autre a soif de l'avenir et s'élance vers l'inconnu! A. de Musset.*, Piper

"Dunkle Berge, helle Matten" *Schwarzwald*, Goltermann-Finckh

"Ein Hof liegt in der stillen Nacht" *Der stille Hof*, Pfau

"Ein Wändeviereck schlechtvertüncht und alt" *Kreuzgang von Santo Stefano in Venedig*, Engelmann

"Er ging im Dunkel gern, wo schwarzer Bäume" *Er ging im Dunkel ...* , Drasdo

"Er ging im Dunkel gern, wo schwarzer Bäume" *Er ging im Dunkel ...* , Engelmann

"Er ging im Dunkel gern, wo schwarzer Bäume" *Er ging im Dunkel ...* , Goltermann-Finckh

"Er ging im Dunkel gern, wo schwarzer Bäume" *Er ging im Dunkel ...*, Löhnert

"Er ging im Dunkel gern, wo schwarzer Bäume" *Er ging im Dunkel* ... , Pfau
"Er ging im Dunkel gern, wo schwarzer Bäume" *Er ging im Dunkel* ... , Piper
"Es geht ein Wind von Westen" *Der Brief*, Engelmann
"Es giebt so Schönes in der Welt" *Es giebt so Schönes* ... , Goltermann-Finckh
"Es kam ein Tag, der war so schwer" *Mutter*, Goltermann-Finckh
"Es nachtet schon, die Straße ruht" *Nachtwanderung*, Finckh
"Es nachtet schon, die Straße ruht" *Nachtwanderung*, Schoenaich-Carolath
"Es wird dir sonderbar erscheinen" *Es wird dir sonderbar* ... , Engelmann
"Es wird dir sonderbar erscheinen" *Es wird dir sonderbar* ... , Löhnert
"Flüchtig wie auf hellen Matten" *Einer Schönheit*, Engelmann
"Flüchtig wie auf hohen Matten" *Einer Schönheit*, Goltermann-Finckh
"Flüchtig wie auf hohen Matten" *Einer Schönheit*, Piper
"Ich habe keinen Kranz ersiegt" *Müde*, Finckh
"Ich habe keinen Kranz ersiegt" *Müde*, Schoenaich-Carolath
"Ich habe nichts mehr zu sagen" *Der alte Geiger*, Pfau
"Ich habe nur wenig Lieder" *Zigeuner*, Finckh
"Ich habe nur wenig Lieder" *Zigeuner*, Schoenaich-Carolath
"Ich liebe Frauen, die vor tausend Jahren" *Ich liebe Frauen* ... , Piper
"Ich möchte wohl, wie große Dichter thun" *Ich möchte wohl* ... , Drasdo
"Ich möchte wohl, wie große Dichter thun" *Ich möchte wohl* ... Löhnert
"Ich sagte nicht: ich liebe dich" *Rücknahme*, Engelmann
"Ich sagte nicht: ich liebe dich" *Liebesgeschichte II*, Piper
"Ich träume wieder von der Unbekannten" *Mon rêve familier (Aus dem Französischen des Paul Verlaine)*, Drasdo
"Ich weiß: an irgend einem fernen Tag" *Vollendung*, Goltermann-Finckh
"Ich weiß auf Erden keine reinere Lust" *Reine Lust*, Finckh
"Ich weiß auf Erden keine reinere Lust" *Reine Lust*, Schoenaich-Carolath
"Immer wieder gab ich meine Hände" *Müde nun* ... , Piper
"In großen Takten singt das Meer" *Bei Spezia*, Drasdo
"In großen Takten singt das Meer" *Ligurisches Meer*, Finckh
"In großen Takten singt das Meer" *Ligurisches Meer*, Löhnert
"In großen Takten singt das Meer" *Ligurisches Meer*, Schoenaich-Carolath
"ist herb im Grund und dennoch zart" *Der Duft der Narzisse*, Engelmann
"Jedem Tag ein kleines Glück" *Albumblatt*, Goltermann-Finckh
"Jedem Tag ein kleines Glück" *Albumblatt*, Pfau
"Kennst du mich noch? Wir wurden alt" *La belle qui veut* ... , Löhnert
"Kennst du das auch, daß manchesmal" *Kennst du das auch?*, Drasdo
"Kennst du das auch, daß manchesmal" *Kennst du das auch?*, Engelmann
"Kennst du das auch, daß manchesmal" *Kennst du das auch?*, Finckh
"Kennst du das auch, daß manchesmal" *Kennst du das auch?*, Schoenaich-Carolath
"Mein Herz ist müd, mein Herz ist schwer," *Der Abenteurer*, Löhnert
"Meine Seele, tröste dich!" *Tröste dich*, Goltermann-Finckh
"Meine Jugend war ein keckes Spiel" *Ach, du weißt –* , Engelmann
"Meine Liebe ist ein stilles Boot" *Gleichnisse*, Drasdo
"Mit Dämmerung und Amselschlag" *Nacht*, Pfau
"mußt du mit geschlossenen Augen" *Den Duft der Resede*, Engelmann
"Nach einem Bild, das ich vor Jahren sah" *Hafen von Livorno*, Pfau
"Nachsinnend still und ernst bewegt" *Herbst*, Engelmann
"Nacht ... Finsternis ... In müder Hand" *Notturno*, Drasdo

"Nun bin ich lang gewesen" *Heimkehr*, Goltermann-Finckh
"Nun bin ich lang gewesen" *Heimkehr*, Pfau
"Nun ist die Jugend schon verschäumt" *Wende*, Drasdo
"Nun ist die Jugend schon verschäumt" *Wende*, Finckh
"Nun ist die Jugend schon verschäumt" *Wende*, Schoenaich-Carolath
"O reine, wundervolle Schau" *Spätblau*, Engelmann
"O reine, wundervolle Schau" *Spätblau*, Finckh
"O reine, wundervolle Schau" *Spätblau*, Schoenaich-Carolath
"O schau, sie schweben wieder" *Weiße Wolken*, Pfau
"O wie der Sturm so dunkel braust!" *Ähren im Sturm*, Finckh
"O wie der Sturm so dunkel braust!" *Ähren im Sturm*, Löhnert
"O wie der Sturm so dunkel braust!" *Ähren im Sturm*, Schoenaich-Carolath
"Sie schweigt und denkt mit trauervollen" *Meine Liebe*, Engelmann
"Sie schweigt und denkt mit trauervollen" *Meine Liebe*, Goltermann-Finckh
"Sieh, ich verstehe ja dein Fluchen" *Einem Verächter*, Piper
"Soll ich sagen, was ich träume?" *Florenz*, Finckh
"Soll ich sagen, was ich träume?" *Florenz*, Schoenaich-Carolath
"Spätsommer: Meine Birke regt" *Beim Weiher*, Piper
"Über den Himmel Wolken zieh'n" *Über die Felder*, Goltermann-Finckh
"Über den Himmel Wolken zieh'n" *Über die Felder*, Engelmann
"Über den Himmel Wolken zieh'n" *Über die Felder*, Piper
"Über den silbernen Hügeln" *Der Schmetterling*, Finckh
"Über den silbernen Hügeln" *Der Schmetterling*, Schoenaich-Carolath
"Und ringsum Schnee und junges Eis" *Grindelwald*, Finckh
"Und ringsum Schnee und junges Eis" *Grindelwald*, Schoenaich-Carolath
"Und weiter geh'n die Tage" *Pilger*, Engelmann
"Und weiter geh'n die Tage" *Pilger*, Finckh
"Und weiter geh'n die Tage" *Pilger*, Goltermann-Finckh
"Und weiter geh'n die Tage" *Pilger*, Löhnert
"Und weiter geh'n die Tage" *Pilger*, Schoenaich-Carolath
"Vor mir her getrieben" *Das welke Blatt*, Pfau
"Weit aus allen dunklen Thalen" *Frühsommernacht*, Drasdo
"Weit aus allen dunklen Thalen" *Frühsommernacht*, Engelmann
"Wenn du die kleine Hand mir giebst" *Liebesgeschichte I*, Piper
"Wenn mich der fernen Kindertage" *Gedächtnis*, Finckh
"Wenn mich der fernen Kindertage" *Gedächtnis*, Löhnert
"Wenn mich der fernen Kindertage" *Gedächtnis*, Schoenaich-Carolath
"Wie das so seltsam traurig macht" *Fremde Stadt*, Drasdo
"Wie das so seltsam traurig macht" *Fremde Stadt*, Goltermann-Finckh
"Wie eine weiße Wolke" *Elisabeth*, Drasdo
"Wie eine weiße Wolke" *Liebeslied*, Finckh
"Wie eine weiße Wolke" *Liebeslied*, Löhnert
"Wie eine weiße Wolke" *Liebeslied*, Schoenaich-Carolath
"Wie eine Welle, die von Schaum gekränzt" *Wie eine Welle …* , Drasdo
"Wie eine Welle, die von Schaum gekränzt" *Wie eine Welle …* , Goltermann-Finckh
"Wie eine Welle, die von Schaum gekränzt" *Wie eine Welle*, Löhnert
"Wie eine Welle, die von Schaum gekränzt" *Wie eine Welle …* , Pfau
"Wie eine Welle, die von Schaum gekränzt" *Wie eine Welle …* , Piper
"Wir biegen flammend schlanke Wipfel im Wind" *Die Cypressen von San Clemente*,
    Goltermann-Finckh

"Wir biegen flammend schlanke Wipfel im Wind" *Die Cypressen von San Clemente*, Piper

"Wo der gestürzte Gott, von Schatten überschauert" *Tempel*, Drasdo

"Wo der gestürzte Gott, von Schatten überschauert" *Tempel*, Löhnert

"Wolkenflug und herber Wind" *Ausklang*, Finckh

"Wolkenflug und herber Wind" *Ausklang*, Goltermann-Finckh

"Wolkenflug und herber Wind" *Ausklang*, Schoenaich-Carolath

"Wolkenflug und herber Wind" *Wolkenflug und herber Wind*, Engelmann

APPENDIX D-3

Notturni 1902 – Title Plus First Line of Each Poem

Notes: Mileck = Joseph Mileck, *Hermann Hesse, Biography and Bibliography*, volume number, page number, poem listing number; *DG = Die Gedichte*, 1977; 1902 = *Gedichte 1902*; 1921 = *Ausgewählte Gedichte*. Dates in brackets [ ] = *Gedichte 1902*, Hesse's own "dating" – as he entered it in pencil in his own copy of the work. Poems are in the same order as in originals.

Drasdo *Notturni.* Title page: *Verse. Meinem Freunde Otto Drasdo.* Closing page: *Basel 1902*

1. *Notturno* (= *Inspiration, DG*, 347). Mileck, 1: 571 (387)
   "Nacht ... Finsternis ... In müder Hand"
   (= *DG*, lines 1–12 ONLY)
   **Not in 1902, 1921

2. *Bei Spezia* [1902] (*DG*, 198). Mileck, 1: 557 (315)
   "In großen Takten singt das Meer"
   (= 1902, p. 149; = *DG*)
   **Not in 1921

3. *Das fernste Schiff ... (Bei Livorno)* [June 1901] (*DG*, 134). Mileck, 1: 507 (72)
   "Das fernste Schiff, das abendlich besonnt"
   (Textual variations in 1902, different title: *Odysseus Bei Livorno*, p. 145; = *DG*)
   **Not in 1921

4. *Tempel* [1901] (*DG*, 150). Mileck, 1: 624 (622)
   "Wo der gestürzte Gott, von Schatten überschauert"
   (One word different in 1902, p. 118; = *DG*)
   **Not in 1921

5. *Frühsommernacht* [1902] (= *Eine Geige in den Gärten, DG*, 191). Mileck, 1: 610 (562)
   "Weit aus allen dunklen Thalen"
   (Textual variations in 1902, p. 45; = *DG*)
   **Not in 1921

6. *Fremde Stadt* [1901] (*DG*, 163). Mileck, 1: 614 (583)
   "Wie das so seltsam traurig macht"

(One word different in 1902, p. 36; = *DG*)
**Not in 1921

7. *Elisabeth* [1900] (= *Elisabeth I, DG,* 113). Mileck, 1: 521 (140)
"Dir liegt auf Stirne, Mund und Hand"
(Textual variations in 1902, p. 42; *DG* differs from 1902 in one word)
**Not in 1921

8. *Elisabeth* [1901] (= *Elisabeth III, DG,* 114). Mileck, 1: 615 (587)
"Wie eine weiße Wolke"
(Textual variations in 1902, p. 42; = 1921, p. 24; = *DG*)

9. *Fest* [1901] (= *Das Fest, DG,* 136). Mileck, 1: 516 (117)
"Die dunklen Büsche duften schwer"
(= 1902, p. 54; = *DG*)
**Not in 1921

10. *Mon rêve familier (aus dem Französischen des Paul Verlaine)* [1901] (*DG,* 120). Mileck, 1: 548 (276)
"Ich träume wieder von der Unbekannten"
(Textual variations in 1902, p. 44; = *DG*)
**Not in 1921

11. *Gleichnisse* [1901] (*DG,* 171). Mileck, 1: 568 (370)
"Meine Liebe ist ein stilles Boot"
(= 1902, p. 72; = *DG*)
**Not in 1921

12. *Kennst du das auch?* [1901] (*DG,* 151). Mileck, 1: 562 (335)
"Kennst du das auch, daß manchesmal"
(= 1902, p. 85; = 1921, p. 27; = *DG*)

13. *Wende* [1901] (*DG,* 129). Mileck, 1: 576 (409)
"Nun ist die Jugend schon verschäumt"
(= 1902, p. 91; = *DG*)
**Not in 1921

14. *Ich möchte wohl ...* [1902] (= *Ich bin nur Einer, DG,* 207). Mileck, 1: 547 (269)
"Ich möchte wohl, wie große Dichter thun"
(Textual variations in 1902, p. 109; = *DG*)
**Not in 1921

15. *Wie eine Welle ...* [1901] (*DG,* 162). Mileck, 1: 615 (588)
"Wie eine Welle, die vom Schaum gekränzt"
(Textual variations in 1902, p. 195; = *DG*)
**Not in 1921

16. *Er ging im Dunkel ...* July [1901] (*DG,* 182). Mileck, 1: 530 (186)
"Er ging im Dunkel gern, wo schwarzer Bäume"
(= 1902, p. 190; = *DG*)
**Not in 1921

Engelmann *Notturni.* Title page: *Verse. Herrn Dr. Th. Engelmann in Basel am 29. Mai 1902 überreicht.*

1. *Herbst.* Not in Mileck.
"Nachsinnend still und ernst bewegt"
**Never published

2. *Ach, du weißt – .* Not in Mileck.
"Meine Jugend war ein keckes Spiel"
**Never published

3. *Über die Felder* [1900] (*DG*, 91). Mileck, 1: 598 (511)
   "Über den Himmel Wolken zieh'n"
   (= 1902, p. 4; = 1921, p. 14; = *DG*)
4. *L'autre a soif de l'avenir et s'élance vers l'inconnu! A. d. Musset.* Mileck, 1:
   676 (962A)
   "Du mit dem tiefen Glanz im Blick"
   **Never published
5. *Den Duft der Resede* [1900]. Mileck, 1: 718 (360)
   "mußt du mit geschlossenen Augen"
   (= 1902, p. 19)
   **Not in 1921, *DG*
6. *Der Duft der Narzisse* [1900]. Mileck, 1: 718 (360)
   "ist herb im Grund und dennoch zart"
   (Textual variations in 1902, p. 18)
   **Not in 1921, *DG*
7. *Spätblau* [1898] (*DG*, 82). Mileck, 1: 578 (419)
   "O reine, wundervolle Schau"
   (Textual variations in 1902, p. 16; = *DG*)
   **Not in 1921
8. *Frühsommernacht* [1902] (= *Eine Geige in den Gärten, DG*, 191). Mileck, 1:
   610 (562)
   "Weit aus allen dunklen Thalen"
   (Textual variations in 1902, p. 39; = *DG*)
   **Not in 1921
9. *Rücknahme* [1901] (*DG*, 123). Mileck, 1: 548 (271)
   "Ich sagte nicht: ich liebe dich"
   (= 1902, p. 61; = 1921, p. 22; = *DG*)
10. *Einer Schönheit* [1899] (= *Lulu, DG*, 87). Mileck, 536 (213)
    "Flüchtig wie auf hellen Matten"
    (Textual variations in 1902, p. 67; = *DG*)
    **Not in 1921
11. *Meine Liebe* [1901] (*DG*, 126). Mileck, 1: 588 (465)
    "Sie schweigt und denkt mit trauervollen"
    (= 1902, p. 70; = *DG*)
    **Not in 1921
12. *Der Brief* [1902] (*DG*, 208). Mileck, 1: 533 (194)
    "Es geht ein Wind von Westen"
    (= 1902, p. 71; = *DG*)
    **Not in 1921
13. *Es wird dir sonderbar ...* [1901] (*DG*, 117). Mileck, 1: 535 (208)
    "Es wird dir sonderbar erscheinen"
    (= 1902, p. 82; = *DG*)
    **Not in 1921
14. *Kreuzgang von Santo Stefano in Venedig* [August 1901] (= *Der Kreuzgang
    von Santo Stefano. Venedig, DG*, 131). Mileck, 1: 527 (172)
    "Ein Wändeviereck schlechtvertüncht und alt"
    (One word different 1902, p. 160; = *DG*)
    **Not in 1921
15. *Kennst du das auch?* [1901] (*DG*, 151). Mileck, 1: 562 (335)
    "Kennst du das auch, daß manchesmal"
    (= 1902, p. 85; = 1921, p. 27; = *DG*)

16. *Wolkenflug und herber Wind* [1901] (= *Ausklang*, DG, 152). Mileck, 1: 625 (629)
    "Wolkenflug und herber Wind"
    (= 1902, p. 184; = DG)
    **Not in 1921

17. *Einsame Nacht* [1901] (DG, 186). Mileck, 1: 517 (122)
    "Die ihr meine Brüder seid"
    (One word different 1902, p. 179; = 1921, p. 31; = DG)

18. *Er ging im Dunkel ...* [July 1901] (DG, 182). Mileck, 1: 530 (186)
    "Er ging im Dunkel gern, wo schwarzer Bäume"
    (One word different 1902, p. 190; = DG)
    **Not in 1921

19. *Pilger* [1901] (DG, 168). Mileck, 1: 599 (518)
    "Und weiter geh'n die Tage"
    (One word different 1902, p. 196; = DG)
    **Not in 1921

Finckh *Notturni*. Title page: *Frau Agnes Finckh in Reutlingen mit schönen Grüssen!*
Closing page: *Basel 1902 Hermann Hesse*

1. *Spätblau* [1898] (DG, 82). Mileck, 1: 578 (419)
   "O reine, wundervolle Schau"
   (Textual variations in 1902, p. 16; = DG)
   **Not in 1921

2. *Grindelwald* [February 1902] (= *Hochgebirgswinter I, Aufstieg*; DG, 195).
   Mileck, 1: 599 (517)
   "Und ringsum Schnee und junges Eis"
   (Textual variations in 1902, p. 11; = DG)
   **Not in 1921

3. *Reine Lust* [1902] (DG, 209). Mileck, 1: 549 (277)
   "Ich weiß auf Erden keine reinere Lust"
   (Textual variations in 1902, p. 146; = DG)
   **Not in 1921

4. *Florenz* [August 1901] (= *Im Norden*, DG, 127). Mileck, 1: 593 (489)
   "Soll ich sagen, was ich träume?"
   (Textual variations in 1902, p. 141; = 1921, p. 18; = DG)

5. *Kennst du das auch?* [1901] (DG, 151). Mileck, 1: 562 (335)
   "Kennst du das auch, daß manchesmal"
   (= 1902, p. 85; = 1921, p. 27; = DG)

6. *Liebeslied [1901]* (= *Elisabeth III*, DG, 114). Mileck, 1: 615 (587)
   "Wie eine weiße Wolke"
   (Textual variations 1902, p. 42; = 1921, p. 24; = DG)

7. *Ligurisches Meer* [1902] (= *Bei Spezia*, DG, 198). Mileck, 1: 557 (315)
   "In großen Takten singt das Meer"
   (One word different 1902, p. 149; = DG)
   **Not in 1921

8. *Nachtgebet der Schiffer auf dem adriatischen Meer (zur Stella maris.)* [June
   1901] (= *Gebet der Schiffer*, DG, 185). Mileck, 1: 520 (134)
   "Die Stunden eilen – Mitternacht!"
   (Textual variations 1902, p. 147; = DG)
   **Not in 1921

9. *Gedächtnis* (= *Zuweilen, DG*, 101). Mileck, 1: 612 (573)
   "Wenn mich der fernen Kindertage"
   (Textual variations 1902, p. 99; = *DG*)
   **Not in 1921
10. *Wende* [1901] (*DG*, 129). Mileck, 1: 576 (409)
   "Nun ist die Jugend schon verschäumt"
   (= 1902, p. 91; = *DG*)
   **Not in 1921
11. *Ausklang* [1901] (*DG*, 172). Mileck, 1: 625 (629)
   "Wolkenflug und herber Wind"
   (One word different 1902, p. 184; = *DG*)
   **Not in 1921
12. *Einsame Nacht* [1901] (*DG*, 186). Mileck, 1: 517 (122)
   "Die ihr meine Brüder seid"
   (One word different 1902, p. 179; = 1921, p. 31; = *DG*)
13. *Der Schmetterling*. Mileck, 1: 662 (836)
   "Über den silbernen Hügeln"
   **Not in 1902, 1921, *DG*
14. *Nachtwanderung* [1902] (= *DG, Nachtgang*, 205). Mileck, 1: 534 (202)
   "Es nachtet schon, die Straße ruht"
   (Textual variations 1902, p. 21; = *DG*)
   **Not in 1921
15. *Müde* [1899] (= *DG, Wie kommt es?*, 86). Mileck, 1: 545 (255)
   "Ich habe keinen Kranz ersiegt"
   (Textual variations 1902, p. 121; = *DG*)
   **Not in 1921
16. *Zigeuner* [1902] (= *DG, Lieder*, 206). Mileck, 1: 546 (259)
   "Ich habe nur wenig Lieder"
   (Textual variations 1902, p. 123; = *DG*)
   **Not in 1921
17. *Ähren im Sturm* [1902] (*DG*, 215). Mileck, 1: 579 (422)
   "O wie der Sturm so dunkel braust!"
   (Textual variations 1902, p. 6; = *DG*)
   **Not in 1921
18. *Pilger* [1901] (*DG*, 168). Mileck, 1: 599 (518)
   "Und weiter geh'n die Tage"
   (One word different 1902, p. 196; = *DG*)
   **Not in 1921

Goltermann-Finckh *Notturni*. Title page: *[Zweite Ausgabe.] Frau Cornelie Golter-mann-Finckh in Frankfurt mit vielen Grüßen!* Closing page: *Basel Juni 1902*

1. *Pilger* [1901] (*DG*, 168). Mileck, 1: 599 (518)
   "Und weiter geh'n die Tage"
   (= 1902, p. 196; = *DG*)
   **Not in 1921
2. *Über die Felder* [1900] (*DG*, 91). Mileck, 1: 598 (511)
   "Über den Himmel Wolken zieh'n"
   (= 1902, p. 4; = 1921, p. 14; = *DG*)
3. *Die Cypressen von San Clemente* [1901] (= *Die Zypressen von San Clemente, DG*, 153). Mileck, 1: 622 (613)

"Wir biegen flammend schlanke Wipfel im Wind"
(Textual variations 1902, p. 152; = 1921, p. 17; = *DG*)

4. *Heimkehr* [June 1901] (*DG*, 172). Mileck, 1: 576 (404)
"Nun bin ich lang gewesen"
(= 1902, p. 191; = *DG*)
**Not in 1921

5. *Fremde Stadt* [1901] (*DG*, 163). Mileck, 1: 614 (583)
"Wie das so seltsam traurig macht"
(Textual variations in 1902, p. 36; = *DG*)
**Not in 1921

6. *Wie eine Welle* ... [1901] (*DG*, 162). Mileck, 1: 615 (588)
"Wie eine Welle, die von Schaum gekränzt"
(One word different 1902, p. 195; = *DG*)
**Not in 1921

7. *Ausklang* [1901] (*DG*, 172). Mileck, 1: 625 (629)
"Wolkenflug und herber Wind"
(One word different 1902, p. 184; = *DG*)
**Not in 1921

8. *Tröste dich.* Mileck, 1: 688 (1079)
"Meine Seele, tröste dich!"
**Never published

9. *Albumblatt.* Mileck, *Neujahrsblatt ins Album*, 1: 648 (761)
"Jedem Tag ein kleines Glück"
**Not in 1902, 1921, *DG*

10. *Schwarzwald* [1901] (*DG*, 128 – First line: "Seltsam schöne Hügel-fluchten"). Mileck, 1: 587 (462)
"Dunkle Berge, helle Matten"
(Textual variations 1902, p. 5; = *DG*)
**Not in 1921

11. *Einer Schönheit* [1899] ("Lulu", *DG*, 87). Mileck, 1: 536 (213)
"Flüchtig wie auf hohen Matten"
(Textual variations 1902, p. 67; = *DG*)
**Not in 1921

12. *Er ging im Dunkel* ... [July 1901] (*DG*, 182). Mileck, 1: 530 (186)
"Er ging im Dunkel gern, wo schwarzer Bäume"
(= 1902, p. 190; = *DG*)
**Not in 1921

13. *Vollendung.* Mileck, 1: 646 (743)
"Ich weiß: an irgend einem fernen Tag"
**Not in 1902, 1921, *DG*

14. *Es giebt so Schönes* ... [1901]. Mileck, 1: 637 (705)
"Es giebt so Schönes in der Welt"
(Textual variations 1902, two additional lines, p. 33)
**Not in 1921, *DG*

15. *Hochgebirgswinter* [Feb. 1902] (= H. IV, 'Schlittenfahrt', *DG*, 196–97). Mileck, 1: 514 (108)
"Der Schneewind packt mich jäh von vorn"
(= 1902, "Hochgebirgswinter V, 'Gimmelfahrt'", p. 13; *DG*: one word different)
**Not in 1921

16. *Mutter.* Mileck, 1: 679 (993)
    "Es kam ein Tag, der war so schwer"
    **Never published
17. *Meine Liebe* [1901] (*DG*, 126). Mileck, 1: 588 (465)
    "Sie schweigt und denkt mit trauervollen"
    (= 1902, p. 70; = *DG*)

Löhnert *Notturni.* Title page: *Verse Herrn Hermann Löhnert in Bern überreicht.*
No date.

1. *Ähren im Sturm* [1902] (*DG*, 215). Mileck, 1: 579 (422)
   "O wie der Sturm so dunkel braust!"
   (Textual variations 1902, p. 6; = *DG*)
   **Not in 1921
2. *Dunkelste Stunden* [1902] (*DG*, 202). Mileck, 1: 508 (83)
   "Das sind die Stunden, die wir nicht begreifen!"
   (= 1902, p. 194; = *DG*) (FN: In his own copy, Hesse discovered an error,
   corrected it in pencil: "Und" to "Uns" in line 7.)
   **Not in 1921
3. *Ich möchte wohl ...* [1902] (= *Ich bin nur Einer*, *DG*, 207). Mileck, 1: 547
   (269)
   "Ich möchte wohl, wie große Dichter thun"
   (Textual variations 1902, p. 109; = *DG*)
   **Not in 1921
4. *Tempel* [1901] (*DG*, 150). Mileck, 1: 624 (622)
   "Wo der gestürzte Gott, von Schatten überschauert"
   (Textual variations 1902, p. 118; = *DG*)
   **Not in 1921
5. *Der Abenteurer* [1901] (*DG*, 173). Mileck, 1: 566 (362)
   "Mein Herz ist müd, mein Herz ist schwer,"
   (Textual variations 1902, p. 139; = 1921, p. 19; = *DG*)
6. *Ligurisches Meer* [1902] (= *Bei Spezia*, *DG*, 198). Mileck, 1: 557 (315)
   "In großen Takten singt das Meer"
   (One word different 1902, p. 149; = *DG*)
   **Not in 1921
7. *Einsame Nacht* [1901] (*DG*, 186). Mileck, 1: 517 (122)
   "Die ihr meine Brüder seid,"
   (One word different 1902, p. 179; = 1921, p. 31; = *DG*)
8. *Odysseus – Ein Gondelgespräch* [June 1901] (= *Venezianische Gondelge-
   spräche V*, *DG*, 144–45). Mileck, 1: 521 (141)
   "Dort am Horizonte kannst du sehen"
   (Textual variations, two more lines 1902, p. 172; = *DG*)
   **Not in 1921
9. *Liebeslied* [1901] (= *Elisabeth III*, *DG*, 114). Mileck, 1: 615 (587)
   "Wie eine weiße Wolke"
   (Textual variations 1902, p. 42; = 1921, p. 24; = *DG*)
10. *Pilger* [1901] (*DG*, 168). Mileck, 1: 599 (518)
    "Und weiter geh'n die Tage"
    (= 1902, p. 196; = *DG*)
    **Not in 1921

11. *Es wird dir sonderbar* ... [1901] (*DG*, 117). Mileck, 1: 535 (208)
    "Es wird dir sonderbar erscheinen,"
    (= 1902, p. 82; = *DG*) |
    **Not in 1921

12. *Gedächtnis* (= *Zuweilen*, *DG*, 101). Mileck, 1: 612 (573)
    "Wenn mich der fernen Kindertage"
    (Textual variations 1902, p. 99; = *DG*)
    **Not in 1921

13. *La belle qui veut* ... [1902] (*DG*, 749). Mileck, 1: 650 (767)
    "Kennst du mich noch? Wir wurden alt"
    (= 1902, p. 65; = *DG*)
    **Not in 1921

14. *Einer Schönheit* [1900] (= *Elisabeth I*, *DG*, 113). Mileck, 1: 521 (140)
    "Dir liegt auf Stirn und schmaler Hand"
    (Textual variations 1902, p. 40; *DG* differs from 1902 in one word)
    **Not in 1921

15. *Wie eine Welle* [1901] (*DG*, 162). Mileck, 1: 615 (588)
    "Wie eine Welle, die von Schaum gekränzt"
    (Textual variations 1902, p. 195; = *DG*)
    **Not in 1921

16. *Er ging im Dunkel* [July 1901] (*DG*, 182). Mileck, 1: 530 (186)
    "Er ging im Dunkel gern, wo schwarzer Bäume"
    (One word different 1902, p. 190; = *DG*)
    **Not in 1921

Pfau *Notturni*. First page: *Basel 1902*

1. *Albumblatt*. Mileck, *Neujahrsblatt ins Album*, 1: 648 (761)
   "Jedem Tag ein kleines Glück"
   **Not in 1902, 1921, *DG*

2. *Der stille Hof* [1900] (*DG*, 112). Mileck, 1: 526 (164)
   "Ein Hof liegt in der stillen Nacht"
   (Textual variations 1902, p. 26; = 1921, p. 25; = *DG*)

3. *Ist das schon Herbst?* [1901] (= *Dass ich so oft –*, *DG*, 188). Mileck, 1: 509 (88)
   "Daß ich so oft mit dunklem Leid"
   (One word different 1902, p. 180; = *DG*)
   **Not in 1921

4. *Das welke Blatt* [1900] (= *Das treibende Blatt*, *DG*, 104). Mileck, 1: 606 (543)
   "Vor mir her getrieben"
   (Textual variations 1902, p. 25; = *DG*)
   **Not in 1921

5. *Heimkehr* [June 1901] (*DG*, 172). Mileck, 1: 576 (404)
   "Nun bin ich lang gewesen"
   (One word different 1902, p. 191; = *DG*)
   **Not in 1921

6. *Weiße Wolken* [1902] (*DG*, 211). Mileck, 1: 578 (420)
   "O schau, sie schweben wieder"
   (One word different 1902, p. 193; = *DG*)
   **Not in 1921

7. *Nacht* [1901] (*DG*, 125). Mileck, 1: 569 (378)
   "Mit Dämmerung und Amselschlag"

(= 1902, p. 188; = *DG*)
**Not in 1921

8. *Sage* [1901] (*DG*, 187). Mileck, 1: 513 (102)
"Der König mit den Mannen saß beim Mahl"
(One word different 1902, p. 183; = *DG*)
**Not in 1921

9. *Der alte Geiger* [1901] (= *Der Geiger VI, 'Ich habe nichts mehr ... '*, *DG*, 77).
Mileck, 1: 546 (257)
"Ich habe nichts mehr zu sagen"
(= 1902, p. 135; = *DG*)
**Not in 1921

10. *Hafen von Livorno* [1901] (*DG*, 199). Mileck, 1: 571 (386)
"Nach einem Bild, das ich vor Jahren sah"
(One word different 1902, p. 150; = *DG*)
**Not in 1921

11. *Er ging im Dunkel ...* [July 1901] (*DG*, 182). Mileck, 1: 530 (186)
"Er ging im Dunkel gern, wo schwarzer Bäume"
(= 1902, p. 190; = *DG*)
**Not in 1921

12. *Wie eine Welle ...* [1901] (*DG*, 162). Mileck, 1: 615 (588)
"Wie eine Welle, die von Schaum gekränzt"
(Textual variations 1902, p. 195; = *DG*)
**Not in 1902

Piper *Notturni*. Title page: *Herrn Kurt Piper mit herzlichem Gruß!* Closing page:
Basel anno 1902 scripsit Hermann Hesse (Mileck, 1: 469, 4a)

1. *Die Cypressen von San Clemente* [1901] (= *Die Zypressen von San Clemente*,
DG, 153). Mileck, 1: 622 (613)
"Wir biegen flammend schlanke Wipfel im Wind"
(Textual variations 1902, p. 152; = 1921, p. 17; = *DG*)

2. *Einer Schönheit* [1899] ("Lulu", *DG*, 87). Mileck, 1: 536 (213)
"Flüchtig wie auf hohen Matten"
(Textual variations 1902, p. 67; = *DG*)
**Not in 1921

3. *Ich liebe Frauen ...* [1901] (*DG*, 118). Mileck, 1: 547 (266)
"Ich liebe Frauen, die vor tausend Jahren"
(One word different 1902, p. 114; = *DG*)
**Not in 1921

4. *L'autre a soif de l'avenir et s'élance vers l'inconnu! A. d. Musset.* Mileck, 1:
676 (962A)
"Du mit dem tiefen Glanz im Blick"
**Never published

5. *Drüben überm Berge* (*DG*, 288 = *Drüben*). Mileck, 1: 522 (143)
"Drüben überm Berge"
**Not in 1902, 1921

6. *Einem Verächter* [1902]. Mileck, 1: 659–60 (821)
"Sieh, ich verstehe ja dein Fluchen"
(One word, title different 1902 = *Einem Unzufriedenen*, 1902, p. 186 –
included only in first edition, not in 1906 edition)
**Not in 1921, *DG*

7. *Er ging im Dunkel ...* [July 1901] (*DG*, 182). Mileck, 1: 530 (186)
   "Er ging im Dunkel gern, wo schwarzer Berge"
   (One word different 1902, p. 190; = *DG*)
   **Not in 1921

8. *Beim Weiher.* Mileck, *Das Kreuzlein*, 1: 662 (830)
   "Spätsommers: Meine Birke regt"
   **Not in 1902, 1921, *DG*

9. *Über die Felder* [1900] (*DG*, 91). Mileck, 1: 598 (511)
   "Über den Himmel Wolken ziehn"
   (One word different 1902, p. 4; = 1921, p. 14; = *DG*)

10. *Müde nun ....* Mileck, *"Einsamkeit*, 1: 647 (751)
    "Immer wieder gab ich meine Hände"
    **Not in 1902, 1921, *DG*

11. *Certosa di Val d'Ema.* Mileck, 1: 674 (928a)
    "Der Mönch an seiner Pforte thut mir leid"
    **Never published

12. *Wie eine Welle ...* [1901] (*DG*, 162). Mileck, 1: 615 (588)
    "Wie eine Welle, die von Schaum gekränzt"
    (Textual variations 1902, p. 195; = *DG*)
    **Not in 1921

13. *Liebesgeschichte I/II* [1900–1901] (I = *Bitte*, *DG*, 122; II = *Rücknahme*, *DG*, 123). Mileck, 1: (I, 612, 570; II, 548, 271)
    I "Wenn du die kleine Hand mir giebst"
    (= 1902, p. 59; = *DG*)
    **Not in 1921
    II "Ich sagte nicht: ich liebe dich"
    (= 1902, p. 61; = 1921, p. 22; = *DG*)

Schoenaich-Carolath *Notturni.* Title page: *Dem Prinzen Emil zu Schoenaich-Carolath überreicht.* Closing page: *Für den kranken Hermann Hesse geschrieben von Ludwig Finckh. VIII 1902.*

1. *Zigeuner* [1902] (= *DG*, *Lieder*, 206). Mileck, 1: 546 (259)
   "Ich habe nur wenig Lieder"
   (Textual variations 1902, p. 123; = *DG*)
   **Not in 1921

2. *Müde* [1899] (= *DG*, *Wie kommt es?*, 86). Mileck, 1: 545 (255)
   "Ich habe keinen Kranz ersiegt
   (Textual variations 1902, p. 121; = *DG*)
   **Not in 1921

3. *Spätblau* [1898] (*DG*, 82). Mileck, 1: 578 (419)
   "O reine, wundervolle Schau"
   (Textual variations in 1902, p. 16; = *DG*
   **Not in 1921

4. *Grindelwald* [February 1902] (= *Hochgebirgswinter I, Aufstieg*; *DG*, 195). Mileck, 1: 599 (517)
   "Und ringsum Schnee und junges Eis"
   (Textual variations in 1902, p. 11; = *DG*
   **Not in 1921

5. *Der Schmetterling.* Mileck, 1: 662 (836)
   "Über den silbernen Hügeln"
   **Not in 1902, 1921, *DG*

6. *Nachtwanderung* [1902] (= *DG, Nachtgang*, 205). Mileck, 1: 534 (202)
   "Es nachtet schon, die Straße ruht"
   (Textual variations 1902, p. 21; = *DG*)
   **Not in 1921

7. *Reine Lust* [1902] (*DG*, 209). Mileck, 1: 549 (277)
   "Ich weiß auf Erden keine reinere Lust"
   (Textual variations in 1902, p. 146; = *DG*)
   **Not in 1921

8. *Florenz* [August 1901] (= *Im Norden, DG*, 127). Mileck, 1: 593 (489)
   "Soll ich sagen, was ich träume?"
   (Textual variations in 1902, p. 141; = 1921, p. 18; = *DG*)

9. *Kennst du das auch?* [1901] (*DG*, 151). Mileck, 1: 562 (335)
   "Kennst du das auch, daß manchesmal"
   (= 1902, p. 85; = 1921, p. 27; = *DG*)

10. *Liebeslied* [1901] (= *Elisabeth III, DG*, 114). Mileck, 1: 615 (587)
    "Wie eine weiße Wolke"
    (Textual variations 1902, p. 42; = 1921, p. 24; = *DG*)

11. *Ligurisches Meer* [1902] (= *Bei Spezia, DG*, 198). Mileck, 1: 557 (315)
    "In großen Takten singt das Meer"
    (One word different 1902, p. 149; = *DG*)
    **Not in 1921

12. *Nachtgebet der Schiffer auf dem adriatischen Meer (zur Stella maris.)* [June
    1901] (= *Gebet der Schiffer, DG*, 185). Mileck, 1: 520 (134)
    "Die Stunden eilen – Mitternacht!"
    (Textual variations 1902, p. 147; = *DG*)
    **Not in 1921

13. *Gedächtnis* (= *Zuweilen, DG*, 101). Mileck, 1: 612 (573)
    "Wenn mich der fernen Kindertage"
    (Textual variations 1902, p. 99; = *DG*)
    **Not in 1921

14. *Wende* [1901] (*DG*, 129). Mileck, 1: 576 (409)
    "Nun ist die Jugend schon verschäumt"
    (= 1902, p. 91; = *DG*)
    **Not in 1921

15. *Ausklang* [1901] (*DG*, 172). Mileck, 1: 625 (629)
    "Wolkenflug und herber Wind"
    (One word different 1902, p. 184; = *DG*)
    **Not in 1921

16. *Einsame Nacht* [1901] (*DG*, 186). Mileck, 1: 517 (122)
    "Die ihr meine Brüder seid,"
    (One word different 1902, p. 179; = 1921, p. 31; = *DG*)

17. *Ähren im Sturm* [1902] (*DG*, 215). Mileck, 1: 579 (422)
    "O wie der Sturm so dunkel braust!"
    (Textual variations 1902, p. 6; = *DG*)

18. *Pilger* [1901] (*DG*, 168). Mileck, 1: 599 (518)
    "Und weiter geh'n die Tage"
    (= 1902, p. 196; = *DG*)
    **Not in 1921

BIBLIOGRAPHY

HESSE'S WORKS

Collections

Gesammelte Briefe, ed. Volker Michels, co-eds. Heiner Hesse and Ursula Michels. 4 vols. Frankfurt/M.: Suhrkamp Verlag, 1973–1986.
Die Gedichte. 2 vols. Frankfurt/M.: Suhrkamp Verlag, 1977.
Gesammelte Dichtungen. 6 vols. Frankfurt/M.: Suhrkamp Verlag, 1952.
Gesammelte Erzählungen. 4 vols. Frankfurt/M.: Suhrkamp Verlag, 1977.
Gesammelte Werke. 12 vols. Frankfurt/M.: Suhrkamp Verlag, 1970.

Individual Works

Chopins grande valse, eine Phantasie, Deutsches Dichterheim – Organ für Dichtkunst und Kritik (Vienna) 17 (1897), p. 394.
Das Rathaus, Aus Kinderzeiten – Gesammelte Erzählungen, 1. Frankfurt/M.: Suhrkamp Verlag, suhrkamp taschenbuch 347, 1977.
Demian. Gesammelte Werke, 5. Frankfurt/M.: Suhrkamp Verlag, 1970.
Demian, translated by Michael Roloff and Michael Lebeck. New York: Harper and Row, 1965.
Der Städtebauer. Gesammelte Erzählungen, 6. Frankfurt/M.: Suhrkamp Verlag, 1977 and 1993.
Der Steppenwolf. Gesammelte Werke, 7. Frankfurt/M.: Suhrkamp Verlag, 1970.
Eine Stunde hinter Mitternacht (1899). *Gesammelte Werke,* 1. Frankfurt/M.: Suhrkamp Verlag, 1970.
"Einzug in ein neues Haus" (1931). *Gesammelte Werke,* 10. Frankfurt/M.: Suhrkamp Verlag, 1970.
"Erinnerung an Hans." *Gesammelte Werke,* 10. Frankfurt/M.: Suhrkamp Verlag, 1970.
Review of *Fontes Melusinae* (Karl Ernst Knodt). *Neue Zürcher Zeitung,* November 19, 1904. *Hermann Hesse, Helene Voigt-Diederichs. Zwei*

Autorenportraits in Briefen 1897–1900. Köln: Eugen Diederichs Verlag, 1971.

Hermann Lauscher. Frankfurt/M.: Insel Verlag, insel taschenbuch 206, 1976.

Kleine Freuden – Kurze Prosa aus dem Nachlaß, ed. Volker Michels (Frankfurt/M., 1977), 187–98.

Kurzgefaßter Lebenslauf (1924). *Gesammelte Werke,* 6. Frankfurt/M.: Suhrkamp Verlag, 1970.

"Lulu. Ein Jugenderlebnis, dem Gedächtnis E. T. A. Hoffmanns gewidmet." *Die Schweiz* 19 (1906), pp. 1–8, 29–36, 53–57.

Peter Camenzind. Gesammelte Werke, 1. Frankfurt/M.: Suhrkamp Verlag, 1970.

"Romantik und Neuromantik." *Gesammelte Werke,* 10. Frankfurt/M.: Suhrkamp Verlag, 1970.

Steppenwolf, translated by Basil Creighton and updated by Joseph Mileck. New York: Holt, Rinehart and Winston, 1963.

"Über *Peter Camenzind." Gesammelte Werke,* 11. Frankfurt/M.: Suhrkamp Verlag, 1970.

Review of *Unterstrom* (Helene Voigt). *Allgemeine Schweizer Zeitung,* Basel 6, (April 14, 1901 [Sunday supplement]), p. 56.

Zum Gedächtnis unseres Vaters. [Hermann and Adele Hesse.] Tübingen: Rainer Wunderlich, 1930.

OTHER WORKS CITED

Ball, Hugo. *Hermann Hesse – Sein Leben und sein Werk.* Berlin: S. Fischer Verlag, 1927.

Bölsche, Wilhelm. *Das Liebesleben in der Natur.* 3 vols. Jena: Diederichs, 1900.

Böttger, Fritz. *Hermann Hesse – Leben, Werk, Zeit.* Berlin: Verlag der Nation, 1974.

Como, Cesco. "Hermann Hesse. Eine psychische Studie." *Deutsche Heimat* 6, no. 50 (Leipzig/Berlin, September 13, 1903), p. 1672

Dietschy, Marta Dietschy. "Hermann Hesse und das Basler Rathaus." *Basler Woche,* no. 7 (February 11, 1977).

Finckh, Ludwig. *Himmel und Erde.* Stuttgart: Silberburg Verlag, 1961.

———. *Der Rosendoktor.* Munich: Deutscher Volksverlag, 1943.

———. "So fing es an." *Familiennachrichten* [der Familie Finckh], no. 21 (June, 1948).

———. *Verzauberung.* Ulm: Gerhard Hess Verlag, 1950.

Freedman, Ralph. *Hermann Hesse: Pilgrim of Crisis.* New York: Pantheon Books, 1978. Goethe, Johann Wolfgang. *Johann Wolfgang Goethe – Selected Poems,* ed. Christopher Middleton. Boston: Suhrkamp/Insel Publishers, 1983.

Gottschalk, Günther. *Dichter und ihre Handschriften – Betrachtungen zu Autographen des jungen Hermann Hesse im Marbacher Archiv.* Stuttgart: Akademischer Verlag Hans-Dieter Heinz, 1979.

Greiner, Siegfried. *Hermann Hesse – Jugend in Calw*. Sigmaringen: Jan Thorbecke Verlag, 1981.

Hafner, Gotthilf. *Hermann Hesse – Werk und Leben*. Nürnberg: Verlag Hans Carl, 1970.

Hesse, Ninon, and Gerhard Kirchhoff, eds. *Hermann Hesse – Kindheit und Jugend vor Neunzehnhundert*, 2 vols. Frankfurt: Suhrkamp, 1966 and 1978.

Hesse Gundert, Adele. *Marie Hesse – Ein Lebensbild in Briefen und Tagebüchern*. Frankfurt/M.: Insel Verlag, 1977.

Kleine, Gisela. *Ninon und Hermann Hesse – Leben als Dialog*. Sigmaringen: Jan Thorbecke Verlag, 1982.

Knodt, Hermann. *Familiengeschichte der hessischen Pfarrfamilie Knodt*. Limburg/Lahn: C. A. Starke Verlag, 1967.

Knodt, Karl Ernst. *Neue Gedichte*. Mülhheim/Ruhr: Karl Schimmelpfeng, 1902.

Leppmann, Wolfgang. *Rilke – A Life*, trans. by Russell Stockman. New York: Fromm International Publishing Corporation, 1984.

Limberg, Michael. "Hermann Hesse und Ludwig Finckh." *Hermann Hesse und seine literarischen Zeitgenossen*, eds. Friedrich Bran and Martin Pfeifer. Calw: Verlag Bernhard Gengenbach, 1982.

Mauerhofer, Hugo. *Die Introversion – Mit spezieller Berücksichtigung des Dichters H. Hesse*. Bern and Leipzig: Verlag Paul Haupt, 1929.

Michels, Volker, ed. *Hermann Hesse in Augenzeugenberichten*. Frankfurt/M.: Suhrkamp Taschenbuch, 1991.

———, ed. *Hermann Hesse – Sein Leben in Bildern und Texten*. Frankfurt/M.: Suhrkamp Verlag, 1979.

———, ed. *Hermann Hesse – Musik*. Frankfurt/M.: Suhrkamp Verlag, 1986.

Mileck, Joseph. *Hermann Hesse – Biography and Bibliography*, 2 vols. Berkeley: University of California Press, 1977.

———. *Hermann Hesse – Life and Art*. Berkeley: University of California Press, 1978.

———. "The Poetry of Hermann Hesse." *Monatshefte* 46 (1954): 192–198.

Pfeifer, Martin. *Hesse-Kommentar zu sämtlichen Werken*. Munich: Winkler Verlag, 1980.

———. *Julie Hellmann – Hermann Hesses Lulu*. Kirchheim: Schöllkopf Verlag, 1991.

Piper, Kurt. *Vom lebendigen Wissen*, ed. Edwin Fröböse. Stuttgart: J. Ch. Mellinger Verlag, 1975.

Rilke, Rainer Maria. *Die Aufzeichnungen des Malte Laurids Brigge*. Munich: Deutscher Taschenbuch Verlag, 1962.

———. *Briefe und Tagebücher aus der Frühzeit (1899 bis 1902)*. Leipzig: Insel-Verlag, 1933.

Schmid, Hans Rudolf. *Hermann Hesse*. Frauenfeld/Leipzig: Verlag von Huber & Co., 1928.

Schneider, Christian Immo. *Hermann Hesse*. Munich: C. H. Beck, 1991.

Schoenaich-Carolath, Emil von. *Gesammelte Werke*. Berlin/Leipzig: Walther de Gruyter & Co., 1922.

Semmig, Jeanne Berta. *Aus acht Jahrhunderten*. Berlin: Union Verlag, 1975.

Small, William. *Kommentar zu den Aufzeichnungen des Malte Laurids Brigge*. Chapel Hill: University of North Carolina Press, 1983, University of North Carolina Studies in the Germanic Languages and Literatures, no. 101.

Spycher, Peter. *Eine Wanderung durch Hermann Hesses Lyrik*. Bern/Frankfurt am Main/New York/Paris: Peter Lang, 1990.

Stelzig, Eugene. *Hermann Hesse's Fictions of the Self: Autobiography and the Confessional Imagination*. Princeton: Princeton University Press, 1988.

Unseld, Siegfried. *Hermann Hesse, Werk und Wirkungsgeschichte*. Frankfurt/M.: Suhrkamp Verlag, 1985.

Zeller, Bernhard, ed. *Hermann Hesse 1877–1977*. Munich: Kösel-Verlag, 1977.

———. *Hermann Hesse – mit Selbstzeugnissen und Bilddokumenten*. Hamburg: Rowohlt Taschenbuch Verlag, 1963.

INDEX

Names and Hesse's Works (Published and unpublished)

TABOOS IN GERMAN LITERATURE

Edited by **David Jackson,** *Senior Lecturer, School of European Studies, University of Wales College of Cardiff*

An innovative collection that will intrigue all students of German literature and society.

Students of German literature will have asked themselves at one stage or another why certain topics have received saturation treatment over the last two centuries while others have either been ignored entirely or at best grossly neglected. This books tackles this fascinating issue and illuminates why, at various junctures, specific topics and attitudes were regarded by influential sections of society as being either inadmissible or presentable only in particular, prescribed ways. While the presentation of sexual matters such as homosexuality and lesbianism is inevitably at the heart of the book, political, social and ideological issues also loom large. The editor has recruited a team of prominent scholars to provide a penetrating, comprehensive focus that ranges from individual writers and their works, i.e. Goethe, Hölderlin, Kafka, and Thomas Mann, to specific issues, movements and periods.

Contents: M. Swales, Text and Sub-text: Reflections on the Literary Exploration of Taboo Experience – E. McInnes, "Verlorene Töchter": Reticence and Ambiguity in German Domestic Drama in the Late Eighteenth Century – D. Constantine, Saying and Not-saying in Hölderlin's Work – D. Jackson, Taboos in Poetic-Realist Writers – C. Weedon, Of Madness and Masochism: Sexuality in Women's Writing at the Turn of the Century – E. Boa, The Double Taboo: Male Bodies in Kafka's Der Prozeß – T. J. Reed, The Frustrated Poet: Homosexuality and Taboo in Der Tod in Venedig – H. Peitsch, Discovering a Taboo: the Nazi Past in Literary-political discourse 1958-1967 – G. Paul, Inarticulacy: Lesbianism and Language in post-1945 German Literature – J. H. Reid, Sex and Politics: the Case of the GDR.

Available · 224 pages · bibliog., index
ISBN 1-57181-881-2 · hardback · ca. **$45.00/£30.00**
Literature/German Studies

165 Taber Avenue • Providence, Rhode Island 02906
Phone: 401-861-9330 • Fax: 401-521-0046 • E-mail: BerghahnBk@aol.com
For MasterCard and Visa orders, please dial 1-800-540-8663.

TURKISH CULTURE IN GERMAN SOCIETY TODAY

Edited by **David Horrocks** and **Eva Kolinsky,** *Department of Modern Languages, Keele University*

Provides valuable information on the social and cultural life of the Turkish minority in Germany.

For many decades Germany has had a sizeable Turkish minority that lives in an uneasy co-existence with the surrounding German community and as such has attracted considerable interest abroad where this tends to be seen as a measure of German tolerance. However, little is known about the actual situation of the Turks. This volume provides valuable information, presented in a most original manner, which combines literary and cultural studies with social and political analysis. It focuses on the Turkish-born writer Emine Sevgi Özdamar, who writes in German and whose work, particularly her highly acclaimed novel *Das Leben ist eine Karawanserei,* is examined critically and situated in the context of German "migrant literature." An interview with the author and a sample of her work are followed by a sociological survey of the general situation of minorities in Germany today; their views and experiences, official government policy towards, and popular perceptions of them. The volume furthermore includes a study of a particular Turkish community, that of Frankfurt am Main, which is supported by a collection of documents and statistical data. General surveys and detailed analyses thus combine to provide a multi-faceted picture in which the life and cultural activity of the Turks in Germany is set against the background of other minorities in the country.

Contents: E. Kolinsky/D. Horrocks, Between Acceptance and Exclusion: Culture, Society and Minorities in Contemporary Germany – M. McGowan/S. Fischer, The Literature of Ethnic Minorities in Contemporary Germany – D. Horrocks, Turkish Germans, German Turks? Language, Culture and Identity in Emine Sevgi Özdamar's Work – E. S. Özdamar, Living and Writing in Germany – D. Horrocks/F. Krause, Emine Sevgi Özdamar: her Voice and her Life – E. Kolinsky, Non-German Minorities in Germany Today – E. Kürsat-Ahlers, The Turkish Minority in German Society – H.-P. Waldhoff/D. Tan, Everyday Life and Turkish Everyday Culture – Y. Karakasoglu, Turkish Youth between German and Islamic Traditions.

Available · 240 pages · ca. 20 tables and diagrams, bibliog., index
ISBN 1-57181-899-5 · hardback · ca. **$29.95/£22.00**
ISBN 1-57181-047-1 · paperback · ca. **$12.50/£9.95**
Culture and Society in Germany, Volume 1
German Studies/Literature/Sociology

165 Taber Avenue • Providence, Rhode Island 02906
Phone: 401-861-9330 • Fax: 401-521-0046 • E-mail: BerghahnBk@aol.com
For MasterCard and Visa orders, please dial 1-800-540-8663.

FASCISM AND THEATRE
Comparative Studies on the Aesthetics and Politics of Performance in Europe, 1925-1945

Edited by **Günter Berghaus**, *Reader in Theatre History and Performance Studies, University of Bristol*

Since the 1920s, an endless flow of studies has analysed the political systems of fascism, the seizure of power, the nature of the régimes, the atrocities committed and, finally, the wars waged against other countries. However, much less attention has been paid to the strategies of persuasion employed by the régimes to win over the masses for their cause. Among these, fascist propaganda has traditionally been seen as the key means of influencing public opinion. Only recently has the "fascination with Fascism" become a topic of enquiry that has also formed the guiding interest of this volume: it offers, for the first time, a comparative analysis of the forms and functions of theatre in countries governed by fascist or para-fascist régimes. By examining a wide spectrum of theatrical manifestations in a number of States with a varying degree of fascistization, these studies establish some of the similarities and differences between the theatrical cultures of several countries in the interwar period.

Available · 336 pages · 45 photos, index
ISBN 1-57181-877-4 · hardback · ca. **$59.95/£40.00**
ISBN 1-57181-901-0 · paperback · ca. **$24.50/£16.50**
Cultural Studies/ Theatre/History

165 Taber Avenue • Providence, Rhode Island 02906
Phone: 401-861-9330 • Fax: 401-521-0046 • E-mail: BerghahnBk@aol.com
For MasterCard and Visa orders, please dial 1-800-540-8663.